Values and Virtues in Higher Education Research

Values and Virtues in Higher Education Research centres on practitioners studying and researching their practices in higher education settings, in order to improve those practices for the benefit of others and themselves. Making research public is a key aspect of ensuring the quality of educational research and educational practices: *Values and Virtues in Higher Education Research* raises questions and develops conversations about why higher education practitioners should study and improve their work, how this may be done and what might be some of the benefits of doing so. What we do as practitioners is influenced by and linked with what we value, what we believe is good. Improving practices therefore involves becoming aware of and interrogating the values that enter into and inform those practices; a study of practices becomes a study of the relationships between the practices in question and their values base.

From an international group of contributors in this growing field, this book provides strong theoretical resources and case study material that shows how this transformation may be achieved, including topics such as:

- theorising practices to show personal and organisational accountability
- developing inter-professional and inter-disciplinary dialogues for social transformation
- establishing communities of inquiry in higher education and other workplace settings
- reconceptualising professional education as research-informed practice
- locating educational theory in the real world for human and environmental well-being.

Showing the evolution of theory through critical engagement, this text will be a valuable companion for lecturers, students and professional developers in higher education. This book will form core reading for those who are interested in engaging in practice-based research and as additional reading for those whose aim is to broaden their thinking in relation to the role of values and virtues in educational research.

Jean McNiff is an independent researcher and writer, Professor of Educational Research at York St John University, and Visiting Professor at Oslo and Akershus University College, Beijing Normal University and Ningxia Teachers University. She is also the author of key texts *Action Research: Principles and Practice, You and Your Action Research Project* and *Writing Up Your Action Research Project*.

Values and Virtues in Higher Education Research

Critical perspectives

Edited by Jean McNiff

Routledge
Taylor & Francis Group

LONDON AND NEW YORK

First published 2016
by Routledge
2 Park Square, Milton Park, Abingdon, Oxon OX14 4RN

and by Routledge
711 Third Avenue, New York, NY 10017

Routledge is an imprint of the Taylor & Francis Group, an informa business

British Library Cataloguing in Publication Data
A catalogue record for this book is available from the British Library

Library of Congress Cataloging in Publication Data
Names: McNiff, Jean, editor.
Title: Values and virtues in higher education research : critical perspectives / edited by Jean McNiff.
Description: New York, NY : Routledge, 2016. | Includes bibliographical references.
Identifiers: LCCN 2016000807 (print) | LCCN 2016013312 (ebook) | ISBN 9781138916814 (hbk : alk. paper) | ISBN 9781138916821 (pbk : alk. paper) | ISBN 9781315689364 (ebk)
Subjects: LCSH: Education, Higher—Research. | Action research.
Classification: LCC LB2326.3 .V35 2016 (print) | LCC LB2326.3 (ebook) | DDC 378.007—dc23LC record available at http://lccn.loc.gov/2016000807

ISBN: 978-1-138-91681-4 (hbk)
ISBN: 978-1-138-91682-1 (pbk)
ISBN: 978-1-315-68936-4 (ebk)

Typeset in Galliard
by diacriTech, Chennai

Contents

Contributors

Dina Bethere is an associate professor at the Faculty of Pedagogy and Social Work, Liepāja University, Latvia, and a corresponding member of the International Academy of Humanization in Education. She is also a director of bachelor level special education teachers' study programmes and is recognised for her expertise in special education at the national level.

Josephine Bleach is Director of the Early Learning Initiative at the National College of Ireland. She worked formerly as a primary school teacher, Home School Community Liaison Co-ordinator in Darndale, Dublin, and a facilitator with the School Development Planning Support Service (Primary) of the Department of Education and Science. She has published widely about her work in community action research, numeracy, professional development and parental involvement.

Christopher Branson is Professor of Educational Leadership and National Head of Education in the Faculty of Education and Arts at the Australian Catholic University. His research interests include those of the nature and practice of leadership, ethical leadership, educational leadership, personal and organisational values, leadership for social justice, and organisational change.

Alison Buckley is a Senior Lecturer in the Department of Nursing, Health and Professional Practice at the University of Cumbria, having worked as a senior nurse at Manchester and Cambridge hospitals in neurosurgery and acute brain injury services. Alison has particular interests in ethics, law, pharmacology and professional practice. A main research focus is on narrative and phenomenological inquiry, notably in understanding the patient's experience of altered states of consciousness secondary to neuropathology. She is currently registered as a probationary PhD student with Lancaster University.

Andy Cheng is a Senior Associate Research Fellow in the Department of Social Work, School of Education and Social Work, University of Sussex; and a Senior Development Worker for Impact and Evaluation with the Sussex Community Development Association.

Sue Dymoke is a poet, Reader in Education and National Teaching Fellow in the School of Education, University of Leicester. Her research focuses primarily on aspects of poetry pedagogy and curriculum. Her recent publications include *Making Poetry Happen: Transforming the Poetry Classroom* co-edited with Myra Barrs, Andrew Lambirth and Anthony Wilson (Bloomsbury, 2015) and *Moon at the Park and Ride* (Shoestring Press, 2012).

Margaret Franken is an Associate Professor in the Faculty of Education at the University of Waikato. She has recently served as a chairperson of a department for several years and has had a particular interest in learning theory. Her research has included a strong focus on situated learning in particular contexts. This interest has underpinned her writing about leadership with her colleagues.

Cheryl Hunt is Editor of the international *Journal for the Study of Spirituality*, Vice President of the British Association for the Study of Spirituality (BASS) and former Executive Editor of *Teaching in Higher Education*. She recently retired as Director of Professional Doctorates in the Graduate School of Education, University of Exeter, UK, where she is currently a Research Fellow. She has worked and researched in the field of Critical Reflective Practice for over thirty years, developing accredited programmes in higher, adult, community and medical education, and in health and social care. Cheryl is an Honorary Life Member of the Standing Conference on University Teaching and Research in the Education of Adults (SCUTREA).

Lāsma Latsone is a docent at Liepāja University, Latvia, Faculty of Education and Social Work and a research fellow of York St John University, Faculty of Theology and Education. Her research interests are connected with religious and intercultural education.

David Maughan Brown is Professor Emeritus at York St John University, where he served until his retirement as Deputy Vice Chancellor with executive responsibility for the University's academic activities. Born in Cape Town and raised in what was then Tanganyika, he became Professor and Dean of Arts and finally Acting Vice Chancellor at the University of Natal. He has published widely in the fields of African Literature and Colonial fiction and race ideology. From 1992 to 2002 he was involved in the transformation of Higher Education in South Africa, resulting in his appointment to the newly established Board of the South African Higher Education Quality Committee.

Jean McNiff took early retirement from her work as a school teacher and deputy head teacher, subsequently developed a successful retail business and later entered higher education. She is currently Professor of Educational Research in the Faculty of Education and Theology at York St John University, and holds other international visiting professorial positions. Special research interests include ethics in educational research and writing for publication. Recent publications include *Action Research: Principles and Practice* (Routledge, 2013), *Writing and Doing Action Research* (Sage, 2014), *You and Your Action Research Project* (Routledge, 2016) and *Writing Up Your Action Research Project* (Routledge, 2016).

Hugh Mehan is Professor Emeritus of Sociology and Education at the University of California, San Diego. He has dedicated his efforts to improving the academic preparation of underrepresented students through partnerships with K-12 schools. For the past twenty years, he has helped build equitable educational environments (The Preuss School, Gompers Preparatory Academy, the Diamond Educational Excellence Partnership, and Groundwork San Diego in southeastern San Diego) while documenting the processes of organisational change in those institutions. His most recent book, *In the Front Door*, presents his research on the political origins, culture, and organisation of The Preuss School and Gompers Preparatory Academy.

Jon Nixon is Honorary Professor of International Education and Lifelong Learning at the Hong Kong Institute of Education. Recent publications include *Hannah Arendt and the Politics of Friendship* (Bloomsbury, 2015), *Interpretive Pedagogies for Higher Education* (Bloomsbury, 2012), *Higher Education and the Public Good* (Continuum, 2011) and *Towards the Virtuous University* (Routledge, 2008).

Linda Pavītola is associate professor and a Deputy Dean of the Faculty of Pedagogy and Social Work at Liepāja University where she is a director of bachelor and master level teacher training study programmes with responsibility for the development of teacher education. Her research interests are connected with the dimensions of quality in teacher education with particular interest in pedagogical relationships.

Dawn Penney is Professor of Physical Education and Sport Pedagogy at Monash University, Australia, having worked in universities in the UK, Australia and New Zealand. Her experience includes the roles of Associate Dean (Research), Chair of Department, research group leadership and mentoring appointments, and performance management. Her leadership research builds on sustained work in education policy sociology and concerns to pursue issues of equity.

Jane Rand is Head of Department for Children, Young People and Education (CYPE) in the Faculty of Education and Theology at York St John University. Jane joined York St John University having worked as a teacher, and teacher-educator, in Further Education and after completing a professional doctorate at the University of Sheffield. Her research interests are epistemologies, the practices of learning and applied pedagogical research.

Joseph M. Shosh is professor and chair of the Education Department at Moravian College, where he also directs the action research based graduate education program. An initiator of the Action Research Network of the Americas (ARNA), he currently serves as Chair of the Executive Committee of the Coordinating Group. He is a past recipient of the National Council of Teachers of English Paul and Kate Farmer English Journal Writing Award, the James N. Moffett Award for Classroom Research, and Cornell University's Merrill Scholar Teaching Award. He has published widely in the field of teacher action research and is associate editor of the 2016 *Palgrave International Handbook of Action Research.*

Carla Solvason is a Senior Lecturer in the Centre for Early Childhood at the University of Worcester. She teaches on undergraduate routes as well as co-ordinating and delivering the Masters pathway for Early Childhood. A key aspect of her work is supporting and developing student research. Prior to lecturing, Carla worked as a researcher, a Speech, Language and Communication consultant and a primary school teacher. Carla has published work relating to student research, the team around the child, school culture, educational equality, professionalism, ethicality and supporting speech and language development.

Jane Spiro is Reader in Education and TESOL at Oxford Brookes University. Her research interests include the international student experience, higher education pedagogies, writing identities and academic literacies, teacher beliefs and creativity in second language learning. Her publications include *Creative Poetry Writing* and *Storybuilding* (Oxford University Press, 2004, 2007), *Changing Methodologies in TESOL* (Edinburgh University Press, 2013), *Reflective Writing* (with Williams and Woolliams, Palgrave Macmillan, 2013), a novel, two collections of learner stories and a poetry collection, *Playing for Time* (Oversteps, 2015). She has also written and presented six interfaith programmes for Carlton/West Country television.

Julian Stern is Dean of the Faculty of Education and Theology at York St John University and was a schoolteacher for fourteen years prior to working in a number of universities. He has researched and published widely on schools as learning communities (including religious education and spirituality, solitude and loneliness, and homework) and on higher education (including the role of dialogue and virtuous educational practice).

Jonathan Vincent is a lecturer at York St John University and a PhD candidate at Lancaster University. Predominantly taking a participatory action research approach, his research seeks to create opportunities for students on the autism spectrum to articulate their lived experiences of university and transition into employment. He has co-authored articles for *Educational Action Research Journal* and *Good Autism Practice Journal* alongside students on the autism spectrum.

Introduction

Jean McNiff

This book is about practitioners studying and researching their practices in higher education settings, in order to improve those practices for the benefit of others and themselves. This stance itself offers reasons for optimism for the future of higher education. The practitioners in question include researchers, academics, professional educators, administrators and managers. The aim of the book is to raise questions and develop conversations about why higher education practitioners should study and improve their work, how this may be done, and what might be some of the benefits of doing so.

In this introductory chapter I am writing in two capacities, as editor and author. My purpose as editor is to set out the debates regarding values and virtues in higher education research. As author, like the other authors in the book, I engage with the debates. A key point, for me, is the need to recognise that what we do as practitioners is influenced by and linked with what we value, what we believe is good. Improving practices therefore involves becoming aware of and interrogating the values that enter into and inform those practices; a study of practices becomes a study of the relationships between the practices in question and their values base. By studying and researching these relationships we are able to give reasons for why we do what we do, and articulate our purposes in doing it. By offering these values-based kinds of explanations, we are able to show how we hold ourselves accountable to others and to ourselves. This can, and does, lead to important discussions about the need for higher education practitioners to research what we are doing, and to produce public accounts that invite critique about the usefulness of our research and its potential impact in other people's and our own thinking and practice. It intensifies the idea of justification, and moves the focus to a justification for researchers' reasons and purposes: in effect, towards what might be seen as an ethical basis for what we do.

The book aims to engage with these discussions through the production of case studies that show how a group of higher education practitioners, in different settings and across disciplines, have dealt with some of the issues and dilemmas that have emerged. The book comprises twelve studies, including this introductory chapter, which stands as my contribution to the discussion. A main permeating theme emerges that education is informed by educational values, and so should not be seen simply in terms of a narrow conception of instrumental instruction, but more as a form of committed intentional action whose aim is to encourage others to think for themselves and develop capacity in helping yet more others to do the same. This stance involves a commitment to values pluralism which itself requires choosing between the many and frequently competing choices available about which values to espouse to guide educational practices. This in turn requires a consideration of what guiding principles inform our choices, and what kinds of contributions our choices might make for wider personal and social practices. These are of course complex issues, yet they signal what emerges as a distinctive feature of the book, the idea that practitioners themselves should study, reflect on and explain what they are doing.

The importance of practitioners studying the values base of their own work is highly significant for the field of practice improvement, and also represents a significant turn in the study of values and ethics in higher education research. In many traditionalist texts, authors tend to speak about values from an abstract, objectivised stance without inserting themselves into their stories, whereas in this book, authors speak about their own positioning in the study of values and their understanding of the relationship between values and practices. The shift is similar to that discussed by Chomsky in relation to the significance of generative grammar for linguistic enquiry. He commented:

> The study of generative grammar represented a significant shift of focus in the approach to problems of language. Put in the simplest terms, ... the shift of focus was from behavior or the products of behavior to states of the mind/brain that enter into behavior. If one chooses to focus attention on this latter topic, the central concern becomes knowledge of language: its nature, origins, and use.
>
> The three basic questions that arise, then, are these:
>
> 1   What constitutes knowledge of language?
> 2   How is knowledge of language acquired?
> 3   How is knowledge of language put to use? (Chomsky, 1986: 3)

Similarly, the shift in the study of values, from an objectivist perspective to a study of their work by practitioners themselves gives rise to the same kinds of question:

1   What constitutes knowledge of values?
2   How is knowledge of values acquired?
3   How is knowledge of values put to use?

These questions apply equally to the study of practices. When a practitioner says, 'I know what I am doing', they imply that they understand and can articulate why they are doing it and what they hope to achieve. This carries all sorts of implications in terms of accountability, honesty and professional commitment.

In this book, the complexities and significance of addressing such questions are reported in the individual chapters where authors explain how they engaged with understanding the values that inform their practices, why they chose one particular value rather than another, what informed their choices, how they use their knowledge, and some of the possible consequences. Each author does this, individually and collectively with co-authors, and from their own articulated values tradition.

Now speaking as editor, therefore, I offer a summary of the contents of the book and introduce the authors and their chapters.

Contents of the book

The book arose from a series of international conferences on Value and Virtue in Practice-Based Research, at York St John University, York, UK. The sixth conference took place in 2016. Given that the conference was situated in higher education, and that many presenters work in higher education, a main theme emerged as what should be the aims of higher education research, and what values should inform those aims. The theme winds throughout the chapters.

First, in Chapter 1, David Maughan Brown, former Vice Chancellor of York St John, sets the scene by examining how different perspectives on the values base of higher education research may be represented through different government policies, and how this in turn influences understandings of the nature of higher education institutional and research practices.

Ten chapters follow. Each contains ideas about the conceptualisation of the values base of practices, and explains how the values are realised in practice, or, if not, what kinds of constraints prevented this. They also offer explanations for how and why those practices may be justified as virtuous. The chapters are as follows.

- Chapter 2 is by Carla Solvason, who outlines how she and colleagues adopt a speculative attitude to their work, wondering how they can understand more clearly how and why their work with students may be considered ethical.
- Chapter 3, by Cheryl Hunt, considers the importance of autoethnography as a morally committed methodology: it is ethically responsible, she argues, to study oneself before studying others.
- Similarly, in Chapter 4, Julian Stern considers the personal in higher education research, from different perspectives: 'Researching your own students', 'Researching your own colleagues', and 'Researching colleagues in other higher education institutions'.
- Jane Rand, in Chapter 5, explains how she has combined different methodological approaches to form what she calls 'open-logic sense making'.

- In Chapter 6, Linda Pavītola, Lāsma Latsone and Dina Bethere question how the core research values of openness and criticality may be more fully developed in the context of higher education research in Latvia.
- Chapter 7, by Jon Nixon, Alison Buckley, Andy Cheng, Sue Dymoke, Jane Spiro and Jonathan Vincent shows, through its structure and form, what it means to open up a collaborative conversation.
- In Chapter 8, Josephine Bleach shows the potential benefits of developing these kinds of conversations throughout a community.
- Chapter 9 offers an explanation by Joseph Shosh for how he supports under-graduate and postgraduate students in producing their accounts of educational practices.
- In Chapter 10, Christopher Branson, Margaret Franken and Dawn Penney consider how different values enter debates about middle leadership practices; they offer their own stand in relation to new, transrelational forms of middle leadership.
- Finally, in Chapter 11, Hugh Mehan shows how unwavering commitments to egalitarian values can lead to the realisation of more democratic and futures-oriented practices for all.

A note about my own editorial practices

As noted, I occupy two positions in the book, as editor and author of this chapter. As editor I have had the privilege of working with individual authors, mainly through engaging in what I hope have been educational conversations where we have developed increasingly critical insights about the content and form of research texts. I have in turn sent my draft chapter to authors, inviting their critical feedback and acting on it. All authors, including myself, have reached our best thinking to date, though we acknowledge that the thinking will develop through further conversational engagement. This means that the book represents work in progress. A core value of higher education research emerges as a commitment to hold one's ideas open to new influences and insights. Like life, therefore, the production of research texts is always work in progress.

I now re-position myself as author, and set out my personal perspectives.

Personal perspectives on the values base of higher education research

My understanding is that the ideas in the book have important implications for higher education and for educational research in general, specifically in relation to an ongoing debate about the differences between education research and educational research. A formal debate was launched, to my knowledge, in the 1970s, when John Elliott made the point, broadly speaking, that education research refers to research on or about education, whereas educational research (as a form

of real-world research, or research in action) becomes educational for the participants involved. Reflecting on his contribution, he says:

> In various past writings I have argued that ... educational research is best
> viewed as a form of action research directed towards the moral/practical
> ends of education rather than the discovery of disinterested facts about edu-
> cation (see Elliott 1980, ... 1987 ...). (Elliott, 2007: 185)

What is distinctive about the difference, he argues, is that each form is informed
by different kinds of values: 'What the distinction does is highlight the special significance of a form of research which requires the active engagement of
[practitioners] because it is conditioned by educational values' (2007: 186).
(I have substituted 'practitioners' for Elliott's 'teachers', because I think everyone
in every walk of life is potentially a teacher.)

The distinction has been debated over the years, and became a core issue in the
2005 BERA Presidential address by Geoff Whitty who said that:

> [O]ne way of handling the distinction might be to use the terms 'education
> research' and 'educational research' more carefully. ... I have so far used the
> broad term education research to characterise the whole field [of education
> studies]; but it may be that within that field we should reserve the term
> educational research for work that is consciously geared towards improving
> policy and practice. (Whitty, 2006: 173, emphasis in original)

These distinctions are not trivial: they raise issues about what should constitute
the proper focus of research in higher education, and how judgements should be
made about its ethical basis. Further, the debate, in my view, has implications for
how the nature of a new public sphere should be understood, a point debated in
the literatures from often widely different perspectives (for example, Kim, 2011
and Thijssen et al., 2013). My own understanding of a public sphere is that it
provides a space where people may come together, on an equal footing, to debate
issues in a free and untrammelled way in order to take purposeful action in the
social world. Higher education should do just that. This is, in my view, what makes
this book distinctive: it communicates an understanding that, rather than simply
speaking hypothetically about the need for a new public sphere (which is a common stance in the literatures), authors offer their own stories of practice to show
what such a public sphere might look like and how it may be created. The book
thereby comes to represent such a public sphere itself. The perennial question,
'How should we live?' takes on real-life meaning as authors ask questions about
how higher education researchers involved in educational practices should live
and practise. Further, they confront some of the dilemmas involved, including
what emerges as a core problematic – recognising that definitive answers or clear
guidelines about which values to choose are simply not available. While there

are historically many attempts to do this – philosophy is full of them – still no universally agreed, overarching guidelines exist to explain why one value should be adopted rather than another. Nevertheless, all authors explain, as an inherent aspect of their texts, how they work with available intellectual materials to try to understand how to improve their practices for the benefit of others and thereby hold themselves accountable for what they do.

The hope is that this collection of essays may contribute to the emergent body of literatures that do see higher education as an organic form of public sphere, an opportunity for engaged public debate in relation to the values base of practices; but now in terms of what Eikeland (2006) calls 'communities of inquiry' rather than only communities of practice, in that all participants are involved in inquiry. This book represents such a community of educational inquiry: all participants, individually and collectively, show how their work is informed by educational values, how they actively inquire and research rather than position themselves as consumers of others' research. They refuse simplistically to apply others' theories to their own practices; they accept the responsibility of generating their own theories of practice. Each chapter therefore represents a research account that contains explanations for why authors choose to ground their practices in specific values, why they espouse those values and not others, and therefore why they practise as they do.

This returns us to the idea of an emergent conversation, and new questions arise, about what issues the conversation might address. For me, the three questions above, regarding what constitutes knowledge of values and practices, and how this knowledge is acquired and used become main topics, discussed now.

What constitutes knowledge of values?

Values influence every part of our lives: they 'saturate practice', says Nixon (2008: 42) and give meaning to what we do as virtuous researchers (see also Harland and Pickering, 2011; Stern, 2015). This idea, however, begs an explanation for the link between the concepts of values and virtues. My understanding (writing still as author of this chapter and therefore speaking for myself) is that when we accept particular values as part of our everyday practices, we internalise them as virtues. 'Virtues', therefore, should not be seen as decontextualised 'right' or 'appropriate' qualities or characteristics, as presented in some classical and contemporary literatures: the concept of virtue is, for me, part of the process of trying to live by articulated values and finding an appropriate language to communicate the importance of transforming values into virtues. 'Virtue' therefore refers to a process, not an object; it becomes an activity, a process of living in the direction of identified values and, one hopes, living them fully as practices. The task of showing how we justify our choices as researchers then becomes a core virtue: we show how we hold ourselves accountable for our choices.

This is where higher education researchers come under intense pressure to conform to normative understandings and practices, communicated through what have until recently been seen as the dominant, 'authorised' literatures. These normative understandings include the idea that only certain values qualify as proper values, usually socially acceptable values such as hard work, tenacity, compassion, collegiality, dialogue and regard for the other. Those literatures fail to recognise, however, that this represents a false image of real life. As people living in the real world, academics have to acknowledge that there are different kinds of values: everyone can hold nasty values as well as nice, socially acceptable ones, and we have to accept that this is part of our human condition. Most people are, on occasion, greedy and self-serving; we commit at least minor crimes, tell lies, and manipulate others in order to get our own way. Such occurrences do not happen by chance; we make deliberate choices about them. I often wonder why many people tend to position Gandhi as a saint and Al Capone as an out and out sinner. Al held strong family values (see Capone, 2011), believed in rules and good order, and provided sustenance for the needy. The story is told, for example, how Al set up a regular soup kitchen during the dark days of the Depression:

> Though his participation was never firmly established, one soup kitchen attendant told a reporter that Capone was indeed behind the charitable effort. 'Nobody else was doing it,' he said, 'and Mr Capone couldn't stand it seeing so many poor fellows dying of starvation. Not heart failure, mind you, but starvation. ...' (Eig, 2010: 302)

However, a discussion of these kinds of values dilemmas do not easily get into traditionalist educational research literatures, although they do get into the literatures of criminology and pathology. But acknowledging that we occasionally tell lies and manipulate others does not mean we are pathological: it means we are human, trying to improve while having to use our own judgement about what 'improvement' looks like. Further, there is no overarching view of what 'improvement' means or looks like because there is no 'ideal state' that 'improvement' leads to. This raises questions about whether the idea of an 'ideal state' or 'utopia' might itself be damaging to human interactions. This was a core theme in the work of Isaiah Berlin, who spoke, for example, about 'the crooked timber of humanity' (1990): trees do not grow straight; people are not perfect, because there is no such thing as perfection. The imposition of freedom becomes a betrayal of the concept of freedom (Berlin, 2002). The idea of perfection is part of the intellectual tradition that says we are heading in a specific direction, with clear guidelines about how to get there, and we have to make rational choices about these things. Berlin critiques this idea of a utopia, as well as a fundamentalist reliance on rationality, that we can find 'right answers' provided we look hard enough: 'This is to say that, on this traditional view, not only does every genuine question have one right answer, but that all these answers are mutually compatible, or even entailed by one another' (Gray, 1995b: 42).

These issues have special significance for higher education practitioners, set out, for example, by Stephen Rowland's (2006) arguments:

> If the university consists of two cultures (academic and managerial) in conflict, it is to a large extent internalized by all involved. It is not so much a problem of 'us against them', but one of addressing the identity conflict that is experienced by all involved. (p. 118)

How do we resolve the identity conflict when we try to live in the direction of our own educational values while caught in the demand to adopt (usually) very different values of corporate institutions?

Yet other intellectual traditions, while visible over centuries, have actively emerged to challenge old ones, possibly in light of the new social order presented by globalism and a runaway world (Giddens, 2002). Powerful contemporary works (for example from Said (1991), Mouffe (2013), Gray (1995a) and Berlin himself (2002)) hold that, instead of searching for a rational grounding for decisions about how to live, we should instead consider an agonistic approach, where 'agon' refers to a struggle or contest (Gray, 1995b: 100). On this view, there are no single 'right' answers to moral dilemmas: nor is there 'any overarching or undergirding standard whereby the goods and virtues recognized in different cultural traditions can be put in the balance and weighed' (Gray, 1995b: 45). Further, and to introduce another confounding variable, we also need to remember that '[w]e are beings thrown into the world who are always shaped by and shaping the traditions that form us' (Bernstein, 1991: 24). We negotiate and do our best with whatever intellectual and practical resources we have: we need to recognise that what may be simplistically held as 'right' and 'wrong' more often appears as competing rights, as in, for example, questions about who gets the children when parents part; and we always need to bear in mind that we may, after all, be mistaken (Polanyi, 1958).

These different perspectives in the literatures mean that academics need to be critical of their choices. Even so, according to Bernstein, while we always need to exercise tentativeness and critique towards our own thinking as well as that of others, we also need to take a stand, otherwise we will go in ever-repeating spirals of regress until we are paralysed by inaction. We need to recognise that there is no final answer. According to Loy (2010), every story is underpinned by another story. There is no one story that tells us which story is the 'right' story; and this in itself is a story. So perhaps a practical strategy for finding our way of being in the world is to tread cautiously, testing out ideas and influences, and acting with discernment and thought for others. In my view (emphasising again that I am speaking as author, not editor, though I think fellow authors may share some of these views), a commitment to values pluralism means challenging the idea of a monist, one-dimensional view of values, a view that accepts only one specific form of living as valuable, as well as only one form of thinking about values, informed by rational choices about why these should be promoted as virtues. I worry about the idea that only specific forms of life may qualify as part of a 'good' life, and that the idea of 'good' may be understood only in a particular way, usually in terms of achieving a designated end point where human flourishing is guaranteed.

Yet I recognise here a sweet internal irony: in taking my stand I am actually doing the very thing in practice that I disagree with in theory. I note Gray's comment (1995a: 70) that recognising the incommensurability of values is 'a radical denial of the meaning of perfection', yet I appear to be opting for a view of a perfect (or at least more perfect) view of living, in that it is desirable, for me anyhow. How to negotiate one's way through the maze of contradictions with no golden thread to guarantee a return? But we do need to take a stand, as Bernstein says, and this is where I take mine.

However, where I feel on more solid ground is in Berlin's idea of negative and positive freedoms. Berlin proposed, as core to his entire project, the idea that freedom was a requisite for critical thinking. Further, he said, there are two forms of freedom – negative and positive freedom (see his 1969). Positive freedom, he says, enables us to choose between competing sets of values and lay the foundations for creating our lives as we wish. Negative freedom is freedom from the constraint to choose between only a limited number of options. This, for Berlin, was the most basic form of freedom that allows for the positive freedom of creating one's life as one wishes, whether that may be seen as reputable or disreputable, though always in negotiation with others.

This view holds that there is no specified 'end point' to human living: we should act from our own principled decisions rather than follow definitive rules or codes of practice. The idea of a utopia, in my view, needs to be challenged as misleading: it means we are always condemned to leading a life of imperfection if we disagree with the established moral canon. For me, practices, especially research practices, are informed by an understanding that multiple forms of values, and multiple forms of thinking about values, are available and worthy of consideration. It is then the choice of freethinking, thoughtful and informed people to choose wisely and be prepared to explain how they hold themselves accountable for their choices.

These are problematic, often irresolvable issues, which each person has to decide for her or himself. I agree with Hannah Arendt (1970) that the prime task of citizens is to think: this especially applies to people in higher education whose job description includes focused, purposeful thinking, even (perhaps especially) in these days of corporate managerialism. The task, in my view, is to use that thinking to challenge those very managerialist forms that threaten to close it down. Freedom, for me, is both the outcome and the condition for thinking. It is an outcome in that we begin to question why we should go along with the mainstream, and why we should not think against the current, as Berlin (1997) suggests. It is a condition, as set out by Sen (1999), in that development, including intellectual development, has to be rooted in an understanding that we are at liberty to question established ways of being and thinking, and take control of the idea that we can create our own lives in ways appropriate for ourselves, while recognizing that we are always in relation with others, our environment and the planet. Freedom is, to cite George Orwell (2004), being allowed to say, if we wish, in spite of violent efforts to make us say different, that two and two really does equal four.

So ...

How is knowledge of values acquired?

Earlier, I indicated that what might be seen as 'authorised' literatures are gradually losing their privileged status. This may be for several reasons: mainly because the oppositional force of a flood of new texts by new authors, committed to new practice-based forms of knowledge and its production, systematically challenge the stereotypical view of higher education as only about the creation of abstract knowledge and pure theory (Gibbons et al., 1994). As happens when an abundance of rain falls, former tributaries can swell and become a flood, absorbing the main stream and carrying it along as part of a new flow. This appears to be happening today: real-world, practice-based texts, supported by new digital resources, open access technology, self and online publishing and social media networking enable the freer flow of information and new ideas and easier access to peer critique.

This new swell of voices carries implications, including the following.

'Ordinary people' should represent themselves

Those same authorised literatures carry an assumption that only certain people are able or allowed to speak for themselves: see Marx's (1987) critique that so-called 'ordinary people' 'cannot represent themselves: they must be represented' (cited in Said, 1995: xiii). Two examples of this assumption are, first, from Chomsky (1989), reporting on writings from Harold Lasswell and Reinhold Niebuhr:

> Harold Lasswell explained in the *Encyclopaedia of the Social Sciences* that we should not succumb to 'democratic dogmatisms about men being the best judges of their own interests.' They are not; the best judges are the elites, who must, therefore, be ensured the means to impose their will, for the common good. (Chomsky, 1989: 17)

And second, from Berlin (2002), who cites Fichte as saying:

> To men as they are in their ordinary education, our philosophical theory must be absolutely unintelligible, for the object of which it speaks does not exist for them; they do not possess that special faculty for which, and by which, alone this object has any being. It is as if one were talking to men blind from birth; men who know things and their relations only by touch, and one spoke to them about colours and the relations of colours. (cited in Berlin, 2002: 51–52)

These somewhat extreme examples may be supplemented by more mundane contemporary texts that, however, betray much the same attitudes: for example, that 'intellectuals' are to be found only in universities (Corcoran and Lalor, 2012), or that so-called 'practitioners' cannot generate academic theory (Taber, 2013). This is the same kind of thoughtless theorising that was challenged by Sojouner Truth in 1951 when she asked 'Ain't I a woman?', demanding, as a former slave and working-class woman, the same rights as black middle-class women, a claim taken up by bell hooks (1987), who challenged racism and classism within the feminist movement.

Further, critiques of these kinds of imperialist attitudes are challenged from within higher education itself, especially by those academics who have come up through the ranks and retain strong commitments to the practice bases of their earlier workplace professional identities. They also contribute to a new groundswell of literatures of everyday practices. Brinkmann, whose own texts contribute to the field, explains how qualitative inquiry should be seen as 'a vital human activity that all human beings are engaged in' (2012: 15). He reports:

> The term 'everyday life' has entered many corners of the social sciences today. Classical works have investigated 'the presentation of the self in everyday life' (Goffman, 1959), 'everyday life in the modern world' (Lefebvre, 1968) and 'the practice of everyday life' (de Certeau, 1984). More specific approaches, such as ethnomethodology (Garfinkel, 1967) and symbolic interactionism (Blumer, 1969), have also advocated a focus on the mundane details of human interaction as the key to understanding social processes. A focus on our everyday lives becomes particularly central in a postmodern era, when society 'has been broken apart and reconstituted as everyday life' (Ferguson, 2009, p. 160).

This is not to mention my own field of action research, with its broad family of different approaches (Reason and Bradbury, 2001, 2008; Noffke and Somekh, 2009), with overlaps to appreciative inquiry (Cooperrider and Whitney, 2005), autoethnography (Denzin, 2013) and self-study (Samaras, 2011). Everyday life is everywhere, and recognised as such.

The 'New Literacies' movement

Those same new literatures have led to an increased focus on 'the New Literacies' (see for example the New London Group, 1996), the need for social and political literacy in order to 'read the world' (Freire and Macedo, 1987). We need critically to read the social and political Discourses that surround us, as communicated through oral and written texts: see, for example, the analysis by Clark and Ivanič (1997: 30) of how military personnel from different sides are presented in the media, taken from reports in the *Guardian* across one week (Table I.1).

Table 1.1 Extracts from Clark and Ivacič (1997: 30)

We have –	They have –
Army, Navy and Air Force	A war machine
Brave	Fanatical
Pre-emptively	Without provocation
Gallant boys	Overgrown schoolchildren

Stories from real people's experience

There is now recognition of the need to access the stories of real people rather than rely on established authors' privileged interpretations: in media studies, for example, this manifests as the telling of stories from the perspectives of the oppressed rather than the oppressor, as in 'Dances with Wolves'. Everett (2012) learns about the nature of language from real-life experience; Ingold (2011) argues that anthropology should be seen as 'a sustained and disciplined inquiry into the conditions and potentials of human life' (p. 3). Dee Brown's (1991/1970) *Bury My Heart at Wounded Knee* emphasises the importance of accessing primary sources. He writes (p. xv):

> During that time [of the invasion of the American West by white settlers] the culture and civilization of the American Indian was destroyed, and out of that time came virtually all the great myths of the American West – tales of fur traders, mountain men, steamboat pilots, goldseekers, gamblers, gunmen, cavalrymen, cowboys, harlots, missionaries, schoolmarms, and homesteaders. Only occasionally was the voice of an Indian heard, and then more often than not it was recorded by the pen of a white man. The Indian was the dark menace of the myths, and even if he [sic] had known how to write in English, where would he have found a printer or a publisher?

Even so, I learned more from the experience of visiting the memorial site at Wounded Knee and listening to Native Americans there and elsewhere than from reading any text about the need to respect indigenous cultures and ways of knowing.

Academic voices only

And a final critical comment at this point, that texts continue to be written, almost exclusively, by authors in or associated with academia, including myself. While they may speak of the need for 'ordinary people' to speak for themselves, the fact remains that the dominant academic voice denies access by those same 'ordinary people'. This has profound implications for the third question, about how knowledge of values may be put to use.

How is knowledge of values put to use?

In 1967, Chomsky spoke about the responsibility of intellectuals. Intellectuals, he argued,

> ... are in a position to expose the lies of governments, to analyze actions according to their causes and motives and often hidden intentions. In the Western world at least, they have the power that comes from political liberty, from access to information and freedom of expression. (p. 60)

The responsibility of intellectuals, he concludes, is 'to speak the truth and to expose lies' (p. 60). I agree, though I do not think this goes far enough. I also agree with Chomsky (1987) that intellectuals do not work only in higher education settings. Highly critical discussions are conducted daily by persons who call themselves mechanics, hairdressers and laundry attendants; they do not call themselves intellectuals, though they are. However, the popular view remains that intellectuals do work exclusively in higher education settings.

Coming closer to home, to academic settings, Said (1994) argues that the responsibility of intellectuals is to challenge uncritical orthodoxies, while recognising that those same intellectuals must be guided by their own values commitments. 'There are no rules by which intellectuals can know what to say or do: nor for the true secular intellectual are there any gods to be worshiped and looked to for unwavering guidance' (p. xii). Further, 'Intellectual representations are the *activity itself*, dependent on a kind of consciousness that is skeptical, engaged, unremittingly devoted to rational investigation and moral judgment: and this puts the individual on record and on the line' (p.15, emphasis in original). Said communicates his own position as always to be alert to the need for critique:

> I take criticism so seriously that, even in the very midst of a battle in which one is unmistakably on one side against another, there should be criticism, because there must be critical consciousness if there are to be issues, problems, values, even lives to be fought for. (Said, 1991: 28)

Yes – yet, in my view, this capacity for critique must first be directed to oneself. For all kinds of reasons – appeals to democracy, moral and egalitarian impulses – it makes little sense to critique others without critiquing oneself first. Howard Zinn comments on this idea: in justifying his teaching and public lectures he explains:

> I didn't pretend to an objectivity that was neither possible nor desirable. 'You can't be neutral on a moving train,' I would tell [the audience, often students]. Some were baffled by the metaphor, especially if they took it literally and tried to dissect its meaning. Others immediately saw what I meant: that events are already moving in certain deadly directions, and to be neutral means to accept that. (Zinn, 2002: 8)

This capacity for critique, says Zinn, is what qualifies one to call oneself an intellectual: to reflect on what you are doing, and on the thinking and the values that enter into that thinking. He shows this commitment by reflecting on his part in the warfare he critiques; as a trained bombardier he had dropped bombs on cities, killing innocent people, as is happening today around the world. He had not engaged in what Schön and Rein (1994) term 'frame reflection', the capacity to critique one's own thinking while using that form of thinking to do so, a hugely difficult task, as noted throughout, yet essential if one is to engage in debates about values pluralism and the need to make choices about the process of making choices.

These ideas bring me to a consideration of some implications for higher education research.

So what? Significance of the ideas

The views expressed here carry significant implications for higher education academic researchers, including the following (there are many more).

Need to know in a complex runaway world

Appadurai (1996: 168) says that all people have a right to research, to access:

> those tools through which any citizen can systematically increase that stock of knowledge which they consider most vital to their survival as human beings and to their claims as citizens.

It could also be argued that we all have a responsibility to research, to know what is going on in the wider world and to use our knowledge wisely in the service of others as well as ourselves. Sennett (2009: 1) tells the story of how, in 'the days in 1962 when the world was on the brink of atomic war' Hannah Arendt, his former teacher stopped him on a freezing New York street, oblivious to the cold: 'She wanted me to draw the right lesson: people who make things usually don't understand what they are doing.' If you open Pandora's box, he says, you release all the evils of the world as well as the goods. We need to know why we do what we do, and think carefully about some of the consequences.

Demonstrating epistemic responsibility

Similarly, Lorraine Code (1987) outlines a key problem in matters of knowing and knowledge. She argues that ignorance of codes does not excuse a breach of them. For example:

> If a North American motorist rents a car in Britain and proceeds to drive on the right-hand side of the road, thereby causing an accident, the courts will

not accept as an excuse that he or she did not know that one drives on the left in Britain. One who takes the wheel of a car has a responsibility to know the rules of the road. (p. 1)

Analogously, if a higher education researcher undertakes research, they need to know that research is about knowledge creation, and questions arise regarding the uses of the knowledge they create. This idea is especially relevant for higher education researchers: we need to think about the potential consequences of the use of our knowledge and decide how to use it well (see Lilla's 2001 account of Heidegger's 'reckless' use of his knowledge). We also need to consider the possible uses of our knowledge once it is put into the social world and is no longer under our control. How do we build in appropriate safeguards to the potential misuses of our research findings?

Potential for the co-construction of new texts and discourses

The New Literacies movements (above) emphasise that simply knowing how to produce texts is not enough; we also need to know what is happening in wider contexts that affect the everyday lives of people. This kind of reading is essential within the current higher education climate of increasing organisational and intellectual control. There are signs everywhere of the quiet, unobtrusive establishment of cultures that require a uniform commitment to specific ways of thinking (see again Orwell, 2004). Mandated forms of thinking do not require, and often actively disallow critique, let alone self-critique. However, when higher education practitioners join forces with practitioners in other workplaces, new forms of knowledge can emerge through the combination of the different forms of knowledge each party brings to the relationship. It is this idea of the solidarity of intellectuals from multiple workplaces, speaking in unison from within their positioning in an increasingly multicultural and polyphonic world, that carries hope for the future.

Conclusion: Challenging limited choices

The united voices of the book challenge, and thereby destablise, the imposition of those established intellectual traditions that allow us to choose only from the limited choices provided by the gatekeepers of those traditions. To repeat, the task of all humans, says Hannah Arendt (1970), is to think. We hope that our book shows our capacity for thinking, and for thinking about thinking, to find ways of creating, through higher education, a more intellectually turbulent, and thereby a more peaceful and productive world than the one we are living in at present.

References

Appadurai, A. (1996) 'The right to research', *Globalizations, Societies and Education*, 4 (2): 167–77.
Arendt, H. (1970) *Men in Dark Times*. London: Jonathan Cape.

Berlin, I. (1969) *Four Essays on Liberty*. London: Oxford University Press.
Berlin, I. (ed. H. Hardy) (1990) *The Crooked Timber of Humanity*. London: John Murray.
Berlin, I. (ed. H. Hardy) (1997) *Against the Current*. London: Pimlico.
Berlin, I. (ed. H. Hardy) (2002) *Freedom and Its Betrayal: Six Enemies of Human Liberty*. London: Chatto & Windus.
Bernstein, R. (1991) *The New Constellation: The Ethical-political Horizons of Modernity/Postmodernity*. London: Polity.
Blumer, H. (1969) *Symbolic Interactionism: Perspective and Method*. Englewood Cliffs, NJ: Prentice-Hall.
Brinkmann, S. (2012) *Qualitative Inquiry in Everyday Life: Working with Everyday Life Materials*. London: Sage.
Brown, D. (1991/1970) *Bury My Heart at Wounded Knee: An Indian History of the American West*. London: Vintage.
Capone, D. (2011) *Uncle Al Capone*. [No location recorded] Recap Publishing.
Chomsky, N. (1967) 'The responsibility of intellectuals', from *American Power and the New Mandarins* (pp. 23–126), reproduced in N. Chomsky (1987) *The Chomsky Reader* (ed. J. Peck). London: Serpent's Tail: pp. 59–136.
Chomsky, N. (1986) *Knowledge of Language*. New York: Praeger.
Chomsky, N. (1989) *Necessary Illusions: Thought Control in Democratic Societies*. London: Pluto.
Clark, R. and Ivanič, R. (1997) *The Politics of Writing*. London: Routledge.
Code, L. (1987) *Epistemic Responsibility*. Hanover: Brown University Press.
Cooperrider, D. and Whitney, D. (2005) *Appreciative Inquiry*. San Francisco: Berrett-Koehler.
Corcoran, M.P. and Lalor, K. (eds) (2012) *Reflections on Crisis: The Role of the Public Intellectual*. Dublin: Royal Irish Academy.
de Certeau, M. (1984) *The Practice of Everyday Life*. Berkeley, CA: University of California Press.
Denzin, N. (2013) *Interpretive Autoethnography*. Los Angeles: Sage.
Eig, J. (2010) *Get Capone*. New York: Simon and Schuster.
Eikeland, O. (2006) 'Condescending ethics and action research: an extended review article', *Action Research*, 4 (1): 37–47.
Elliott, J. (1980) 'Educational action research', in J. Nesbit and S. Nesbit (eds) *Research, Policy and Practice*. London: Kogan Page. Chapter 18.
Elliott, J. (1987) 'Educational theory, practical philosophy and action research', in *British Journal of Educational Studies*, 25 (2): 149–160.
Elliott, J. (2007) *Reflecting Where the Action Is: The Selected Works of John Elliott*. Abingdon: Routledge.
Everett, D. (2012) *Language: The Cultural Tool*. London: Profile Books.
Ferguson, H. (2009) *Self-Identity and Everyday Life*. Abingdon: Routledge.
Freire, P. and Macedo, D. (1987) *Literacy: Reading the Word and the World*. Westport, CT: Bergin and Garvey.
Garfinkel, H. (1967) *Studies in Ethnomethodology*. Cambridge: Polity.
Gibbons, M., Limoges, C., Nowotny, H., Schwartzman, S., Scott, P. and Trow, M. (1994) *The New Production of Knowledge*. London: Sage.
Giddens, A. (2002) *Runaway World*. London: Profile Books.
Goffman, E. (1959) *The Presentation of Self in Everyday Life*. New York: The Overlook Press.
Gray, J. (1995a) *Enlightenment's Wake: Politics and Culture at the Close of the Modern Age*. London: Routledge.
Gray, J. (1995b) *Berlin*. London: Fontana.

Harland, A. and Pickering, N. (2011) *Values in Higher Education Teaching.* Abingdon: Routledge.

hooks, b. (1987) *Ain't I a Woman? Black Women and Feminism.* London: Pluto.

Ingold, T. (2011) *Being Alive: Essays on Movement, Knowledge and Description.* Abingdon: Routledge.

Kim, S. (2011) *Theology in the Public Sphere: Public Theology as a Catalyst for Open Debate.* London: SCM Press.

Lefebvre, H. (1968) *Everyday Life in the Modern World.* London: Penguin.

Lilla, M. (2001) *The Reckless Mind: Intellectuals in Politics.* New York: The New York Review of Books.

Loy, D. (2010) *The World Is Made of Stories.* Boston, MA: Wisdom.

Mouffe, C. (2013) *Agonistics: Thinking the World Politically.* London: Verso.

Nixon, J. (2008) *Towards the Virtuous University.* New York: Routledge.

Noffke, S. and Somekh, B. (eds) (2009) *The SAGE Handbook of Educational Action Research.* London: Sage.

Orwell, G. (2004) *Nineteen Eighty-Four.* London: Penguin.

Polanyi, M. (1958) *Personal Knowledge.* London: Routledge & Kegan Paul.

Reason, P. and Bradbury, H. (eds) (2001) *Handbook of Action Research, Participative Inquiry and Practice.* London: Sage.

Reason, P. and Bradbury, H. (eds) (2008) *Handbook of Action Research, Participative Inquiry and Practice* (2nd edn). London: Sage.

Rowland, S. (2006) *The Enquiring University.* Maidenhead: Society for Research into Higher Education and Open University Press.

Said, E. (1991) *The World, the Text and the Critic.* London: Vintage.

Said, E. (1994) *Representations of the Intellectual. The 1993 Reith Lectures.* London: Vintage.

Said, E. (1995) *Orientalism.* London: Routledge & Kegan Paul (new Afterword edition).

Samaras, A. (2011) *Self-Study Teacher Research.* Thousand Oaks, CA: Sage.

Schön, D. and Rein, M. (1994) *Frame Reflection.* New York: Basic Books.

Sen, A. (1999) *Development as Freedom.* Oxford: Oxford University Press.

Sennett, R. (2009) *The Craftsman.* London: Penguin.

Stern, J. (2015) 'Soul-searching and re-searching: action philosophy alone', *Educational Action Research*, 23 (1): 104–115.

Taber, K. S. (2013) 'Action research and the Academy: seeking to legitimise a 'different' form of research', *Teacher Development*, 17 (2): 288–300.

The New London Group (1996) 'A pedagogy of multiliteracies: designing social futures', *Harvard Educational Review*, 66 (1): 60–92.

Thijssen, P., Weyns, W., Timmerman, C. and Mels, S. (eds) *New Public Spheres: Recontextualzing the Intellectual* (2013) Farnham: Ashgate.

Whitty, G. (2006) 'Education(al) research and education policy making: is conflict inevitable?', *British Educational Research Journal*, 32 (2): 159–176.

Zinn, H. (2002) *You Can't Be Neutral on a Moving Train: A Personal History of Our Times.* Boston: Beacon Press.

Chapter 1

Values in higher education

Articulation and action

David Maughan Brown

Introduction

The *Magna Charta Universitatum*, signed by several hundred university Presidents and Rectors from around the world in Bologna in 1988, on the 900th anniversary of the founding of the world's oldest university, is probably the closest one can get to a globally recognised reference for the fundamental values and principles of the university. This kind of recognition of the core values and principles of the university is essential, because these contribute to an understanding of how the purposes of higher education research may be construed and how research should be supported.

In discussing universities' contemporary 'responsiveness and responsibilities' in the light of the *Magna Charta Universitatum*, Luc Weber comments:

> Because society is changing, it needs references and frames for social, political and economic debate, construction of meaning, identity and consensus on policies. The universities have a key role in providing these. ... Some of the duties that higher education is entrusted with can quite easily conflict with each other. In these cases higher education must exercise its sense of responsibility vis-à-vis society, by adopting solutions that maintain and reassert the intellectual, ethical and social values on which it is built. (Weber, 2002: 63)

The general thrust of this chapter will be a reflection on the extent of UK higher education's success or otherwise in maintaining those intellectual, ethical and social values in the face of mounting pressures. My reflections are based on three decades of higher education (HE) experience in South Africa – twenty-one years in a Department of English under apartheid and eleven in university management following the unbanning of the African National Congress – and eleven years in university management in the UK. They lead me to conclude that in the face of relentless external pressures it is just as important for universities in the UK in 2016 to keep the intellectual, ethical and social values on which HE is built to the forefront of their institutional consciousness as it was for universities in South Africa to do so under the apartheid regime in the 1970s and 1980s.

The political context of South Africa in the 1970s and 1980s under the Nationalist government bears little comparison with that of the UK over the past fifteen years, even if they have started to become significantly less dissimilar since 9/11 than one would have hoped. But the extent to which government and media pressures have been brought to bear on HE in the UK over the past decade to shape it to ideological ends is not unlike the way the Nationalist government tried to use HE to serve its ideological ends in South Africa. In both instances the ideological ends have been in tension with, if not actively hostile to, the core values of a liberal higher education. This requires a consideration of what those values might be.

What are the core values of a university?

In exploring this question it is perhaps best to start with what individual higher education institutions publicise as the institutional values that inform their activities. These can be read off from their mission statements. However different the contexts, the values underpinning such statements will usually be found to share a great deal in common.

For example, the Mission Statement of York St John University (the host institution for the series of conferences on Value and Virtue in Practice-Based Research, where the paper that was to become this chapter was first presented) is distinctive mainly in the active assertiveness of its commitment 'to the provision of excellent, open and progressive higher education that embraces difference, challenges prejudice and promotes justice, and is shaped by York St John's Church foundation'. Building on this foundation, the statement goes on, the university will, among other things: 'Foster a supportive, creative, critical and reflective community which promotes personal and professional development for both students and staff'.

The values being articulated here are easily discerned: openness, diversity, equity, inclusiveness, community, creativity and self-reflexiveness. The university is a community of scholars; its role is to enable the personal and professional development of its students and staff. 'Personal' implicitly involves both intellectual and spiritual development. Personal and professional development is generally agreed to involve equipping graduates for productive and ethical employment after they leave university.

However, these values are finding themselves increasingly at odds with the values that have come to inform the dominant discourse about HE in the UK. Further, a sector-wide consideration about 'the kind of university education which is worthwhile, ethical and advances a democratic society' that Melanie Walker identifies as having characterised HE in South Africa over the past forty years (Walker, 2012: 49) seems to have been almost entirely missing from the debate about HE in the UK over the past decade.

In apartheid South Africa in the 1970s and 1980s the central value on which the liberal English language universities set out their stall was academic freedom, articulated in terms of the freedom to choose who should be taught, what they should be taught and who should do the teaching. All three strands of this perspective were anathema to apartheid's segregationist ideologues. Beyond that, the object of the exercise was seen as being to enable each individual student to achieve his or her potential to the fullest.

The concomitant benefits to society were understood along the lines later articulated so well for the UK by Bill Taylor in the Taylor Report, *New Directions for Higher Education Funding*. Taylor argued that good higher education enhances the quality of life, helps to create a more responsible and informed electorate, encourages longer time perspectives and assists in raising cultural tolerance and understanding. This last was particularly important in a South African society deeply divided along ethnic and cultural lines. Higher educational levels also, for Taylor, 'encourage creativity, imagination and the visual and performing arts' (Universities UK, 2001: 2–3).

However, the Afrikaans language universities did not share the same interpretation of academic freedom as the English language universities and were willing to be used by the government as vehicles for the furtherance of Afrikaner Nationalism. It was from these universities that the Nationalists drew their political philosophers, historians and theologians as well as their politicians and the high level functionaries of the apartheid state. History had to be shaped to accord with the segregationist narrative of Nationalist Afrikanerdom; a 'Christian' rationale for racial discrimination needed to be mined from the Bible and apartheid needed to be theorised. Consequently, 'Coloured' and 'Indian' universities were established and universities for Africans set up in the 'Bantustans' – the supposedly 'independent' 'Homelands' – in line with the philosophy of 'separate development'. Universities were thereby perceived as, and used as, key instruments for the furtherance of the Nationalist government's apartheid ideology. All the while, government ministers declared an unwavering commitment to university autonomy, even as they manipulated the funding formulae to the severe disadvantage of universities that opposed their policies.

A comparison between the South African and the UK situation reveals a disturbing parallel. While the ideological ends to which universities are being directed are clearly not the same, there has been in the UK over the past fifteen years a deeply disconcerting descent into an equivalent instrumentalism in the discourse around higher education. This is best exemplified via a brief comparison of the Dearing and Browne reports. For Dearing (as for Taylor) the main purposes of higher education are:

- to inspire and enable individuals to develop their capabilities to the highest potential levels throughout life, so that they grow intellectually, are well-equipped for work, and can contribute effectively to society and achieve personal fulfilment;
- to increase knowledge and understanding for their own sake and to foster their application to the benefit of the economy and society. (Dearing, 1997: 5.11)

Being well-equipped for work and benefiting the economy are explicitly second-order imperatives: what universities are for is 'to play a major role in shaping a democratic, civilised, inclusive society'. It is, says Dearing: '... a hallmark of a civilised society that it pursues knowledge at the highest levels for its own sake and that it seeks knowledge for altruistic, and not only commercial, ends' (Dearing, 1997: 5.44).

Dearing, as recently as 1997, could assert that 'there are values shared throughout higher education and without which higher education, as we understand it, could not exist'. He lists among such values:

- a commitment to the pursuit of truth;
- a responsibility to share knowledge;
- freedom of thought and expression;
- analysing evidence rigorously and using reasoned argument to reach a conclusion;
- a willingness to listen to alternative views and judge them on their merits;
- a commitment to consider the ethical implications of different findings or practices. (Dearing, 1997: 5.39)

In 1997 Dearing identified the main beneficiaries of higher education and, concluding that 'the costs of higher education should be shared among those who benefit from it', identified three: the individual, the employers of graduates, and the State (Dearing, 1997: 18.26).

Fifteen years later, by contrast, Browne starts off by asserting that 'a strong higher education system is an important element in the economy and culture of a leading nation' (Browne, 2010: 14). The precedence given to 'economy' over 'culture' is symptomatic. The discourse, in keeping with the dominant discourse of the UK government over the past decade, is instrumentalist and, although it makes passing and somewhat token reference to the wider value of HE to society, the dominant value – that of economic growth – invariably shows through, as in: 'Higher education institutions (HEIs) generate and diffuse ideas, safeguard knowledge, catalyse innovation, inspire creativity, enliven culture, stimulate regional economies and strengthen civil society' (Browne, 2010: 14).

Any non-financial benefits that might accrue to graduates are therefore always subordinate to a much fuller elaboration of the economic benefits to individuals than had characterised the Dearing Report. According to Browne:

Higher education matters because it transforms the lives of individuals. On graduating, graduates are more likely to be employed, more likely to enjoy higher wages and better job satisfaction, and more likely to find it easier to move from one job to the next. Participating in higher education enables individuals from low income backgrounds and then their families to enter higher status jobs and increase their earnings. (Browne, 2010: 14)

'Transforming the lives of individuals' is seen in purely economic terms. Higher education is transformative for the individual because it enables people to make more money and, for society: 'Higher education matters because it drives innovation and economic transformation' (Browne, 2010: 14). It could, of course, be argued that graduate employment is important, but HE doesn't exist solely to give students the certificates they need to get jobs.

We are told by Browne at some length that HE helps to produce economic growth and output through innovation. The core of the argument goes:

> These benefits are captured in the premium employers pay to employ graduates. A degree provides graduates with an entry to employment as well as a habit of learning. Over the course of a working life the average graduate earns comfortably over £100,000 more, in today's valuation and net of tax, than someone with A levels who does not go to university. (Browne, 2010: 15)

So where Dearing recognised the three main beneficiaries of HE as the State, the individual and employers, it comes as no surprise after this that Browne's focus is entirely on the individual. He downplays the benefit to the State, and while acknowledging that the economy and the employers benefit, he can't think of a way of making employers contribute beyond their employment of graduates. Employing graduates is hardly altruistic. And the current situation is that, with the notable exception of a minimum academic threshold for admission to HE, almost every one of Browne's recommendations has been implemented.

The dominant values are economic and individualistic – shared no doubt with a great many contemporary bankers who have had them reinforced by their university experience. Universities are understood as being about equipping graduates with higher-level skills, and they are expected to put 'employability' at the top of their agendas. Further, universities that wish to aspire to the liberal HE values articulated so well by Dearing are, like the liberal universities in apartheid South Africa, likely to find themselves increasingly isolated. Informed by a dominant ideology that is highly elitist and, for all lip service to the contrary, highly exclusive, UK governments this century have, like the Nationalist government in South Africa, been wholly unashamed in using funding levers to shape the sector to their ideological ends.

Contrast the values inherent in both reports. For Dearing a university education was a public good, though individuals clearly benefit and should share some of the cost. The values imbued in the university include truth, community and public responsibility; virtue resides, among other things, in ethical behaviour. For Browne a university education is overwhelmingly a private good and values are overwhelmingly economically orientated; virtue consists in earning over one's lifetime £100,000 more than people who didn't go to university.

One can only agree with Mark Cleary's comment that there '... is a sense that the role of universities in providing for and building the "public good" is in danger of disappearing with the increased ferocity of a competitive, market driven rhetoric in which individual employability and the graduate premium is the ultimate measure of what a university does' (Cleary, 2011: 41).

One brief example must suffice by way of illustration of the kind of outcome one can expect if governments are going to manipulate higher education evaluation processes and funding mechanisms to narrowly focussed and politically expedient ideological ends. November 2013 saw the deadline for submissions to the 2014 Research Excellence Framework (REF) which determined universities' research funding for the six years after 2015. The increasing instrumentalism that characterised Browne's vision of higher education has resulted in a Treasury-driven insistence that a significant portion of the future funding of research should be based on its measurable economic, social and cultural 'impact'. In the process, blue-sky research – the increase in knowledge and understanding for their own sake – has been drastically devalued.

So in seventeen years we have moved a long way away from Dearing's '… a hallmark of a civilised society [is] that it pursues knowledge at the highest levels for its own sake and that it seeks knowledge for altruistic, and not only commercial, ends'. If it is, as the Dearing report suggests, 'a distinctive feature of an advanced civilisation to seek the advancement of knowledge for its own sake …' (Dearing, 1997: 5.24), the utilitarian instincts of twenty-first century UK governments have clearly set our civilisation on a regressive path. It may have been salutary for the architects of the REF 'impact' agenda to pause for a moment over one of Britain's greatest recent scientific accolades – the Nobel Prize for Physics awarded to Professor Peter Higgs for his theorising of the Higgs-Bosun particle – and to consider whether it would meet the criterion of demonstrating impact. While the award of the Nobel Prize would seem on the face of it to indicate that Higgs's research must have had some impact, it would be difficult thus far to identify any social, economic or cultural benefit. A further disqualifying factor would have been the fact that the key paper was published sixty years ago, since the REF regulations insisted that any 'impact' worth recognising must happen within an arbitrary sixteen years of the research having been undertaken. Professor Higgs's research has served to confirm global understandings of the basis of human life. Sadly it appears that it just hasn't had any 'impact'.

So, what are universities for?

In spite of the commonality, and implicitly the shared values, to be found across University mission statements, the higher education sector as a whole in the UK has been wholly ineffectual in maintaining a coherent collective view on the fundamental question: 'What are universities for?' Universities are not going to be able to provide society with Weber's 'references and frames' (see above) for the 'construction of meaning, identity and consensus on policies' if they are unable to reach a consensus on HE policy. And, if they can't agree on policy, they will certainly not be able to act in concert in striving to achieve the best outcomes for HE as a whole.

Currently too many conflicting sectional interests inform the different groups of universities in the HE sector, as represented by the different 'mission groups', for consensus on the central purpose of HE to be arrived at. While university mission statements might seem to suggest a commonality of underlying values, the discourses of different 'mission groups' often suggest that they are at loggerheads with one another – the most obvious divide being that between the 'research-intensive' universities and the rest.

In South Africa under apartheid, 'divide and rule' was a key dimension of the Nationalist government's political philosophy and strategy. While it seems unlikely that the same degree of conscious political manipulation has characterised the approach to higher education of different UK governments this century, the simple expedient of creating a wholly artificial divide between teaching and research via the allocation of funding from two entirely separate pots to these two inextricably interwoven dimensions of university activity has proved a highly effective divide and rule strategy. The effectiveness of the strategy has been greatly assisted by the passivity of most university leaders in the face of the vagaries of UK government HE policy.

I suspect the general inertness of the sector can be attributed mainly to a desire on the part of university leaders to be seen to be playing the tune that those paying the piper have been calling for, compounded at times by an understandable befuddlement as to exactly what that tune is supposed to be. This last has been at times anything but clear. Government rhetoric promotes a diverse HE sector whereas the funding mechanisms drive towards homogeneity. The rhetoric promotes internationalisation; the practice panders to populist xenophobia. The rhetoric promotes collaboration; the drivers are all towards competition. The rhetoric promotes equal opportunity and pleads for social mobility; wizard wheezes like 'AAB' (not counting students with two As and a B at A-level towards universities' capped numbers) promote elitism and exclusiveness and militate against social mobility.

Even if universities found themselves unable to reach consensus on the broader question of what universities are for, one might reasonably have expected the leaders of the sector to be heard standing up much more assertively in the public square when it came to such matters as a governmental disregard for the findings of scientific research. Universities invariably identify the undertaking of research – the generation of new knowledge – as the core function that distinguishes them from other post-secondary institutions. They would all espouse the values articulated by Dearing as 'a commitment to the pursuit of truth' and 'analysing evidence rigorously and using reasoned argument to reach a conclusion'.

Yet at the national level in the UK, the findings of scientific research, whether practice-based or otherwise, do not appear to have a strong record when it comes to influencing government policy, and university leaders are seldom, if ever, heard trying to intervene. This is most obviously evidenced by any research that runs counter to the emotive prejudices of whatever section of the electorate the ruling party is most anxious not to alienate when the next election comes around. Obvious examples would be research into the importance and safety of GM crops, research that demonstrates that current drug classification in the UK is informed by popular hysteria rather than science, and economic research that demonstrates the extent to which, as Mark Blyth puts it, 'austerity remains an ideology immune to facts and basic empirical refutation' (Blyth, 2013: 226).

If HE is unable to arrive at a consensus, or to provide society with references for debate about the identity and purposes of HE itself, it is not going to be able 'to exercise its sense of responsibility vis-à-vis society, by adopting solutions that maintain and reassert the intellectual, ethical and social values on which it is built' on the wider social and political fronts.

Ethical dilemmas in higher education and in higher education research

Universities are constantly encountering ethical dilemmas of one sort or another that test their adherence to the values espoused in their mission statements. One of the major ethical dilemmas currently being posed for universities in the UK relates to the Boycott, Disinvestment and Sanctions (BDS) campaign currently being promoted in an attempt to further a peaceful and just solution to the ongoing conflict between Israel and Palestine. The cancellation in March 2015 by the University of Southampton of an academic conference on 'International Law and the State of Israel' in response to political pressure, including a 6,400 strong petition, is just one example (Siddique, 2015).

York St John University organised a conference on Peace and Reconciliation at the Hebrew University in Jerusalem in November 2012. The University came under a great deal of pressure to cancel the conference. There was no disagreement whatever between the York St John organisers of the conference and those advocating BDS with regard to the policies and behaviour of Israel in relation to Palestine. But, as is so often the case with moral dilemmas, the choice was between two goods: the good, on the one hand, of active engagement with Israeli academics to demonstrate moral support for the difficult and often dangerous work of those who actively oppose their government's policy and behaviour towards Palestine; and the good, on the other hand, of sending a strong message to the Government of Israel about just how unacceptable those policies are perceived to be by joining the BDS campaign and cancelling the conference. The University Ethics Committee opted for the former and the conference went ahead.

My own position as then Deputy Vice Chancellor was conflicted, as someone who had actively supported a boycott of South African universities – and thereby of my university as an institution and myself as an individual academic – in South Africa during the 1970s and 1980s. There is no question that much of what is happening in Israel and Palestine at present bears strong comparison with apartheid South Africa: land dispossession, the destruction of homes, severe restrictions on movement with consequent unemployment and poverty, targeted extra-judicial assassinations, and so on. One would have expected the liberal values espoused in university mission statements to lead to a principled stand and some kind of action, as they had done where apartheid was concerned. But, unlike the academic boycott of South Africa in the 1970s and 1980s, none of the bodies formally representing the university sector in the UK, such as Universities UK, has formally endorsed an academic boycott. There seemed little point in an individual university undertaking an apparently lone boycott.

The absence of an academic boycott of Israel universally agreed by all UK universities, similar to that of South Africa in the 1970s and 1980s, in spite of the similarities between both contexts and the manifest suffering, seems to me to be symptomatic of the extent to which 'the university', in Weber's terms, has had its attention distracted in the intervening years from the intellectual, ethical and social values on which it is built. This must be attributable, at least in part, to UK government HE policy over the past twenty years – in particular to the ideological fixation on 'competition', which brings with it the requirement for 'differentiation'.

The active promotion of competition between universities in terms of student choice must inevitably serve as a disincentive to collaboration, whether it be in terms of the sharing of resources or the articulation of common purpose. Another of Weber's comments is highly pertinent in this context: 'The climate of strongly increased competition is pushing the public sector to pay more attention to its efficiency, and less to social justice, nationally and internationally' (Weber, 2002: 65).

Weber argues in the essay from which I took the quotation at the beginning of this paper that universities need to be simultaneously 'responsive' and 'responsible'. They clearly need to be responsive to the changing needs of their societies in terms of access, appropriate curricula, funding for students, and keeping up with technological advances. But they also, he argues, have to assume a crucial responsibility towards society because 'they remain practically the only institution able to secure and transmit the cultural heritage of a society, to create new knowledge and to have the professional competences and the right status to analyse social problems independently, scientifically and critically'. To exercise this responsibility, universities need to be autonomous and 'should have the ambition to guide reflection and policy-making in society' (Weber, 2002: 63).

Further, for Weber the idea of 'professionalism' needs to be treated with considerable caution as it carries implications of the economic instrumentalism that has dominated UK government discourse about HE. Weber recognises that HE needs to be 'responsive' to the 'market' and needs to be aware that young graduates will be anxious to find jobs, but he asserts that universities should not 'reduce or abandon the disciplines providing a general education without specific professional knowledge or … transform their teaching programs to make them more professionally oriented' (Weber, 2002: 68). They should not do this, he says, because they have a 'long-term responsibility towards society': 'The welfare and cohesion of a society depends ... on knowledge, the rate of return of which cannot be evaluated in terms of economic growth.' He goes on to say:

> ... ethical issues raised by the development of science, the consequences of economic development on the environment, or the increasing divide between those who have and can and those who have not and cannot, require that programs aim not only at providing knowledge to the students, but also a better general education and a sense of their responsibility towards the long term interest of society and not only the essentially short term targets of the business world. (Weber, 2002: 68)

Weber's view of the role of the university in society is clearly much closer to those of Lord Taylor and Lord Dearing than they are to those of Lord Browne. It is comforting to note that while being a Lord would appear to be an eligibility requirement of those appointed to produce major policy documents on higher education in the UK, not all eligible Lords are required to think alike.

There is, of course, no inevitable congruence between enhancing professionalism and a narrowly instrumental focus on higher education as the engine of the economy. HE in professional subject areas such as teaching and the caring professions does not have to focus on short-term targets and would, one would hope, aim to inculcate in students a sense of their responsibility towards the long-term interest of society. But it is important to note the caveat implicit in Weber's use of the term in this context.

Weber clearly conceives of HE as a sector capable of providing coherent intellectual and ethical leadership and of exercising a responsibility to society based on consensus. The English language universities in South Africa were able to provide something resembling such leadership in the final decade of apartheid, though very much less so in the previous three decades. As I have suggested in relation to the BDS campaign, when it comes to many of the moral issues facing individual universities in the sector a consensus across the sector is crucial. Universities in the UK have shown themselves entirely unable to arrive at the kind of consensus that could have informed effective resistance to the wilder vagaries of government policy.

The failure of the HE sector in the UK to put forward a persuasive consensual argument in rejecting the instrumentalism of the government's approach to HE and reasserting the values and aims of a liberal higher education has led to a situation that has been summed up very well by J.M. Coetzee, the Nobel Prize winning South African novelist:

> The response of the political class to the university's claim to a special status in relation to the polity has been crude but effectual: if the university, which, when the chips are down, is simply one among many players competing for public funds, really believes in the lofty ideals it proclaims, then it must show it is prepared to starve for its beliefs. I know of no case in which a university

has taken up the challenge. The fact is that the record of universities, over the past 30 years, in defending themselves against pressure from the state has not been a proud one. Resistance (has been) weak and ill organized. (Coetzee, 2013)

In the UK case there is no question that the university would have had to starve. While it would be quixotic for an individual university to take up the challenge, the sector as a whole could do so to considerable effect, if only it were able to act in unison. Government rhetoric is constantly asserting the importance of university graduates to the 'knowledge economy'; the government clearly recognises the extent of the contribution UK universities themselves make to the economy and the lasting damage that would be occasioned by leaving the university sector to starve. Had the universities been able to speak with one voice, and had that voice been backed by a determination to take collective action, the government would have had to take heed.

To revert to the 'impact' example by way of illustration, the university sector as a whole could have taken a stand in insisting, with Lord Dearing, that it is the '... hallmark of a civilised society that it pursues knowledge at the highest levels for its own sake and that it seeks knowledge for altruistic, and not only commercial, ends'. It would have been entirely possible for the universities to agree among themselves that they would be happy to submit the outputs of their research to REF 2014 for peer review but that they would under no circumstances submit 'Impact Case Studies'.

There would have been nothing whatever that HEFCE (Higher Education Funding Council for England), or HEFCE's Treasury masters, could realistically have done about it. It would not have been either practical, or politically or economically sensible, to cut research funding to the universities by the 25 per cent originally earmarked for allocation on the basis of 'impact'. But rather than forming a united front in resisting that particular ideological whim, with the massive and extremely costly burden of work it brought with it – wholly unrelated in any way to the quality of the research which the whole REF exercise was supposed to be evaluating – some universities concluded that they could gain competitive advantage over their rivals by enthusiastically embracing the 'impact' agenda.

One could list many other areas where any attempt by an individual university to hold back the tide would be ineffectual and damaging but concerted protest and collective action on the part of the universities working together could still make a very significant difference. I will mention just two.

First, the funding for tertiary education in the UK in 2010 stood at a princely 1.4 per cent of GDP, below the OECD average of 1.6 per cent, less than half that of the USA and below that of Russia, Brazil and any Western European country for which data are available. These data from the OECD, published in *Education at a Glance 2013* (OECD, 2013), were published on 25 June 2013. The following day George Osborne in his capacity as Chancellor of the Exchequer announced yet further cuts to higher education teaching funding in the Spending Review.

The President of Universities UK, Professor Sir Eric Thomas, responded to this in somewhat less than outraged terms: 'In very difficult economic times, this government has shown its commitment to science and innovation. We welcome this continuing with the maintenance of the science budget in cash terms through to 2015–16 …'.

There was no protest beyond a slightly plaintive, 'This cut to the teaching grant will have real effects in our universities' from the Chair of Universities UK. There was no reference whatever to the OECD data, and no analysis of the lasting damage being done to HE in the UK by this under-spending relative to other countries competing for students with the UK (Universities UK, 2013). These data should be a serious embarrassment to government, but no one is going to feel embarrassed until authoritative persons stir themselves collectively to do the embarrassing.

Second, universities obviously have an immediate interest in the education offered by schools. I have always been puzzled as to why the HE sector in England tolerates an organisation (Ofsted) whose Thursday morning telephone call or whose knock on the door is anticipated by those who suffer its inspections with a dread reserved in totalitarian countries for the secret police, as was the case in South Africa under apartheid. Alex Quigley comments:

> When you couple the impact of league tables and a bad Ofsted inspection the results can be catastrophic for a school and any school leader. The sense of trauma is real and it inhibits the real progress of our education system. It is enough to drive people into fearful disarray. Not only that, it serves as a gross distraction from what should be our core focus: improving teacher quality and improving the quality of student learning. With the time invested in sheer protective measures to escape such a perilous fate, students indeed suffer. (Quigley, 2013)

What kind of 'quality enhancement' agency is it that appears to think that quality is enhanced by the traumatizing of those it is supposed to be supporting? This is another area of direct import to UK universities where their collective action – easily exercised by the simple expedient of asserting their right of selective entry onto their campuses – could surely make a salutary difference.

Resisting the instrumentalism of the Lord Browne approach to HE and upholding the informing values identified by Lord Dearing involves being sceptical about language usage. Just as we should resist labelling our students as 'customers' when they are co-producers of knowledge rather than passive recipients of a purchased qualification, so we need to retain some intellectual distance from, if not scepticism of, the concept of an HE 'market' in general.

Martin Hall makes an important point when he says:

> To insist that an educational qualification is a commodity to be traded on price in a competitive market is to encourage the use of a university degree as a positional good – a signifier of status rather than a record of the value that

a person has gained from higher education … a place at university comes to be a reward for prior advantage and attainment, rather than recognition for the potential to succeed. (Hall, 2011: 33)

A degree from what those in government and the media choose to refer to as a 'top university' may, thanks to its value as a positional good, be a ticket to employment by employers uncritically accepting of the 'top' epithet. But there is no virtue whatever to be found in admitting A* A-level students and turning them out three years later with wholly predictable first and upper second class degrees. The potential to succeed cannot automatically be read off from A-levels. Nor is 'the value that a person has gained from higher education' encapsulated in the final classification of his or her degree. That value is to be found in students' entire experience of university life and the way that experience enhances their lives as graduates and the lives of those around them.

Conclusion

I would like to conclude this discussion of higher education values (and their implications for research practices) by quoting a passage from Bill Williamson and Frank Coffield that poses two questions that have haunted me since I first read them some nineteen years ago:

> Forced into a market place in which the services they provide have to be tailored to the needs of powerful stakeholders in government or industry, universities could well lose their ability to question critically the society in which they function. Who would then fill that small but essential critical space on which the fragile values of democracy depend? Which voices then would speak loudest in the already shrunken public realm of modern societies? (Williamson and Coffield, 1997: 122)

In recent years representative institutional voices in UK higher education have been almost totally silent when it comes to the critical questioning of the society in which they function. Universities have found themselves cast as atomistic stall-holders in a marketplace where the services they provide have had to be tailored to the needs of the powerful stakeholder in government. Upholding the liberal values that informed many of their mission statements, let alone the 'fragile values of democracy', has become subordinate to meeting the accountability requirements for continued government funding.

What is different now, in comparison with the situation ten years ago, is that the powerful stakeholder in government has in large measure given away the right to call the tune by deciding to withdraw from directly subsidising university teaching in most subjects. This hasn't stopped it, of course, from continually increasing the regulatory burden it demands in exchange for the money it is no longer giving.

One might ask in passing what other government of a developed country provides no direct subsidy whatever for the university teaching of the Arts, Humanities, Social Sciences, Commerce and Law. But this effective privatisation of large parts of the HE sector should have the salutary effect of enabling the universities both to feel less constrained in fulfilling their role in questioning critically the society in which they function and of rethinking their level of necessary subservience to the ideology of whatever political party happens to be in power.

At a critical moment in the post-apartheid transformation of the University of Natal twenty years ago I found myself suggesting to the University Senate that if the University allowed itself to be pushed into abandoning the values and principles it had tried to stand by for the previous forty or more years it would lose its soul as a university. In the event, the University refused to abandon those values and principles, successfully weathered that moment of crisis and went on by the end of the 1990s to be heralded by senior representatives of the post-apartheid government as the best example in the country of successful HE transformation. That success can be attributed to a commitment on the part of staff to an understanding of what universities are about, and the values that should inform them, which coincided with Lord Dearing's view that universities exist 'to inspire and enable individuals to develop their capabilities to the highest potential levels throughout life, so that they grow intellectually, are well-equipped for work, can contribute effectively to society and achieve personal fulfilment'.

If the university sector in the UK is not ultimately to lose its soul it needs collectively to reaffirm its commitment to those same values – which will almost always be found to inform the mission statements of the individual universities – and to resist the instrumentalism that characterises contemporary government thinking about HE, if necessary via collective action. Universities have many purposes beyond churning out functionaries to lubricate the cogs of economic development, and it is the responsibility of the leaders of the sector collectively to tell that particular truth to power.

References

Blyth, M. (2013) *Austerity: The History of a Dangerous Idea*, Oxford: Oxford University Press.

Browne, J. (2010) *Securing a Sustainable Future for Higher Education: An Independent Review of Higher Education Funding and Student Finance*, www.gov.uk/government/uploads/system/uploads/attachment_data/file/31999/10-1208-securing-sustainable-higher-education-browne-report.pdf (accessed 18/3/14).

Cleary, M. (2012) 'The role of universities in the education sector: can they act collectively?' in *Inequality and Higher Education: Marketplace or Social Justice?* Leadership Foundation Stimulus Paper 2012: pp. 40–41, www.salford.ac.uk/_data/assets/pdf_file/0015/76110/Inequality-and-Higher-Education-published-Jan-2012.pdf (accessed 18/3/14).

Coetzee, J.M. (2013) 'Universities head for extinction', foreword to J. Higgins *Academic Freedom in a Democratic South Africa*, Johannesburg: Wits University Press, http://mg.co.za/article/2013-11-01-universities-head-for-extinction (accessed 3/8/15).

Dearing, R. (1997) *National Committee of Inquiry into Higher Education*, https://bei.leeds.ac.uk/partners/ncihe/ (accessed 18/3/14).

Hall, M. (2011) *Inequality and Higher Education: Marketplace or Social Justice?* Leadership Foundation Stimulus Paper 2012, www.salford.ac.uk/_data/assets/pdf_file/0015/76110/Inequality-and-Higher-Education-published-Jan-2012.pdf (accessed 18/3/14).

OECD (2013) *Education at a Glance 2013: OECD Indicators*, www.oecd.org/edu/eag.htm (accessed 18/3/14).

Quigley, A. (2013) 'The Ofsted Stockholm syndrome', *Guardian Professional*, 22 October 2013, www.theguardian.com/teacher-network/teacher-blog/2013/oct/22/school-ofsted-stockholm-syndrome (accessed 18/3/14).

Siddique, H. (2015) 'University event questioning Israel's right to exist is cancelled', *Guardian*, 31 March 2015, www.theguardian.com/uk-news/2015/mar/31/southampton-university-cancels-event-questioning-israel-existence (accessed 2/12/15).

Universities UK (2001) *New Directions for Higher Education Funding: Funding Options Review Group Final Report*. London: Universities UK.

Universities UK (2013) 'Universities UK response to Spending Round announcement', www.universitiesuk.ac.uk/highereducation/Pages/SpendingRoundannouncement2013.aspx#.UodUquBy_0c (accessed 18/3/14).

Walker, M. (2012) 'The value of a broadly based approach', in *Inequality and Higher Education: Marketplace or Social Justice?* Leadership Foundation Stimulus Paper 2012: pp. 48–50, www.salford.ac.uk/_data/assets/pdf_file/0015/76110/Inequality-and-Higher-Education-published-Jan-2012.pdf (accessed 18/3/14).

Weber, L.E. (2002) 'Universities' responsiveness and responsibilities in an age of heightened competition' in W. Z. Hirsch and L. E. Weber (eds) *As the Walls of Academia Are Tumbling Down*. London: Economica.

Williamson, B. and Coffield, F. (1997) 'Repositioning higher education' in F. Coffield and B. Williamson (eds) *Repositioning Higher Education*. Buckingham: SRHE and Open University Press.

Chapter 2

Ethicality, research and emotional impoverishment in a technological era

Carla Solvason

In this chapter I explore ideas about the teaching of ethics in higher education professional education programmes. I ask whether this should or even can be done; and if so, why it should be done and what dilemmas might emerge from the experience. I also raise issues about the varied discourses and representations in the literatures regarding 'ethical practice'. A main assumption in the literatures appears to be that it is enough to write in abstract terms about what counts as ethical practice without demonstrating how real-life practices may be understood as ethical. This situation is compounded by the fact that, within the current technological era, students are encouraged to look for quick answers rather than ask considered questions (Carr, 2010). These matters, I feel, should be a matter of priority for professional educators, who also need to ask themselves whether they are modelling the practices they endorse or whether they fall into the trap of making recommendations without showing how they live those recommendations in their real-life practice.

The chapter provides an account of how our team in a university Centre for Early Childhood reflected upon the embedded nature of ethical practice within our programmes, individually and collectively, in order to help student teachers learn to do the same. This, we hoped, would help them raise the quality of their research and, more importantly, of their overall practice in relation to children, parents and the wider community. I also argue that it is not enough to develop ethicality in research practices only: ethicality needs to be a feature of all personal and social practices if the practices in question are to be understood as 'good'.

First here is a context for the study.

Context

I am a member of a team of sixteen early years lecturers with backgrounds in teaching, health, social work and law, and with a wide range of expertise. Significantly, every one of us believes in a caring approach to pedagogical practices. My role is to lead on student research, with responsibility for student independent studies (their research projects, or dissertations). Until recently our centre, following the wider institutional culture, adopted a traditional social sciences perspective to the students' dissertations. This meant that the students observed, critiqued and offered advice about their work to professional colleagues in practice settings, though they did this from a traditional outsider perspective. This somewhat detached and 'cold' approach did not reflect the values of our team, though it went largely unquestioned or problematized by tutors, and therefore the students. This was because, at that time, our team did not have the confidence or feel sufficiently qualified to raise questions about established institutional practices that were generally accepted as normative. The situation troubled me, sufficiently so that I began to hold conversations with colleagues about how we could make the experience of doing their research projects more meaningful for students and also for the people in the early years settings where the projects were carried out. The idea of 'purpose' became prominent in our discourses to do with this area. However, I still could not fully articulate why the situation presented a problem for me and needed to understand why I felt so uneasy about our existing approaches.

A turning point happened when I attended the 2011 Value and Virtue Conference at York St John University: this helped me begin to develop my ideas and find an appropriate language for what I was experiencing. Whilst I already understood that research should not be about criticising others, I did not fully appreciate the idea of critique, especially the importance of critiquing one's own practice. Two conference presentations in particular influenced my thinking: McNiff's (2011) presentation about how research could act as a vehicle for improving oneself when conducted in respectful collaboration with others; and Stern's (2011) explanations of a research approach that incorporated notions of self-interrogation, respect, sensitivity and even love towards those with whom we research. These were values that I unwittingly held, but had not been able, until the conference, to recognise, or to communicate. Having gained a clearer conceptualisation of how values may transform into living practices, and an appropriate language to communicate this idea, I was able to clarify and articulate my vision of what 'caring practitioner research' should look like, both for myself and subsequently for the team at my university.

These insights led to many practical changes in our teaching practices and programme delivery. During a team meeting shortly after the conference, I presented ideas about how care, respect and sensitivity should be integral to the students' research studies, and the team fully embraced the theoretical framework proposed. I had anticipated no challenge to these notions, as I knew that they were already part of our team's shared values. It then became a matter of embedding these ideas within the teaching preparation for the students' research projects (a module on which I led) and also within all the support materials for their independent study, which, as lead in the area, I also developed. These materials were shared with colleagues for their critical responses before being published. All support materials are stored and accessed through a single virtual resource bank which is now available to all students and staff. A significant feature of these materials emerged as the assessment criteria: as a staff it was important to clarify for students exactly what we valued in their work. As a staff team we worked together to produce these criteria; we also sought the opinion of students about the validity of the criteria, and acted collaboratively on their feedback to refine our understandings and documentation about the nature and purposes of our collective work. We continue to reflect upon and discuss the nature of the independent study, through ongoing deliberations about the purpose and value of the students' research and our work as professional educators.

But knowledge is always troubling, and just as I was beginning to feel confident that we were effectively engaging in appropriate pedagogies regarding the ethical nature of students' research, I began to feel discomfort that this approach was isolated from other aspects of the students' learning experience. Although it was relatively straightforward to enable students to develop ethical approaches to their *research* within a self-contained module, it was a different matter to help them appreciate that ethical deliberation should permeate all their studies and their practice. At regular points throughout their degree course our students will interact with children and families on an everyday basis. Students on an Early Childhood degree have blocks of full-time practice experience within settings (including nurseries, children's centres, schools and related early years sites) during the academic year, all of which have unique and complex cultures. My growing understanding about the need for ethical practice therefore led me to question whether our responsibility as tutors was not only to ensure that our students develop ethical perspectives to doing research, but whether it also extended to helping them learn how to interact with others in practice settings in an ethically sensitive manner. This then raised the further question of whether this 'formation of character' was something that was actually achievable through teaching. Finally this led me to consider the issue of whether the contemporary increasingly desensitised technologised culture in which students now learn (Czarniawska, 2013) would, to some extent at least, impede the development of such emotions and values.

Engaging with these issues became the starting point for a new topic for collaborative staff enquiry. What follows is an account of the steps we took to achieve new understandings about the nature of our own pedagogy and how these, in turn, had potential for influencing students' understandings and practices.

Embedding ethicality within student research

As I have already explained, embedding ethicality and sensitivity within our approach to supporting student research was reasonably straightforward for a team that genuinely tries to embody the values of care and respect in their practices. Here I discuss how we modified our approaches to teaching and learning, encouraging students to adopt a curious and contemplative (Dadds, 2002) approach to a research area that would provide them with an arena for professional improvement. In previous years, before being introduced to the concept of practitioner research and its implications for self-development, students were likely to choose a research topic in which they already felt competent and comfortable: their aim was generally to demonstrate understanding of a topic and produce convincing evidence to persuade others to believe that their hypothesis was correct. Conversely we now encourage students to choose an area they know little about. We emphasise that research is about improving their own knowledge and practice by drawing on insights from appropriate literatures and the expertise of others. There is an inextricable link between their research approach and the reflective practice they develop throughout their studies. We emphasise throughout our teaching sessions the importance of students sharing what they learn through their research for the benefit of others, and of their not losing sight of the idea that the aim of their research is to benefit the children in their care. We have moved away from studies concluding with a list of recommendations for others, and instead encourage students to reflect critically on what they have learned and how they might incorporate their learning into their practice settings in an ethically sensitive way.

Consequently, traditional approaches which included disengaged hypotheses and recommendations have now been replaced by meaningful conversations between the student and participants in the setting about the topics and approaches that would be both useful and relevant to all. We encourage students to see participants in settings as research partners and themselves as learners rather than subject knowledge experts. This approach recognises the fragile and transient nature of knowledge, and the students readily embrace McNiff's (2010: 106) advice to 'hold your knowledge lightly, and be aware that what you know today may change tomorrow. Always remember that you may, after all, be mistaken'. This idea has become a part of student discourses and is used regularly in their written assignments. A sense of not-knowing, and an appreciation for the diverse knowledge and experience of others has now become embedded in the research approach adopted by staff and students. This acceptance of a transformative educational approach is a large step for students, many of whom come into their first year of studies having experienced a predominantly transmission approach to education.

As testimony to the above, here are some extracts (slightly edited with permission) from the reflective conclusions of students' independent studies, undertaken in the third year of their undergraduate study. The comments clearly reveal affirmative attitudes towards research as a process of ongoing, experiential enquiry, enabled through a carefully planned programme and a shared values-based pedagogy.

> Student 1: Doing my research has helped me deepen my understandings of Active Learning, and I now see how motivation can impact on children's learning and development. I have observed children's involvement, perseverance, and achievement as they engage in play. Before doing my research, I struggled to articulate Characteristics of Effective Teaching and Learning

in meaningful ways with colleagues and parents. I knew this learning was important but couldn't explain it clearly. Having researched the literature and begun to theorise my practice more closely, I can now do this confidently.

Student 2: Through the analysis of data and the reading of material connected with autonomy I have come to realise that my original question did not fully encompass the many hidden aspects of practice. Holding such strong convictions about the place of autonomy in children's learning experiences, I took it for granted that all practitioners agreed with me and also understood the practical elements necessary to assist children in achieving this. Carrying out this research has made me realise that if we want to find answers to a question we must first take account of the beliefs, knowledge and practical experience of all those involved.

Student 3: The most important point that I have taken away from this study has been to appreciate the differing opinions of the professionals and parents I am working with. Whilst I've read in the literatures and explored in lectures the benefits of integrated working I have found during the data collection process that this has further embedded my understanding of the importance of working in partnership with parents and practitioners. The more perspectives I have gained throughout this study the clearer the picture I have built. I hope that the skills I have gained will be transferable to future situations requiring integrated working with other professionals and parents.

So far so good. However, whilst we, as tutors, considered ways to tackle practical issues, such as how to encourage students to develop greater appreciation of others' perspectives, it also became evident that we needed to rethink our own pedagogical methodologies, and explain to students how this methodology might influence their research approaches. We therefore focused upon two key theoretical frameworks: practice-based critical action research (McNiff, 2011) and appreciative inquiry (Cooperrider and Whitney, 2005). We selected these approaches because action research encourages students to consider an area of practice they would like to develop and, allied to this, appreciative inquiry gives them a constructive way in which to do so. Cooperrider and Whitney (2005) describe appreciative inquiry as an approach based on an exploration of the positive and successful elements of what works within the research area, with the aim of also reflecting upon why these work. This analysis of why an initiative should be deemed successful then provides opportunities to build upon 'the good', to review what is in place and to consider what else might be achieved. This affirming approach aligns itself particularly well to our programme as it starts from a positive and supportive position, scaffolding positive relationships between student and participants in the setting, rather than intimating that there is a 'problem' to be resolved, as is often the case in educational research. These two theoretical frameworks enable students to establish a positive research relationship with their settings from which all can benefit.

This shift in the focus of students' research has led to new discourses in our centre where ethicality is recognised as central. Our students are now far more aware that they are researching *with people*, rather than doing research *on partici-pants* (Reason and Rowan, 1981; Reason and Bradbury, 2001, 2008), and that relationships, trust and respect must take priority over data collection. Below, a third year undergraduate student explains the importance of sensitive relationships in planning her research:

> Student 4: It is the strong relationship with the setting that enabled me to be transparent and honest when discussing the direction I planned to take the research in and when clarifying the topic. The trustworthy relationship with the setting enabled effective communication with the practitioners: I could discuss in more depth the positive impact the research could have on their practice and ensure an approach to the research which allowed perspectives to be seen from the inside of the organisation, thus hopefully improving the research outcomes.

Students have engaged with the idea that, regardless of the care and sensitivity they take in their approach, their research will inevitably impact upon others' lives, so their responsibility is to make sure that the impact is constructive and worthwhile. A sense of purpose has now become central to our students' research. They have adopted the views of Munford et al. (2008: 64) that research should not only be about avoiding harm whilst researchers extract the evidence they require, but also about discovering how to make a positive difference. We begin our research module with reference to Bloor's (2010) work that states that we should not only aim to do 'good research' that will be academically recognised, but, more importantly, we should strive to 'bring about good' in our research locales. Students have taken ownership of this responsibility, recognising their moral duty towards the individuals they work with.

By developing the concept that research is about individual improvement, developed in collaboration with others in the setting, the values of honesty and the need for the respectful positionality of the student researcher have become central aspects of the independent study. Students are now required to start their research projects by explaining the ideas and beliefs that frame their work and the origins of those beliefs. We refer to this as their 'theoretical framework', recognising that their own personal theory of practice is as valuable as any other they cite. It can be a struggle for students to accept their own subjectivity, given that the idea of subjectivity tends to be deemed as 'bias' in traditionalist research texts, something to be eliminated, or at least hidden. Contrary to this, Munford et al. (2008: 57) emphasise that '[r]esearchers need to be explicit about their research intentions, the values that inform their research work and the positions they occupy within the research process'. They encourage students to share the life experiences, significant readings and professional encounters that have informed the evolution of their beliefs and to contextualise their understanding of research topics. However, a number of popular research textbooks still assume that the research will be conducted from an objectivised stance, so students can become confused by these mixed messages. When preparing students for their study we emphasise that unless they clearly establish their starting point they will be unable to show transformations in their thinking. Dadds (2002: 12) argues that 'passions and humanity' are 'inexorably locked into practice-based research'. She cites Stenhouse (1975), Noddings (1994) and Hargreaves (1999) who all stress that the subjective and inter-relational aspect of practitioner-research is a strength, not a weakness. Such research is based upon emotions and 'human bonds' (Dadds, 2002: 13). This leads on to the impact upon self and on other.

Once they have grasped the notion of self-improvement the students will often ask: 'If my independent study is about improving my own knowledge and under-standing, then how can it have a positive impact upon settings?' In response they are reminded that any setting is only the sum of the individuals that comprise it. Processes can be developed only through the enrichment of individuals' under-standing, and only through the development of individuals' knowledge can ideas be shared. Through their research they can develop, create and share knowledge. This may be done through informal discussions with fellow practitioners, chil-dren or parents, through more formal means, such as newsletters or presentations at staff meetings, or through the 'subtle accumulation of nuances, a hundred things done a little better' (Kissinger, cited in Peters and Waterman, 1982: 107). Consequently, knowledge becomes seen as a collective endeavour, generated by research participants for mutually beneficial use.

These pedagogical approaches, aimed at embedding a deeper understanding of ethicality and a greater sensitivity and responsibility towards the setting, have enabled our students to develop new, other-oriented, perspectives towards their research, as the excerpts above show. We believe we have successfully changed the research culture in our centre to one of sensitive and respectful collaboration. But what has also happened, and what I would like to explore more fully now, is that the staff's concerns to embed a more caring approach to student research has highlighted other gaps in our course. While it has been reasonably straight-forward to develop pedagogies that have raised the status of ethicality in *research*, what we really need to do is to embed ethicality throughout the students' entire study programme, for the reasons mentioned earlier. For our students the estab-lishment of trusting relationships, sensitivity and empathy are central to their professional development and not just a facet of their research projects. My own research has led me to question how we, as educators, might do this, but also whether teaching someone to be 'ethical' is an achievable or even desirable task, and whether this may be seen as an ethical procedure in itself.

Embedding ethicality in all teaching

Whilst as a team we have broadened and deepened our understanding of ethics in our development of research approaches, we have also moved away from a focus only on the abstract concept of professional ethics, or ethics as procedure, and towards more effectively nurturing ethical practices within our students' professional lives. Banks (2009: 59) explains that we can do this by 'broadening the scope of focus from codes, conduct and cases to include commitment, character and context'. One aspect of the professional expectations presented in Early Education's *Code of Ethics* (2011: no page) is to 'Undertake ... reflection, critical self-study [and] continuing professional development and engage with evidence based theory and practice'. But this 'theory and practice' is not just about a single piece of research: it is about the moral obligation that early years practitioners have to review their practice regularly. Ethics, reflection and practice are interwoven and, as a result, ethicality needs to be embedded within all our teaching. As a team we have long made ethicality visible in our generic marking criteria and have highlighted the need for ethical practices within each of our module outlines. We have reconsidered the ethical nature of all data collection as a key aspect of student research training and have emphasised the need for professional respect and sensitivity in the scripts our first year students produce for their study skills module. Within their reflections and their writing we have encouraged students to take a responsible, proactive stance and, as importantly, a kind and caring approach to those whose behaviours they consider need modification. When they reflect upon instances when collaboration with peers or colleagues has been difficult, we have encouraged them always to try to consider their colleagues' perspectives through drawing on theoretical resources such as Brookfield's (1995) concept of Lenses and Luft's (1963) concept of a Johari Window. We have encouraged them to attempt to formulate their own, positive solutions that will, we hope, enable them to cope more appropriately with similar situations in the future. These small changes have made a difference to the quality of sensitivity and self-awareness demonstrated in the reflective writing that students have submitted. An example, written by an undergraduate student in her second year of study, is the following:

> Student 5: The third value that has really changed the way I will approach my research is the ability to be open-minded, to not let my own research plan affect the overall outcome. I have always tried to have an open mind, but it wasn't until a lecture on 'Theory into Practice' that I realised an important aspect of being open-minded is the ability to admit when you're wrong. It is important to be self-critical and to recognise that my knowledge, no matter how useful, is limited and so what I have to say will never be more important than another person's view. I have pointed out that the needs of children are constantly changing and the aim of research is ultimately to benefit the child. To do this the research must be capable of meeting the ever-changing needs of the child. It needs to be flexible and adaptable; this can be achieved by listening to the views of the people involved, which may lead me in directions that I had not yet considered.

However, the question now arises about whether it is possible to teach and develop in adults a characteristic, quality or value such as self-awareness, or whether, as educators, our responsibility extends only as far as the teaching of process. Should our aim be to produce 'ethical individuals', or simply to teach our students how to follow an ethical code and be able to make ethical decisions from a fairly technical perspective? Here are some reflections about possible ways forward, while recognising some of the problematics involved.

'Teaching' ethicality

Haddad (2005) refers to the importance of *understandings* in ethics, supporting her arguments by recounting simulated ethical dilemmas that she has used as part of her teaching in pharmacy. Her ideas led me to consider how different the concept of ethics is for those who understand 'practice' as something to work towards when fully qualified, as is the case with the pharmacy students, rather than an embedded strand of training, as is the case for our early years students. Haddad's students were preparing for situations that might potentially occur after completing their training. In contrast to this a large measure of our students' training is actually spent within settings, dealing directly with children, families and colleagues, from the first weeks of their training. Early years students could, potentially, encounter a range of small-scale, practice-based dilemmas from their first term at university: from concerns about individual children to difficulties with professional colleagues. There is a significant stretch of time between these early encounters and the students' mid-course consideration of ethics within their research module, and I wonder how well we prepare them for day-to-day exposure to the ethical quandaries of professional life.

Montgomery (2012: 171) commented that 'One barrier to training in professional ethics is a ubiquitous provincialism. ... There is no willingness to understand that professional ethics is generic'. He discusses 'conflict of interest' and why it applies to his own area of environmental practice, just as it does to the world of business. But such ethical dilemmas, including conflicts of interest, equally apply to those training in the early years. Students need to consider what they should do when their concerns for a child's needs conflict with the parents' wishes, or how they respond when Governors push for a course of action that they know will be detrimental to the experience of the children. Or, a phenomenon we have encountered a number of times, what they should do when they are drawn into a friend's social network conversation that discusses one of their colleagues, a tutor or a parent in a less than favourable light. These are all genuine conflicts of interest and I wonder whether we support our trainee professionals sufficiently in making appropriate decisions from the beginning of their studies, or even if we really can.

Some key phrases from Haddad in relation to her theoretical concerns about ethics resonated with me; these were 'human dignity' (2005: 74) and 'mindfulness and self-awareness' (p. 77). Her use of these terms led me to reflect upon the form of language we use with students concerning matters of ethics. We frequently use the terms 'ethical' and 'sensitive', but after reading Haddad's article I wonder whether we should be broadening the range of our ethics-related terminology and embedding it more specifically within our teaching. James et al. (2005: 19) ask, 'How can the prospective teacher be ethical when he or she does not know with any certainty what it is to be ethical?' So perhaps we should be aiming to explore this thorny concept far more thoroughly and to develop a more public discourse of ethicality within our teaching. Possibly we need to explore with the students what, exactly, it means to be 'mindful', or to be 'self-aware,' or how to recognise 'human dignity' when they consider their reflections on practice. I would also argue that reflections on the types of real-life complications that they have experienced are necessary, in order to be aware of the multiplicity of shifting and complex contexts. Noddings (1984) explains why the discussion of real experiences is vital for those working with others in a position of care:

> It seems likely ... that the actions of one-caring will be varied rather than rule-bound; that is, her actions, while predictable in a global sense, will be unpredictable in detail. Variation is to be expected if the one claiming to care really cares, for engrossment is in the variable and never fully understood other, in the particular other, in a particular set of circumstances. (Noddings 1984: 24)

Campbell (2003: 30) adds that 'In the practical world of the teacher, differing orientations to the moral agency role complicate considerably any chance of developing a singular or unified conception of professional ethics'. Individuals will perceive their responsibility quite differently and this will be dependent upon their personal context. The culture of each situation is unique, fluid and ever changing. It is impossible to teach uniform responses, as no one moment is ever duplicated. So although Haddad's (2005) teaching approaches may enable her students to consider a multiplicity of possible approaches, those approaches cannot provide a ready-made solution to any one actual scenario they may encounter. Therefore, if the diversity of context and character means that we cannot provide our students with operational strategies, should we instead focus upon strength of character for dealing with challenges?

James et al. (2005) suggest that those who teach must have a 'good character' if they are to shape the character of the young. This is a huge responsibility for our trainee professionals, many of whom are still in their late teens, and so comparatively 'young' themselves. James et al. argue that although teachers share the moral obligations of any 'ordinary' person, those 'ordinary' people do not always share the moral obligations of public service that a person in a position of professional education and care holds. Dadds (2002: 2012) explains how, '[a]s members of one of the caring professions, our work is a moral enterprise'. It is with some irony, then, that Cummings et al. (2001) discovered that within their institution students who were trainee teachers had lower levels of 'moral reasoning' than those majoring in any other subject areas. They came to the conclusion that teaching courses were often 'skill oriented and devoted to technical competence' and did not sufficiently explore 'more abstract, theoretical content requiring students to stretch themselves cognitively' (Cummings et al., 2001: 153). Although this may be the case with some skills-based teacher training courses, I would argue that such is not the case on our Early Childhood course, which prides itself on being underpinned by reflective practice and personal values. But I do wonder whether an understanding and acceptance of these values is something that we sometimes take for granted with our students and whether this should, as mentioned earlier, be more explicitly recognised and explored through our pedagogical discourses.

Exploring the literature makes it clear that 'morality' has been thoroughly explored in some cultural contexts (for example, Cummings et al., 2001; Fleischmann, 2006; Tuana, 2007) but is under-researched in others. The research of Cummings et al. (2001) in the field of teacher education (cited above) followed on from Tuana's (2007), which discovered the absence of 'moral literacy' from the education of some US teenagers. Tuana argues that moral literacy should be placed on an equal standing with literacy or numeracy, yet she found that it was hardly touched upon within secondary schooling in the United States. This observation prompted me to question the experiences that our students bring to university in the UK. I wonder whether, at any point, previously, they have needed to consider their ethical reasoning skills or develop the moral literacy that Tuana discusses? Our centre provides a year-long module developing new students' academic skills and a year-long research training module that ensures our students acquire the academic skills and understanding necessary to tackle their independent studies; but I wonder to what extent we provide our students with the skills and knowledge they need to cope with daily ethical dilemmas, and how we might embed this in our courses.

Modelling ethicality

Engen and Kaha (2000) suggest that students learn far more from the way that tutors act than from any formal curriculum. They comment that, 'In short, our messages in the classroom do much more than simply transmit information, they build – or disrupt – community, and they teach about citizenship and moral vision in ways we too often ignore' (Engen and Kaha, 2000: 22). Jarvis (1995: 25) makes a similar point when he says that 'the manner through which teachers interact with learners is probably more important than the actual teaching methods employed'. If this is the case then perhaps we should give more credit to the ethical behaviours and values that we model as tutors, and be less concerned about the ethical content we teach. Perhaps showing how we realise our values as real-life practices is enough. And this seems a good point to stop and consider 'whom' rather than 'what' we teach. Just as we encourage our students to remember that their research is about relationships, that it is about dealing with people rather than respondents, we, as tutors, need also to remember that we are dealing with individuals, not cohorts of learners. In our results-driven society

Jarvis (1995: 25) advises that we 'must be prepared to respond to the current social pressures and retain the ethic of concern for persons that forms the very essence of education itself'. Let us 'challenge the single story and offer alternative readings' (Dadds, 2002: 15). Rather than focusing upon *teaching* Haddad's (2005) concepts of mindfulness, self-awareness and human dignity, in a formulaic way, to be ticked off when achieved, perhaps we should acknowledge that some aspects of pedagogy are most effectively delivered through example, through listening, through building relationships and through the naturally unfolding discussion of situations and events.

Modern technology – a barrier to ethicality?

This brings me to my final, and, I would suggest, most troubling point. The students we work and learn with live in a society that does not always run at a speed appropriate for encouraging the careful and sensitive consideration of situations and others' perspectives. Regardless of the emotionally laden skills of reflection and research that form the core of our Early Childhood course, in our Snapchat and Twitter age speed is everything. In a conference presentation Czarniawska (2013: no page) discussed how within the electronic generation thoughts are often 'burped' out without temperance. She used the simple illustration of a man who was walking, slowing down in order to try to remember something, and the opposite example of someone walking at speed to try to forget. How do we encourage our students to slow down and take time to consider their thoughts and their actions, to take the *time* to act mindfully? As tutors we regularly have to deal with students' frustration if we do not respond within hours to an email sent late the previous evening or over a weekend. It seems that living in today's technological era does not nurture patience, nor does it always acknowledge the parameters of the 'working day'. How then, can we encourage our students to slow down and take time to think through an issue, or to remember, in a world of instant information and instant responses?

Within the field of science, Fleischmann's (2006) exploration of teaching ethics in an American university's school of engineering also deserves attention. She unpacks many of the issues I have just begun to touch upon in my own reflections, such as the 'problem' of living for and in the present, influenced by the rapid technological shift over recent times. Fleischmann explores a move away from embedded historical principles 'towards a culture rooted only in the present and without the standards for excellence and honourable living' (2006: 382) of the last century. She touches upon Bloom's (1987) depiction of young people today living in an 'impoverished present' whereby, she says, they are starved of 'an understanding of the past and a vision for the future, both of which come out of the human tradition that is passed from generation to generation in the form of shared values and standards of human behaviour' (Fleischmann, 2006: 383). She concludes that in a world where students desire only answers, not the reasons for the answers, the teaching of ethics has become more difficult than ever. I would argue that, with our teaching of students, the issue is not the lack of desire so much as lack of time. As a team of tutors our experience suggests that students *do* value 'reasons'; our difficulty involves finding the time and space to enable a sufficient and appropriate consideration of the values underpinning those reasons, and signals a new priority for our further consideration.

Fleischmann (2006) also refers to the work of Moore (1993), particularly the challenging points raised in his article 'Care of the Soul'. Moore discusses how education and spirituality have become increasingly separated: intellect and emotion, he says, are now mutually exclusive. He mourns the loss of a 'relationship between information and wisdom' and for the desire for human contact (Moore, 1993: 30). The relationship between the 'problem' of lack of emotional connectedness and the experiences of our trainees within the caring profession of Early Childhood is, I hope, clear. Moore (1993: 30) states that:

> We have a spiritual longing for community and relatedness and for a cosmic vision, but we go after them with literal hardware instead of with sensitivity of the heart. We want to know all about people from far-away places, but we don't want to feel emotionally connected to them.

Early years educators cannot be effective by just 'knowing all about children'; one cannot be a carer without the engagement of emotions. Moore (1993: 30) refers to this situation of emotional isolation as 'psychological modernism', involving 'an uncritical acceptance of the values of the modern world'. Increasingly, the request for our Early Childhood trainees to imagine how someone might *feel* within a certain scenario, or to be 'mindful', to use Haddad's (2005) phrase, becomes more difficult. Within the continued industrialisation of education (Rudduck et al., 1996: 68) emotions are rarely seen to play a role within educational professionalism, which is assumed to be 'about skills and information, not about depth of feeling and imagination' (Moore, 1993: 30). As tutors in the field of Early Childhood education I believe it is our duty to ensure that feelings and mindfulness remain at the core of everything we do. Although I contend that ethical values are more effectively modelled than taught, we should aspire to extend the discourses of ethicality that arise within our teaching and discuss situations and dilemmas explicitly, rather than accepting these matters implicitly, as we often do, assuming a shared understanding between student and tutor.

The language of sensitivity, care and respect for others should not be reserved only for research projects, but should be embedded throughout all areas of our teaching. Within this exploration I have definitely arrived at 'different knowledge from that which [I] initially sought' (Dadds, 2002: 20). Through exploring the most effective ways of teaching ethicality I have reached the conclusion that it is not something to be *taught*; rather it is something to be acknowledged and embraced. By modelling the purposeful creation of time and space to explore emotions and feelings within our teaching sessions we are demonstrating that these features are just as worthy of consideration as other professional skills and knowledge. They are part and parcel of the 'moral enterprise' (Dadds, 2002: 12) of the early years practitioner. We model these values in our relationships with students, but perhaps not clearly enough within our content-driven (and sometimes assessment-driven) teaching sessions. Regardless of the ever-mounting pressures of a market education (Ball, 2006: 12), we should not lose sight of what Jarvis (1995: 25) terms 'the ethic of concern for persons that forms the very essence of education itself'.

With special thanks to Lauren Hunt, Ruth Tedstone, Cari Amos and Charlotte Forrester for allowing me to cite their work.

References

Ball, S.J. (2006). *Education policy and social class: the selected works of Stephen J. Ball.* London: Routledge.

Banks, S. (2009) 'From professional ethics to ethics in professional life: implications for learning, teaching and study', *Ethics and social welfare,* 3 (1): 55–63.

Bloom, A. (1987) *The Closing of the American Mind: How Higher Education Has Failed Democracy and Impoverished the Souls of Today's Students.* New York: Simon & Schuster.

Bloor, M. (2010) 'The researcher's obligation to bring about good', *Qualitative Social Work,* 9 (17): 17–20.

Brookfield, S. (1995) *Becoming a Critically Reflective Teacher.* San Francisco, CA: Jossey-Bass.

Campbell, E. (2003) 'Moral lessons: the ethical role of teachers', *Educational Research and Evaluation: An International Journal on Theory and Practice,* 9 (1): 25–50.

Carr, N. (2010) *The Shallows: How the Internet Is Changing the Way We Read, Think and Remember.* New York: W.W. Norton and Company.

Cooperrider, D.L. and Whitney, D. (2005) *Appreciative Inquiry: A Positive Revolution in Change.* San Francisco, CA: Berrett-Koehler.

Cummings, R., Dyas, L., Maddux, C. D. and Kochman, A. (2001) 'Principled moral reasoning and behavior of preservice teacher education students', *American Educational Research Journal,* 38 (1): 143–58.

Czarniawska, B. (2013) 'Cyberwork: cybernization and cyborgization in news agencies'. Paper presented at the 8th Researching Work and Learning Conference, Stirling.

Dadds, M. (2002) 'Taking curiosity seriously: the role of awe and Wanda in research-based professionalism', *Educational Action Research,* 10 (1): 9–26.

Early Education (The British Association for Early Childhood Education) (2011) *Code of Ethics.* London: Early Education, www.early-education.org.uk/sites/default/files/Code%20of%20Ethics.pdf (accessed 03/07/13).

Engen, D.E. and Kaha, C. W. (2000) 'Moral conversations', *College Teaching,* 48 (1): 22–22.

Fleischmann, S.T. (2006) 'Teaching ethics: more than an honour code', *Science and Engineering Ethics* 12 (2): 381–89.

Haddad, A. (2005) 'Teaching for enduring understandings in ethics', *Journal of Physical Therapy Education* 19 (3): 73–77.

Hargreaves, D. (1999) 'The Knowledge-Creating School', *British Journal of Educational Studies* 47(2): 122–44.

James, A., Davison, J. and Lewis, M. (2005) *Professional Values and Practice: Achieving the Standards for QTS*. London: Routledgefalmer.

Jarvis, P. (1995) 'Teachers and learners in adult education: transaction or moral interaction?' *Studies in the Education of Adults* 27 (1): 24–36.

Luft, J. (1963) *Group Process: An Introduction to Group Dynamics*. California: The National Press.

McNiff, J. (2010) *Action Research for Professional Development*. Poole: September Books.

McNiff, J. (2011) 'Where the wonderful things are: a celebration of global interconnectedness for professional accountability through action research', *Keynote presentation at the Value and Virtue in Practice-Based Research Conference*. York.

Montgomery, J. (2012) 'Letter from the editor: would it be ethical?', *Environmental Practice* 14 (3): 171–72.

Moore, T. (1993) 'Care of the soul: the benefits – and costs – of a more spiritual life', *Psychology Today*, May-June, pp. 28–30; 76–77.

Munford, R., Sanders J., Mirfin, B., Conder, V. and Conder, J. (2008) 'Ethics and research: searching for ethical practice in research', *Ethics and Social Welfare*, 2 (1): 50–66.

Noddings, N. (1984) *Caring: A Feminine Approach to Ethics*. London: University of California Press.

Noddings, N. (1994) 'An ethics of care and its implications for instructional arrangements', in L. Stone (ed.), *The Education Feminist Reader*. New York: Routledge.

Peters, T. and Waterman, R.H. (1982) *In Search of Excellence*. New York, NY: Harper and Row.

Reason, P. and Bradbury, H. (eds) (2001) *Handbook of Action Research: Participative Inquiry and Practice*. London: Sage.

Reason, P. and Bradbury, J. (eds) (2008) *Handbook of Action Research: Participative Inquiry and Practice* (2nd edn). London: Sage.

Reason, P. and Rowan, J. (1981) *Human Inquiry: A Sourcebook of New Paradigm Research*. Chichester: John Wiley and Sons.

Rudduck, J., Chaplain, R. and Wallace, G. (1996) *School Improvement: What Can Pupils Tell Us?* London: David Fulton Publishers.

Stenhouse, L. (1975) *An Introduction to Curriculum Development*. London: Heinemann.

Stern, J. (2011) 'From negative ethics to positive virtues in research', *Presentation at the Value and Virtue in Practice-Based Research Conference*. York.

Tuana, N. (2007) 'Conceptualizing moral literacy', *Journal of Educational Administration*, 45 (4): 364–78.

Chapter 3

Why me? Reflections on using the self in and as research

Cheryl Hunt

Introduction

> People travel to wonder at the height of the mountains; at the huge waves of the seas; at the long course of the rivers; at the vast compass of the ocean; at the circular motion of the stars; and yet they pass by themselves without wondering.
>
> (Saint Augustine, 354–430AD)

> Autoethnography is somewhat unique in research in that it is particularly likely to be warranted by the quest for self-understanding. ... The kind of self-understanding I am talking about lies at the intersection of biography and society: self-knowledge that comes from understanding our personal lives, identities, and feelings as deeply connected to and in a large part constituted by – and in turn helping to constitute – the sociocultural contexts in which we live.
>
> (Anderson, 2012: 372)

I have begun this chapter with the two quotations above since they provide both a 'flavour' of the chapter itself and an indication of my position as its author. The focus of the chapter is on the place and function of autoethnography in education, particularly in doctoral programmes and educational research. My own experience in both fields suggests that developing an understanding of one's 'self' can greatly enhance one's engagement with the processes of learning and researching. Underpinning the chapter, however, is my concern that powerful gatekeepers, whilst apparently upholding an evidence-base of research that demonstrates 'quality', 'rigour' and so on, have effectively been excluding the 'self' of the researcher from the public discourses of educational research. This has had a knock-on effect not only on what is perceived to be 'good' research but also on how and what it is deemed appropriate to teach at all levels of education. I think – hope – that a recent surge of interest in autoethnography represents a backlash against, as well as a challenge to, the impersonal regulatory practices and values associated with neoliberalism, especially the ways in which these are currently being enacted within higher education.

Autoethnographic research and writing often provide stark contrast to traditional research methodologies and ways of representing data, including (perhaps especially) the relationship between the researcher and the researched. The purpose of this chapter is to try to illustrate the personal and social value of autoethnographic research and writing – and to suggest that these are 'virtuous' processes because, as Adams and Holman Jones (2008) argue, they treat research as a political, socially-just and socially-conscious act where the goal is 'to produce analytical, accessible texts that change us and the world we live in for the better' (p. 764).

Bochner (2011: 1), too, has suggested that autoethnography is 'a response to the desire for a more personal social science that centres on identifying what it means to live a good and virtuous life'. Whether or not that goal is central to, or even articulated in, autoethnographic research and writing, I believe that these processes have value in their own right as transformative tools in the lexicon of professional education and lifelong learning; and that, potentially, they also have the power to challenge and disrupt the values now embedded in the neoliberal policies and practices of higher education institutions.

There are many different forms of, and approaches to, autoethnography (Ellis et al. [2011: paras 15–24] provide a useful overview). Here, I have primarily adopted a 'personal narrative' approach in an attempt to create congruence between the content and style of the chapter.

Getting started

Ellis et al. (2011: para 39) note that, 'The questions most important to autoethnographers are: who reads our work, how are they affected by it, and how does it keep a conversation going?' In the interests of opening the conversation(s) that I hope this chapter will prompt – and with 'Why Me?' as its title – I should probably begin by saying something about myself. However, that is not quite as easy as it sounds. As qualitative researchers know only too well, the 'story' someone chooses to tell about her/himself varies according to myriad factors such as place, time, audience, mood, or simply what is uppermost in the storyteller's mind at that moment. Right now, for example, I could tell you about the 'me' who is a grandma; or the 'me' who identifies as an adult educator; or as a researcher or journal editor; or who has recently spent time in hospital; or – where should I begin – or stop? To use Didion's (1979: 11) poetic imagery: 'We live … by the imposition of a narrative line upon disparate images, by the "ideas" with which we have learned to freeze the shifting phantasmagoria which is our actual experience'.

The question of how people 'freeze the shifting phantasmagoria' of their experiences and make sense and meaning out of them has been central to my professional life. For a large part of that, I have been involved in facilitating critical reflective practice with practitioners in a variety of settings, including doctoral and professional development programmes (see Hunt, 2016).

Looking at a birthday card I received recently, I wondered whether I have become rather tiresome to my friends in pursuing the question of meaning-making. The cartoon on the card depicts a woman lying in bed with a 'thought bubble' over her head. Inside the bubble is written: '*Another day in the great narrative of life, another chance to impose structure and significance on human experience, another …*'. A second bubble contains the words of someone who is not in view but who cuts into the woman's thoughts with the words: '*Are you getting up or not?*' (see Figure 3.1).

The card made me laugh out loud not only because it was an affectionate dig at one of my passions by someone who knows me well, but also because it sums up perfectly the difficulty I have often encountered in academia in convincing certain people that the 'inward journey' to the source of personal meaning-making is an appropriate focus for research. There are signs that this is now better understood: for example, Sage has recently published a four-volume set of books on autoethnography as part of its 'Benchmarks in Social Research Methods'

Figure 3.1 'Are you getting up or not?' © Judy Horacek

series (Sikes, 2013); and in May 2014, the Eleventh International Congress of Qualitative Inquiry called for expressions of interest in forming a Special Interest Group on Autoethnography (see the Appendix to this chapter). Nevertheless, I am mindful of the fact that my own research and writing within the genre of autoethnography has sometimes elicited comments from reviewers such as: 'I find this an entirely uncongenial approach ... very self-indulgent and navel gazing'. The autoethnographic aspects of my work were also deemed (I quote) 'too risky' by a former Director of Research and Head of School to be entered into the Research Excellence Framework (REF), the system for assessing the quality of research in UK higher education institutions. They advised me fairly strongly that, in career terms, choosing to research/write in such a style was not wise.

When I look at the card, theirs is the voice I hear from off-stage demanding 'Are you getting up or not?' It carries a strident message that not only cuts across a personal life-world to which autoethnography seeks to give expression in examining the 'structure and significance' of that world, but expects a completely different kind of engagement with a 'reality' that the off-stage voice has the power to determine. In most UK higher education institutions the current reality can perhaps best be described as an 'audit culture' (see Sparkes, 2007: 522).

At a certain point in one's career one has the luxury of being able to choose whether or not to remain within a culture where the dominant voices and values seem to have become increasingly incompatible with one's own. After much consideration, I eventually decided that, no, I *wasn't* 'getting up' in terms of changing the direction and style of much of my research and writing, but that I would, instead, leave my full-time post in the institution that wanted me to do so. I now pursue my interests in the 'inward journey' in other contexts (in particular as a Director and Trustee of the British Association for the Study of Spirituality [www.basspirituality.org.uk], as Editor of the *Journal for the Study of Spirituality* [www.tandfonline.com/loi/yjss], and in freelance work).

But I get ahead of myself. As I said, my purpose here is to raise questions about the place and function of autoethnography in education and educational research, and about the power of certain gatekeepers to exclude the 'self' of the researcher from the discourses of research and education. So, let us turn first to the question of what autoethnography 'is'. In that context I will also say something about my own inadvertent involvement in autoethnographic work, and about both the emergence and exclusion of autoethnography as 'signs of its times'. I will conclude by focussing on autoethnography in higher education, particularly in relation to professional doctorates.

Autoethnography and me

I had been writing and publishing for many years before I recognised that much of my work could be labelled autoethnographic. I think I first came across the term at an adult education conference where the late Valerie-Lee

Chapman (1999: 30), in a paper poignantly entitled 'A woman's life remembered: autoethnographic reflections of an adult/educator', pointed out that: 'Autoethnography has been inspired by feminist autobiography to risk writing about the everyday, about lives that were once not accounted as important enough for the researchers to bother with …'.

This statement alludes to pioneering work within the feminist movement such as that of Betty Friedan (1963). Friedan identified what she called 'the problem that has no name' – the vague, chronic discontent in the early 1960s of many white middle-class American women who, whilst leading ostensibly comfortable lives as 'housewives', felt isolated and depressed in ways that they were unable to articulate properly but which centred on the possibility of having an identity beyond that of wife and mother. Friedan (p. 20) said that, as a mother of three young children herself, she understood the 'groping words' of other women 'long before I understood their larger social and psychological implications'. By bringing the stories of many women together, Friedan's work not only had a much-needed therapeutic effect but it gave a massive jolt to conventional thinking about gender roles, helped to instigate the Women's Movement, and led to significant cultural change. I first came across Friedan's book in the 1970s when I had three young children of my own. It had a major impact on the way in which I then worked as an adult/community educator and subsequently engaged in research.

There has been much debate about how to define autoethnography, but the most commonly agreed understanding seems to be that it is a form of self-narrative that places the self in a social context (Reed-Danahay, 1997). Burdell and Swadener (1999: 22) argue that it is 'both a method and a text'. Essentially, it enables the researcher to draw consciously on her/his embodied self as both agent and subject of research and writing processes.

Ellis and Bochner describe the processes of how researchers create autoethnography as follows:

> As they zoom backward and forward, inward and outward, distinctions between the personal and the cultural become blurred, sometimes beyond distinct recognition. Usually written in the first-person voice, autoethnographic texts appear in a variety of forms – short stories, poetry, fiction, novels, photographic essays, personal essays, journals, fragmented and layered writing, and social science prose. In these texts, concrete action, dialogue, emotion, embodiment, spirituality, and self-consciousness are featured, appearing as relational and institutional stories affected by our history, social structure, and culture, which themselves are dialectically revealed through action, feeling, thought, and language. (Ellis and Bochner, 2000: 739)

Although I am a firm advocate of this process, it is important to note that autoethnography can be an ethical minefield. It helps to know what you are getting into, rather than blundering in blindly as I did! For example, in an editorial for *Qualitative Health Research*, Morse writes:

> With due respect to autoethnography, I usually discourage students from writing about their own experience. There are many reasons for this. First, the narrative is rarely their own. It includes information about others who are, by association, recognizable, even if their names have been changed. As such, writing about others violates anonymity. If these 'others' do not know about the article, it still violates their rights, for they have not given their permission and they do not have the right of withdrawal or refusal that informed consent provides. (Morse, 2002: 1159)

Notwithstanding such necessary caution, I advocate autoethnography as both a valuable and a virtuous process. It is what Pelias (2004: 1) calls a 'methodology of the heart' that is located within the researcher's own body: 'a body deployed not as a narcissistic display but on behalf of others, a body that invites identification and empathetic connection, a body that takes as its charge to be fully human'.

When I first studied psychology in the mid-1960s, it would have been almost impossible to write something like that. The quotation from Saint Augustine at the beginning of this chapter is evocative of the research culture in which I worked as a student (see Hunt, 2009: 78–79). Then, what was to be researched and understood lay in a world 'out there' that was quite separate from the researcher 'in here' – even when that world was constituted by one's fellow human beings as well as by the vastness of the Earth and stars.

My final-year undergraduate dissertation was influenced by Michael Argyle's (1970) work on interpersonal behaviour, especially the ways in which eye contact was used in social encounters. I filmed numerous different two-person discussions in which the relative 'status' of the two people varied. After analysing hundreds of film stills, I was able to demonstrate that 'higher status' individuals looked more often at their 'lower status' counterparts, who looked downwards for more of the time. The discussants' perceptions, feelings and observations on the process did not enter into the data. I moved into the field of education soon after graduation, sensing, but not yet able to articulate, concerns about 'objectivity' and measurement in human relationships (they play out still in my personal aversion to the audit culture and its consequences).

Nearly thirty years later, as an established adult/community educator undertaking a PhD that had strayed into the realm of spirituality, I was both startled and delighted to read John Heron's (1996) introduction to *Co-operative Inquiry*. It contains striking parallels with my dissertation experience – and suggests that my unarticulated concerns about that naive research process might unconsciously have shaped my otherwise apparently serendipitous career in adult/community education and interests in spirituality. Heron writes:

The co-operative inquiry model was born, in my world, in 1968–69 when I started to reflect on the experience of mutual gazing in interpersonal encounters. ... I also made the point that the conventional social scientist cannot properly inquire into the nature of the gaze by doing experiments on and gathering data from other people. The status and significance of the gaze can only be explored fully from within, by full engagement with the human condition.

... I felt that the human condition within myself, in relating with others, and on the wider canvas, was about increasing self-direction in living, in co-operation with other persons similarly engaged. And that this quest for personal and social transformation, for the interacting values of autonomy and co-operation, was at the heart of any truly human social science. (Heron, 1996: 1–2)

I now believe that this 'quest into the human condition' underpins both adult/community education and contemporary understandings of spirituality. The latter often focus on the ways in which people seem driven to search for meaning and purpose, including how they express a sense of 'interconnectedness' or relationship with what lies within, and beyond, themselves (Hunt, 2001; Hunt and West, 2007). As English and Gillen (2000: 2) point out, the pioneers of adult education sought to integrate spiritual and material needs and, in so doing, built their work on clear values concerning 'justice, service, caring, cooperation and the dignity of the person'.

I see autoethnography as an ideal vehicle in which to conduct inquiries into the spiritual and material aspects of the human condition. It enables us to 'wonder about ourselves', to locate that wonder within our sociocultural contexts, and to share our embodied experiences with others. As Ashton and Denton point out, autoethnography:

[E]xpands the horizons of our consciousness [Ellis, 2004]. The researcher/writer's interior inquiry and reflection mirror a larger human landscape, blurring the distinctions between the personal and the cultural. Such writing calls forth the possibility of dialogue, collaboration and relationship. (Ashton and Denton, 2006: 4)

Emergence/exclusion of autoethnography: signs of the times?

Anderson (2006: 375–378) claims that qualitative sociological research has always contained an autoethnographic element. He traces it back to Robert Park's encouragement of his students at the University of Chicago in the 1920s to conduct research in settings where they had 'a significant degree of self-identification' but notes that, despite this, students' reports rarely contained evidence of 'explicit and reflexive self-observation'. Research associated with the so-called Second

Chicago School and the work of Everett Hughes in the 1940s–1960s often focused on students' workplace settings and were 'analytically more sophisticated' but, in general, continued to 'downplay or obscure the researcher as a social actor in the settings or groups under study'. As in my own early encounter with research in psychology, these researchers focused on 'observing and analysing others in the settings studied, they had no "language of qualitative method" … that assigned particular merit to self-observation'. From the mid-1960s to 1970s, there was some experimentation with self-observation and analysis, but it was not until 1979 that a clear case was argued, in an essay on 'Auto-ethnography' by David Hyano, for self-observation in ethnographic research.

The emergence of autoethnography and other forms of engaging with the self as, and in, research (through life-histories and later auto/biographical methods) mirrored other 'signs of the times' in the late 1970s and 1980s: in the field of adult/community education, Freirean ideas about critical pedagogy were encouraging adults to understand their own experiences better in order to be able to participate in, and change, policies and services that powerful others had hitherto created for them; Schön (1983) was developing his case for professionals to reflect on, voice, and take ownership of their own knowing; and feminist writers were exploring the notion of the 'personal as political'.

As Valerie-Lee Chapman indicated in the conference presentation that first alerted me to the nature of autoethnography, feminist writers were especially influential in subsequently creating a turn towards what has become known as 'evocative autoethnography'. Denzin (1997: 228) notes that this invokes 'an epistemology of emotion, moving the reader to feel the feelings of the other'. Ellis and Bochner (2000: 744) elaborate, pointing out that, within this particular genre, 'the mode of story-telling is akin to the novel or biography and thus fractures the boundaries that normally separate social science from literature … the narrative text refuses to abstract and explain'. As Anderson (2006: 377) observes, evocative autoethnographers have published fairly extensively during the past two decades, including in what he calls 'traditionally realist qualitative-research journals' but 'they remain largely marginalized in mainstream social science venues, due to their rejection of traditional social science values and styles of writing'. In my experience, higher education has generally remained one such venue.

As if to verify Anderson's observation, in 2007 Andrew Sparkes published a highly evocative 'story' *about* higher education (specifically the impact of the then-ongoing Research Assessment Exercise [RAE] on people's lives and identities) not *in* a higher education journal but in *Qualitative Research* (and even there Sparkes felt obliged to acknowledge the journal's editors 'for giving the paper a chance even though they are not enamoured with the genre' [p. 546]). The story is a direct response to Pelias's (2004: 10–11) observation of a 'crisis of faith' amongst academics who had begun to feel 'empty, despondent, disillusioned … spiritually and ethically bankrupt', and his subsequent plea for a 'methodology of the heart' which allows greater connection between mind, body and emotions, and with others. Sparkes says of his own story that it 'seeks to speak from the heart about the embodied struggles of a composite and mythical (perhaps?) academic at an imaginary (perhaps?) university in England that is permeated by an audit culture' (p. 522). It deliberately provides no analysis but 'simply asks for your consideration'.

At the end of the story, Sparkes adds examples of 'moments of consideration' from a number of readers, including the anonymous reviewers. One reviewer notes that, although 'I am usually not much of a fan' of this kind of writing, 'I resonated with this'. S/he goes on to say:

> To overturn and overflow the received idea of 'acceptable' scholarship in a largely social science arena ... is a worthy goal IF the enactment allows something to be seen that could not otherwise be seen. Somewhere Foucault calls this 'increasing the circumference of the visible'. (p. 541)

The second reviewer refers specifically to the effects this 'powerful' story had on her/him and asks:

> [H]ow have we let our institutions of higher education become what they are? How have we ever allowed arbitrary quantitative measures to determine value? ... Forgive my rant, but the essay ... made me think about how legislative policies have genuine consequences for individual lives. It allowed me to see more fully the complexity, both conceptually and emotionally, of the problem. ... It persuaded me that change is needed. (*ibid*)

Another reader refers to the way in which 'the brutal and bullying aspects of an audit culture are exposed. ... It speaks of the things that matter to those that care. What more impact could it have than that?' Hunt, (*ibid.*)

My personal 'moment of consideration' was triggered by a section of the story called 'Tears of the Big Fellah' (pp. 529–530) which, although it evoked painful resonances of the 'Are you getting up?' conversation with my erstwhile Director of Research and Head of School, also offered a valuable piece of advice. The section takes the form of a dialogue between Jim, who is Director of Research in the School of Performance Studies (what nice irony in that title!), and the 'Big Fellah', Paul, an experienced colleague from the School of Educational Studies who, despite many years' service, a huge teaching load, innovative curriculum development, excellent student evaluations, and the publication of three articles in refereed journals, is about to lose his job. Paul tells Jim:

> 'They say my history here doesn't count for anything. They now say my research is not good enough. Not the right quality. Just not good enough.'

> His voice thins and trails off.

> He gasps, 'I'm not good enough.'

Jim gives Paul a hug and, repeatedly reassuring him that he *is* 'good enough', advises: 'Don't let them tell you otherwise. Don't believe the shit they are giving you. ... You are so much more than your CV.'

The reactions of Sparkes's readers indicate clearly why it is in the interests of the current audit culture to exclude a 'methodology of the heart' and its expression in autoethnographic writing. West (2001: 430) observes, in relation to auto/biographical methods more generally, that: 'They offer enriched and nuanced insights into processes of learning and into the human subject: in short, into ourselves as well as the other'. Thus, as Sparkes's reviewers noted, such methods do, indeed, increase the circumference of the visible and this can reveal and/or resonate with the uncomfortable emotional consequences of our own actions and/or the institutional policies to which we subscribe – and they can persuade us that change is needed. Whilst this would seem to be in keeping with 'really useful research' of a Freirean kind, it seems to be a sign of our present times that an evidence-base comprising shared personal accounts of the often-wounding impacts of policies and practices – and the need to change them – may struggle to 'count' within institutional league tables as a measure of 'good' research or academic writing.

Does that matter?

I will leave the question open for conversations beyond these pages – but I want to think about it for a moment just in the context of professional doctorates. I am most familiar with the Doctorate in Education (the EdD) so it is that to which, in conclusion, I will now turn.

Autoethnography, pedagogy and the Doctorate in Education (EdD)

Some years ago, I attended a conference organised by the Higher Education Academy in conjunction with the Quality Assurance Agency and other bodies. Its purpose was to examine the changing nature of the UK doctorate. I felt quite excited that there seemed to be a consensus that the process in which doctoral students engage is equally as important as their product, the thesis itself. Sadly, the bureaucracy of Research Councils and universities seems largely to have interpreted this in terms of the need to record/measure the kinds of skills training and supervision that students now receive. However, if we think about the process of learning to 'be' a researcher, I would suggest that that involves the embodiment of knowledge and, therefore, that the 'self' of the researcher is central to the research process.

Indeed, Willis (2004: 323) has argued that doctoral learning is precisely about 'deeper changes in the inner self of the learner/researcher. It is, to a greater or lesser extent, a road of transformation ...'. He outlines three kinds of transformation which a student may undergo on the doctoral journey: organic, unitary and critical. The first involves growing to maturity as a scholar. The second concerns the way in which '"self stories" or personal myths' may be identified and worked with or rejected: the transformative process here requires the embracing of one's own and others' subjectivities, including the associated struggles and epiphanies. Critical transformation is often a consequence of the first two and involves a different way of looking at, and relating to, the world.

One of my adult education colleagues once described how he was working towards an 'autoethnographic pedagogy' in his teaching (Armstrong, 2008). Drawing on an account by Pennington (2007: 99), he noted how, in order to teach a critical perspective on race, she had explored her personal thoughts on race, broken her own silence, and encouraged her students to do the same. This is undoubtedly risky business. However, as West (2001: 429) has noted in another context, 'it is a capacity to learn emotionally, including from "otherness" within – which lies at the heart of becoming more fully human' and which underpins 'good practice, both professionally as well as in personal life'.

I think there is a strong case for the use of an autoethnographic pedagogy within EdD programmes where the majority of students are themselves educators, not least because, as Sullivan points out:

> Our intellectual acts are inextricably embedded in and influenced by the life that accompanies them. The particular and complex combination of attitudes we bring to observation, critique, reflection and scholarship will colour, even to some extent condition, our discoveries, insights and reconstructions of reality. (Sullivan, 2003: 134)

In the EdD programmes that I have directed, I have encouraged colleagues to acknowledge Sullivan's point by sharing their personal research/life stories with students as well as the theories and methods underpinning their research. This is not only congruent with the values of adult education that have continued to shape my own professional practice, but it also works well: students have commented repeatedly on their high levels of satisfaction with the approach, which many say is 'inspirational'. I think this is because, in the words of one of Sparkes's readers, 'It speaks of the things that matter to those that care'.

Unfortunately, there often seems to be a disjuncture between this kind of modelling of the complex inter-relationship between scholarship and self and how research is presented in much published educational literature and report writing. As I have said, I think this is essentially a gatekeeping problem. While what Sparkes's reader called 'the brutal and bullying aspects of an audit culture' are allowed to dominate what is valued as educational research, the 'Are you getting up or not?' voices will continue to cut across – and to cut out from public view – the things that matter most in the personal life-world: the things that touch the heart.

In my final years as a full-time academic, as those neoliberal voices of the audit culture echoed around our research seminars, I do not think I was the only person who sometimes almost lost the will to live as we attempted to evaluate one another's research papers and to allocate them a score from 1-star to 4-star. As Saint Augustine might have pointed out, by focussing on those stars we were too easily forced to pass by the 'selves' of the writers/researchers and research participants that I believe lie at the core of the educational enterprise.

As I hope I have made apparent, I find the values of the audit culture, particularly when applied to education and educational research, very difficult to reconcile with my own view of what these processes are 'for'. I am much influenced by Carr's (1995) argument that educational theory and research should not be *about* education but *for* education, and they require a reflexive understanding of education. Staking a claim for a critical educational science, Carr demonstrates how this would produce 'the kind of educative self-knowledge that would reveal to practitioners the unquestioned beliefs and unstated assumptions in terms of which their practice was sustained' (p. 118).

Parker Palmer makes a similar plea for self-knowledge in a much-quoted passage that has also had a major impact upon my own work:

> The question we most commonly ask is the 'what' question – what subjects shall we teach?
>
> When the conversation goes a bit deeper, we ask the 'how' question – what methods and techniques are required to teach well?
>
> Occasionally, when it goes deeper still, we ask the 'why' question – for what purposes and to what ends do we teach?
>
> ... seldom, if ever, do we ask the 'who' question – who is the self that teaches? How does the quality of my selfhood form – or deform – the way I relate to my students, my subject, my colleagues, my world? How can educational institutions sustain and deepen the selfhood from which good teaching comes? (Palmer, 1998: 4)

As I have tried to demonstrate, I think the 'who' question lies at the heart – almost literally – of the educational enterprise. The time now seems ripe for it to be voiced clearly and unequivocally in the teaching and research processes of our institutions of higher education. The self matters.

Postscript

In terms of evaluating the specific contribution of autoethnography to research, I find Richardson's (2000: 15–16) description of the factors she uses when reviewing personal narrative papers helpful. I hope I have met at least some of them in this chapter. They are:

a   *Substantive contribution.* Does the piece contribute to our understanding of social life?
b   *Aesthetic merit.* Does this piece succeed aesthetically? Is the text artistically shaped, satisfyingly complex, and not boring?

c   *Reflexivity.* How did the author come to write this text? How has the author's subjectivity been both a producer and a product of this text?
d   *Impactfullness.* Does this affect me emotionally and/or intellectually? Does it generate new questions or move me to action?
e   *Expresses a reality.* Does this text embody a fleshed out sense of lived experience?

Acknowledgement

This chapter draws on a presentation I gave at the 39th Annual Conference of the Standing Conference on University Teaching and Research in the Education of Adults (SCUTREA): 'Really useful research? Critical perspectives on evidence-based policy and practice in lifelong learning', Downing College, Cambridge, 2009.

Appendix

The following is reproduced from a Call for Participation in a Special Interest Group on Autoethnography during the Eleventh International Congress of Qualitative Inquiry (May 2014) at the University of Illinois at Urbana-Champaign, USA. It provides an excellent summary of the values, virtues – and difficulties – of autoethnographic research and writing.

Writer Joan Didion [1979: 11] notes simply and powerfully, 'we tell stories in order to live'. Autoethnographic stories — stories of/about the self told through the lens of culture — enable us to live and to live *better*. Autoethnography allows us to lead more reflective, more meaningful, and more just lives by:

• Critiquing, making contributions to, and/or extending existing research and theory.
• Embracing vulnerability as a way to understand emotions and improve social life.
• Disrupting taboos, breaking silences, and reclaiming lost and disregarded voices.
• Making research accessible to multiple and diverse audiences.

To meet these goals, autoethnographers must balance the inward work of introspection with the outward work of social, cultural, and political critique. In the current moment, autoethnographers must seek ways of:

• Engaging deeply and explicitly with existing qualitative research and theory, showing what innovative and interdisciplinary critiques, contributions and/or developments autoethnographic stories can make to existing research conversations and traditions.

- Doing the vulnerable work of personal storytelling as a demonstration of a commitment to the larger goals and responsibilities of creating greater understanding with, empathy for, and improving the lives of others. In other words, asking and answering the question: what work does my story do in the world, for whom, and with what risks and possibilities?
- Working collaboratively with other scholars, as well as with the persons we study, live and work with, and love in our research and writing, demonstrating how autoethnography can expand the boundaries and possibilities of critical qualitative research both inside and outside of the academy.
- Creating work that not only names experiences of loss, exclusion, degradation and injustice but also showing how the stories we tell, the orientation we take to our research and our writing, and responsibility we assume as authors embody the change we seek to make in the world.
- Seeking new and nuanced ways to ethically engage in autoethnographic research that does not separate the experiences we are writing about from the goals of the work, the judgments we make of a story's impact or success, or the persons we become as storytellers; in other words, providing an example of how to engage qualitative research from a position of engagement and humility with and for ourselves, our interlocutors, and our readers/ audiences.

(International Congress of Qualitative Inquiry, 2016)

References

Adams, T. E. and Holman Jones, S. (2008) 'Autoethnography is queer', in N. K. Denzin, Y. S. Lincoln and L. T. Smith (eds) *Handbook of Critical and Indigenous Methodologies* (pp. 373–390). Thousand Oaks, CA: Sage.

Anderson, L. (2006/2012) 'Analytic autoethnography', *Journal of Contemporary Ethnography*, 35 (4): 373–395 (2006). Reprinted in J. Goodwin (ed.) (2012) *Biographical Research (Vol 1)* (pp. 357–378). London: Sage.

Argyle, M. (1970) *Psychology of Interpersonal Behaviour*. London: Penguin.

Armstrong, P. (2008) 'Toward an autoethnographic pedagogy', in J. Crowther, V. Edwards, V. Galloway, M. Shaw and L. Tett (eds) *Whither Adult Education in the Learning Paradigm?* (pp. 43–50). University of Edinburgh: SCUTREA.

Ashton, W. and Denton, D. (2006) *Spirituality, Ethnography and Teaching*. New York: Peter Lang.

Bochner, A. (2011) 'Beyond pleasure and pain: on the virtues of autoethnography', Paper presented at the annual meeting of the Seventh International Congress of Qualitative Inquiry, University of Illinois at Urbana-Champaign, USA.

Burdell, P. and Swadener, B. (1999) 'Critical personal narrative and autoethnography in education', *Educational Researcher*, August-September, pp. 21–26.

Carr, W. (1995) *For Education: Towards Critical Educational Inquiry*. Buckingham: Open University Press.

Chapman, V.-L. (1999) 'A woman's life remembered: autoethnographic reflections of an adult/educator', in B. Merril (ed.) *The Final Frontier: Exploring Spaces in the Education of Adults* (pp. 28–33). University of Warwick: SCUTREA.

Denzin, N. (1997) *Interpretive Ethnography*. Newbury Park, CA: Sage.

Didion, J. (1979) *The White Album*. New York: Simon & Schuster.

Ellis, C. (2004) *The Ethnographic I*. Walnut Creek, CA: AltaMira Press.

Ellis, C. and Bochner, A. (2000) 'Autoethnography, personal narrative, reflexivity: researcher as subject', in N. Denzin and Y. S. Lincoln (eds) *Handbook of Qualitative Research* (2nd edn). Thousand Oaks, CA: Sage

Ellis, C., Adams, T. E. and Bochner, A. (2011) 'Autoethnography: an overview', www.qualitative-research.net/index.php/fqs/article/view/1589/3095 (accessed 15/06/2015).

English, L. and Gillen, M. (eds) (2000) *Addressing the Spiritual Dimensions of Adult Learning: New Directions for Adult and Continuing Education*, 83. San Francisco: Jossey-Bass.

Friedan, B. (1963) *The Feminine Mystique*. New York: W. W. Norton & Co.

Heron, J. (1996) *Co-operative Inquiry: Research into the Human Condition*. London: Sage.

Hunt, C. (2016) 'Spiritual creatures? Exploring an interface between critical reflective practice and spirituality', in J. Fook, V. Collington, F. Ross, G. Ruch and L. West (eds) *Researching Critical Reflection: Multidisciplinary Perspectives* (pp. 34–47). London: Routledge.

Hunt, C. (2009) 'A long and winding road: a personal journey from community education to spirituality *via* reflective practice', *International Journal of Lifelong Education*, 28 (1): 71–89.

Hunt, C. (2001) 'Climbing out of the void: from chaos to concepts in the presentation of a thesis', *Teaching in Higher Education*, 6 (3): 351–367.

Hunt, C. and West, L. (2007) 'Towards an understanding of what it might mean to research spiritually', in L. Servage and T. Fenwick (eds) *Learning in Community* (pp. 301–306). Halifax, Canada: AERC/CASAE.

Hyano, D. (1979) 'Auto-ethnography: paradigms, problems, and prospects', *Human Organization*, 38: 99–104.

International Congress of Qualitative Inquiry (2016) Call for Participation from the Special Interest Group (SIG) on 'Autoethnography: Manifesting the Future of Autoethnography' for the 12th International Congress of Qualitative Inquiry, http://icqi.org/sig-in-autoethnography (accessed 15/06/2015).

Morse, J. (2002) 'Editorial: Writing my own experience ...', Qualitative Health Research, 12 (9) 1159–60

Palmer P. J. (1998) *The Courage to Teach: Exploring the Inner Landscape of a Teacher's Life*. San Francisco: Jossey-Bass.

Pelias, R. (2004) *A Methodology of the Heart*. Walnut Creek, CA: AltaMira Press.

Pennington, J. (2007) 'Silence in the classroom', *Race, Ethnicity and Education*, 10 (1): 93–113.

Reed-Danahay, D. (1997) *Auto/Ethnography: Rewriting the Self and the Social*. Oxford: Berg.

Richardson, L. (2000) 'Evaluating ethnography', *Qualitative Inquiry*, 6 (2): 253–255.

Schön, D. (1983) *The Reflective Practitioner*. London: Basic Books.

Sikes, P. (ed.) (2013) *Autoethnography (Sage Benchmarks in Social Research Methods: 4 Volumes)*. London: Sage.

Sparkes, A. (2007) 'Embodiment, academics and the audit culture: a story seeking consideration', *Qualitative Research*, 7 (4): 521–550.

Sullivan, J. (2003) 'Scholarship and spirituality', in D. Carr and J. Haldane (eds) *Spirituality, Philosophy and Education*. London: RoutledgeFalmer.

West, L. (2001) 'Journeying into auto/biography: the changing subject of lifelong learning', in L. West, N. Miller, D. O'Reilly and R. Allen (eds) *Travellers Tales: From Adult Education to Lifelong Learning – and Beyond* (pp. 427–430). University of East London: SCUTREA.

Willis, P. (2004) 'Mentorship, transformative learning and nurture: adult education challenges in research supervision', in C. Hunt (ed.) *Whose Story Now? (Re)generating Research in Adult Learning and Teaching.* University of Sheffield: SCUTREA.

Chapter 4

Personalism and the personal in higher education research

Julian Stern

Introduction

By their nature, personal issues are difficult to understand from the outside. What does it take to explore aspects of people's personal and private lives, in ways that generate a genuine understanding of those people, whilst at the same time avoiding unnecessary distress? It is an exploration of research into the personal, which also shows how the personal and the relational are themselves central to an understanding of how research is carried out in higher education. Higher education institutions have of course been centres for research since their inception. And research about higher education itself, and reflection on research processes in higher education, has grown hugely over recent times. This idea of research on, rather than in, higher education dates back particularly to Newman's 1858 work on 'the idea of a university' (Newman, 1907). In more recent decades, a third phase of higher education research has emerged within the traditions of action research and practitioner research. Sometimes referred to as 'pedagogic research', or the 'scholarship of teaching and learning in higher education' (Healey, in Barnett, 2005: 69), this appears to have developed alongside an increasing self-consciousness in higher education (Boyer, 1997), and alongside increasing pressures on all staff, including those with heavy teaching responsibilities, to be active empirical researchers (e.g. as a result of research audits such as HEFCE, 2011).

This increasingly popular practice of research within and on higher education brings with it a number of challenges. There are numerous difficulties of positionality, related to the authority relations amongst those involved. There is a possibility of a tension between the professionalism of those involved in the research (as researcher and researched) and the research virtues of honesty or sincerity. The research may be regarded as self-indulgent or as lacking in extended applicability or reliability. This chapter does not provide 'solutions' to all the problems, but explores the personal aspects of such research: the tensions between honesty and professionalism, between sincerity and humility, and between engaging people in your research and exploiting people for your personal and career benefit. Based on three examples from two decades of my own research projects in/on higher education, I provide examples of problems – not examples of 'good practice' – in the hope of informing other researchers. I explore approaches to personal and professional challenges, and ways of building up appropriate levels of trust – notwithstanding the pain and the risk of researchers being far from virtuous. Underpinning the research is the philosophical tradition of 'personalism', and the chapter's conclusion links personal aspects of research to personalism itself.

Example 1: researching your own students

The first example is of research I carried out more than twenty years ago (and published as Stern, 2001), in my first substantial piece of educational research. Working three days a week as a schoolteacher, and two days a week in teacher education, I was interested in how schools worked as communities that are hierarchical. My research interest was not in the processes of research, but in how schools supported learning. As a matter of convenience, the school in which I taught, and the small group of schools with which I was working as a teacher educator, were the most straightforward choices of places in which to complete the research. And, as I was setting tasks for student teachers working in the group of schools, it seemed that those students would provide additional insights into how those schools worked. The study would be informed by the community theory of Macmurray (1946, 2012), the learning theory of Lave and Wenger (1991), and the theories of power and hierarchy of Aristotle (1976). Although the literature inevitably informed the research questions, it did not initially influence the detail of the empirical research methods to be used. However, as the research project progressed, the theories returned and ended up informing the methods far more than I had expected.

Research problems resulting from researching your own students (both university teacher education students, and school students) include the professional ethical problems of, potentially, exploiting power relationships for your own advantage, and the research ethical problems of, potentially, generating biased data, as respondents would feel obliged to respond in ways suited to a tutor/teacher who has a responsibility for assessing and providing reports and references for them. Research instruments used included versions of relatively standard school improvement instruments describing 'real' and 'ideal' characteristics of the school (derived from Dalin and Rust, 1983; Dalin et al., 1993) for student teachers, school staff and school students, and some activities for the student teachers involving creating maps of statements on school organisation. One way of mitigating the professional and research problems would have been to make the research as separate as possible from the professional context, complemented by making participation entirely voluntary. Another was to build the work into the legitimate 'normal' activities of the participants. I decided on the second approach. The activities were all integrated into the teacher education programme (for the student teachers) and into personal and social education lessons (for the school students). Participation in the activities was not voluntary, but permission was sought for the outcomes to be used for research purposes. The framing of the research was thought to be the most significant mitigation of the problems. Younger participants were invited to take part in research intended to help the school improve, and adult participants were invited to take part in research intended to help schooling in general improve, through increasing understanding of schools as communities.

As the research project progressed, the theories began to gain prominence. From the philosophy of Macmurray came an account of the distinction between telling the truth (i.e. selecting from your valid thoughts) and being sincere. Avoiding telling falsehoods is all very well, he says, '[b]ut sincerity in the mind is much more than this', as '[i]t is positively expressing what you do think and believe' (Macmurray, 1995: 76). Sincerity emerged as central to the research ethic. In order to try to elicit 'sincere' responses, the research was structured in such a way as to attempt to give respondents good reasons for being both 'truthful' in the narrow sense of avoiding lying, and also 'sincere' in Macmurray's sense. An illustration of this approach was that, when introducing the questionnaire to school students I asked, 'Do you think you know, better than the teachers, how this school could be run?' The school students answered, in a loud and immediate chorus, 'Yes'. They had been invited to take part in the research, and their sincerity was encouraged through framing the research as helping the school improve. Through convincing them that I, as a researcher, understood that their views were valued by themselves as well as by me, I was demonstrating a sincere confidence in the value of their views. The virtue of sincerity, in this form, became the central quality in the account of the ethics of the research project.

A second way in which the theorising came to take over elements of the methodology was with respect to the choice of participants. In the first instance, the choice of inviting participation from staff and students of each school (along with student teachers placed in some schools) was a simple pragmatic choice. It was a way of getting a larger number of participants, as I only had direct access to a small number of schools. As I came to understand more of the school improvement literature, and even more the learning communities literature, I realised that participation of all members of the school community was itself a quality that would help determine the community nature of the school. The research process, by being 'about' and 'for' the school, was also contributing to school improvement (i.e. how the school as a whole developed or 'learned') and to its nature as a learning community. Lave and Wenger (1991) described learning as, typically, a process of 'situated learning'. Learning, they said, is primarily a process of induction into social practices, and therefore it takes place not simply 'with' society or 'through' society but as a way of coming to be 'in' society. Hence, when 'I' learn, I am gradually coming to be, at first, a legitimate peripheral participant in a social practice, and then a central participant in that practice. As Hanks says in his foreword to the book, learning is an activity and not simply an accumulation of knowledge: 'learning is a way of being in the social world, not a way of coming to know about it' (Lave and Wenger, 1991: 24). The process of research, involving school students and staff (and student teachers), was not only a form of learning for me (that is, it was my research), it was also a form of learning for the school students and staff individually and, I hoped, a form of learning for the school collectively. I was not in control of all the forms of learning, or the interpretation of the research, within the schools, and I was upset to find that one headteacher insisted that my research 'proved' what he had long believed, that the teachers' trade union had 'literally destroyed this school' such that 'there was nothing of joy in the school' (Stern, 2001: 94–95). He introduced the research findings to the staff of the school with this interpretation, and, upsetting as it was for me, it was a good illustration of the difficulty of someone who was something of an 'outsider' attempting to contribute to school development, as described by McDonald (1989). McDonald's view is that an outsider must believe that change is possible, but must also 'have a sense of the immense complexities and staggering ambiguities of life on the inside and of how all outside interventions of policy, curriculum, and method are transformed by inside culture' (McDonald, 1989: 207).

Along with sincerity and participation in learning communities, the third way in which theorising came to underpin methodology was through the hierarchical theories of Aristotle. Initially used by me to explain aspects of school leadership, Aristotle's description of leadership virtues and the 'crown of the virtues', magnanimity (Aristotle, 1976: 153–158), became, somewhat surprisingly, significant for my understanding of the research process itself. Aristotle does not have a straightforward preference for one leadership structure over another, and writes positively about what might be referred to as monarchy (rule by one person), oligarchy (rule by an elite group of people), and democracy (rule by all, albeit usually meaning only adult male citizens). The way he explores the ethics of leadership, in any of these structures, is to look at the attitude of the leaders. Are they leading for their own benefit, or for the sake of the led? For example, in a literally paternalistic account of leadership, he says that a good monarch will act for the led in the way that a good father will act for his children, 'because he is concerned for the welfare of his children' (Aristotle, 1976: 276). A tyrant (i.e. a 'bad' monarch), in contrast, will treat the led like slaves, and justice and friendship, along with magnanimity, will be absent (Aristotle, 1976: 278). Concern for the led, or its absence, determines the ethical quality of leadership, with magnanimity being the virtue that leaders may and should exhibit when they have the other good leadership qualities. (A bad leader who tries to act in a magnanimous way will simply be exhibiting arrogance.) This is interesting in the analysis of school hierarchies, especially as schools are all too rarely democratic and therefore need an account of ethical if non-democratic leadership (as argued in Stern, 2002). But for research methodology it is also significant. Researchers may be in positions of power over those researched, as I was – with respect to school students and teacher education students. And the approach to research in those circumstances should – I came to understand – exhibit suitable care for those being researched. The care might be, as Aristotle suggested, like that of a parent for a child or a (good) political leader for the led. Or, to draw on a more modern philosopher, parents, teachers, leaders or friends could be described as exhibiting 'care ethics' (Noddings, 1984, 2012). I felt a need to 'care for' the school students and teacher education students – as a teacher and tutor – and that care ethic came to be associated with my research too. Not only this, but I realised that I had attempted to convince the students of this ethic. By asking, for example, whether school students knew more than others about how the school might be run, as an introduction to asking whether they were willing to take part in research, I was hoping to exhibit my sincerity, participation, and care or magnanimity. It is worth saying that I might also have been exhibiting manipulation, trying to get the students on my side against the teachers, and kidding myself that I was being sincere. But as I was content explaining the approach to teachers, none of whom questioned my motives, I believed the first explanation was more valid.

In the final write-up of the research (Stern, 2001), theorising and methodology and methods intertwined. The traditional research genre goes from literature to methodology to methods to findings to conclusions. On this occasion, the literature review continued long after the empirical research had been carried out, so that the methodology was rewritten regularly after the methods had been applied. That particular topsy-turvy approach is easy to justify and explain. The next example is a little tougher.

Example 2: researching your own colleagues

When I started working in universities, initially alongside schoolteaching, I found that some were full of intellectual, research-oriented discussions over lunch or coffee. Others, however, were not: it was as though research were entirely a private affair, at best a hobby, and often seen as either a distraction from functional teaching concerns or a cruel burden laid on staff by unsympathetic managers. These experiences influenced my work as a university manager. I became head of a large department in 2003, and dean of a faculty in 2005 – and I have continued as a dean, albeit of different faculties, since then. Throughout that time, I have wanted to encourage research as a normal part of conversation, and to support the idea of universities as – amongst other things – intellectual learning communities. As Barnett says, '[c]ommunity is not given in university life; it has to be worked at', and '[a]n academic ethic is not a matter of rules and regulations but has to be lived, and lived collectively' (Barnett, 2005: 107). He gives significant responsibility for this ethic to university leaders, as '[a] task of university leadership … is that of infusing a university with energy, with spirit' and it is '[i]deas [that] help to enflame' as 'they can give a university more life' – '[m]ore becoming even' (Barnett, 2011: 153).

For more than a decade, I have therefore been trying to keep the conversation going, as a colleague and as a manager. This was and continues to be a matter of everyday activity, discussing research with people over lunch, or making connections between an apparently functional issue (such as a discussion of optimum turnaround time for assessment feedback) and theorising and research (such as the potential for assessment feedback to be dialogic in the sense implied by the philosopher Buber, as in Stern and Backhouse, 2011). However, it also involved somewhat more formal annual 'research conversations' carried out in the two universities in which I have been a manager. These were carried out by myself and one or two other experienced researchers with individual academic staff across the faculty. Along with thousands of more informal research-related conversations with colleagues in my own universities, and universities I have visited and worked with around the world, I have taken part in several hundred of the more formal research conversations. I wrote and presented a conference paper that described, in outline, some of the issues raised by those conversations (Stern, 2011), and I was later invited to write a journal article on the same topic. This was eventually published (Stern, 2014), but not without a great deal of rather difficult discussion. Before getting on to that, it is worth considering the substance of the conversations.

In all the informal and formal research conversations I attempted to take part in what Buber referred to as 'genuine' dialogue, in contrast to 'technical' dialogue (the exchange of information, aiming at 'objective understanding') and 'monologue disguised as dialogue' (Buber, 2002: 22). In genuine dialogue, Buber says, 'each of the participants really has in mind the other or others in their present and particular being and turns to them with the intention of establishing a living mutual relation between himself [*sic*] and them' (Buber, 2002: 22). It is not enough, in other words, to attempt to avoid wholly artificial dialogue, i.e. monologue disguised as dialogue. And the conversations would need to go beyond merely seeking information or understanding. They should attempt to establish *a living mutual relation.* (Mutuality is not the same as equality: there can be mutuality within relationships that include power inequalities.) The questions asked in the more formal conversations focused on research already completed, research planned for the future, and how we – the researchers leading the conversations – could help with the research. It would have been easy to have asked such questions, but to have done so in order to fulfil other purposes. The greatest risk seemed to me to be confusing the conversations with an audit of research performance. As a manager, I had a responsibility for various performance audits, including individual staff performance reviews and collective disciplinary, university-level or national research audits (as in HEFCE, 2011). In order to avoid such audits dominating the conversations, it was made clear that staff involved in the conversations might use the conversations towards their own performance reviews, or towards discussions about wider research audits, but that I would not 'report' the conversations to their line-managers, or record what was said for other management purposes. I also avoided setting performance targets, although I was happy to discuss how I might support any targets set by members of staff.

These were attempts to demonstrate sincerity, but they were somewhat negative attempts – through the absence of linking the conversations to external targets. In order to demonstrate sincerity positively, I wanted to demonstrate my own real interest in the research being discussed, trying to find the genuinely interesting elements, trying to explore its intellectual properties, key concepts, and links to other research – including my own research and the research of other colleagues. By doing this, I was myself inviting conversationalists in to the learning community of researchers, to participate in the community to which the senior researchers leading the conversations already belonged. Each of the researchers leading the conversations also took turns as conversationalists: inviting ourselves into participation in the intellectual learning community. A single discussion, without any evidence of continuing mutuality, might have been regarded as insincere. The more formal conversations were therefore intentionally followed up informally by the conversationalists, and the more formal conversations were repeated each year, each time referring back to the content and the expectations described in previous years. This was accomplished through a mixture of memories (of all participants) and the notes that I took myself of key issues raised. The communal nature of the conversations was also demonstrated, I hoped, by annual reports offered after each set of more formal conversations. Those reports explored some of the common issues raised in the conversations, without naming participants. They were reported to the relevant faculty research committee, and were sent to all participants. Making connections between people and their research, and following up questions and comments after the conversations, were – it was hoped – also demonstrations of the care ethic that I and the other conversational leaders had for staff. As with earlier interpretations, I might have been kidding myself. What transpired does indeed suggest that my interpretation of my work was not congruent with the interpretation of some colleagues. I will continue with the account of the project, drawing out these differences of interpretation.

A question that hangs over many conversations about research in universities is 'why do we do research?' Because we are curious, I believe. It is curiosity – the wish to learn, to find out, to create new knowledge or understanding or insights – that should drive research. Not external audits, not finance, not status or power or influence over policy, but curiosity. Of course those other purposes of research will rightly be taken into account. Succeeding in an audit, generating finance that makes research more sustainable, or gaining promotion or influence, are all valuable and important for individuals and for institutions. Yet they are secondary benefits of research, I suggested to colleagues. And by repeating this, I hoped to affirm my own – and their – wish to learn, to be curious, and to do this in part through genuine dialogue in the various research conversations.

After writing a conference paper on the issues raised (Stern, 2011), and being invited to contribute an article on the topic, I realised that my own and others' image of the conversations might not be quite aligned. In 2013, my annual report to the faculty research committee was in the form of a draft of a possible article, based both on the more formal conversations held that year in that institution, and also on all the more and less formal conversations held in several UK institutions, and in institutions in Germany, China (Hong Kong), and the US. I also said that I hoped to publish the report, and because I had that intention, I was asked to make a request for ethical approval of the research. One of the difficulties that then emerged was that retrospective ethical permission appeared to be ruled out, not least by the question on the ethics form 'Will it be necessary for participants to take part in the study without their knowledge or consent at the time?' The various conversationalists did not know *at the time* – as I did not know – that I might wish to publish the research, and so no prior consent was sought. I was, nevertheless, allowed to seek retrospective permission. Permission was sought – coordinated by the research ethics committee – and all participants in the faculty were also sent a copy of the draft article for their approval and asked to indicate any revisions or corrections they felt were needed. However, once that had been completed, it became clear that I would need to know who had or had not given consent, in order to adjust the article to take account only of the conversations held with people who had given consent. And that putative list was itself regarded by the research ethics committee as a potential source of concern for participants. There might, it was thought, be negative effects on manager–staff relationships. The solution offered was that I might submit the article for publication if I were to protect anonymity, write in general terms, and not quote any conversationalists or provide any other specific data (such as quantitative date) that might be attributed to a particular group of staff.

This was not simply a procedural problem. I had not thought that the reports on the conversations were sensitive, or that making public the issues arising from the conversations might possibly be regarded as coercive or as damaging relationships. Indeed, I had – as explained above – intentionally attempted to make the conversations genuinely dialogic, and to invite participation both in the individual conversations, and also in wider conversations within and beyond the institution. So people expressing their concerns was a rather upsetting surprise. Upsetting, that is, because my own view of the conversations was not shared by (some) others, and because I had not realised that. Researchers, like students, are used to submitting work to others, and are used to receiving it back with critical comments, and perhaps rejection or failure. All are expected to have sufficient humility to take on board any critical comments, and to have sufficient self-confidence to persevere. I was certainly prepared to revise my plans in response to the issues raised by the research ethics committee, particularly as the original draft of the article included no quotations, so all I had to do to make the article 'general' was to take out reference to how many conversationalists there had been in any institution, or any patterns specific to any institution. That was the easy part, and took no more than a few minutes to achieve. The harder part was the self-examination needed, to explore how the research conversations – or making public an analysis of them – might be regarded as coercive or otherwise damaging. Was I experiencing what Serres describes as the penalty of power, of reason?

> [W]hoever wields power … never encounters in space anything other than obedience to his power, thus his law: power does not move. When it does, it strides on a red carpet. Thus reason never discovers, beneath its feet, anything but its own rule. (Serres, 1997: xiii)

Since the article has been published (Stern, 2014), following the normal process of peer review (and revision to take account of the reviewers' criticisms), there has been no further reaction, and the research conversations, both informal and more formal, have continued with no change noticeable to me. This suggests either that no further damage to relationships resulted from the whole correspondence leading to the publication, or perhaps – and more worryingly – that staff were already sufficiently suspicious of a manager taking part in a research conversation, that the levels of suspicion have simply remained steady.

One of the difficulties, therefore, of 'insider' research and how it is reported by the insider is clearly the possibility of self-delusion. In terms of the published research, I was sufficiently confident in the mitigation of potential 'management bias', through the use of conversations across a number of institutions in several countries (in most of which I had no management role), and through the lack of any suggested revisions to the draft article (when it was sent around to conversationalists). However, the sense of my being unaware of concerns, until they were raised, remained troubling. I was sufficiently interested in the 'trouble' with this project, to start a whole new project, exploring the challenges that other researchers found in their own research. This is the basis for my third example.

Example 3: researching colleagues in other higher education institutions

As I write this chapter, I am in the middle of research for a book on 'virtuous educational research' (Stern, 2016). This involves conversations with educational researchers around the world, about the 'research challenges' and 'personal challenges' they have faced, and how they have dealt with those challenges. The first two examples given in this chapter have challenges resulting from my institutional 'insider' status, and from my hierarchical power relationship to some participants. For the virtuous educational research project, there are few such examples, as the participants are almost all based in other institutions, are all – like me – experienced researchers, and are all – except for two people – independent of me in terms of management relationships. Are there examples from this research of the kinds of challenges I have described earlier in this chapter, or of others? I would like to provide an account of one of the conversationalists, Chris Sink, an American specialist in school counselling (Sink, 2005).

Sink is a researcher on 'making meaning, and social and emotional learning', and he is keen that, through his research, he can fulfil his 'strong desire to and passion to actually make a difference not only in schools, but in the broader community as well'. (All quotations are taken from transcriptions, but with ellipses and interruptions and hesitations edited out, and changes in the text indicated by square brackets.) The challenges he faces are wide-ranging, and many are related to the professional responsibilities of researchers. Although his research is not primarily on higher education, it does – like my first example – involve work with his students and colleagues as co-researchers and/or participants. One of the challenges is to 'maintain integrity and discipline within the research thing rather than submitting to publish or perish, but to do things that actually mean something to [a] broader population'. This could, in turn, help 're-envision school culture, and re-envision or re-imagin[e] the way we see children and our interaction with children'. This is not only of value in itself, but also because 'the exercise of thinking and writing and communicating whether it be to a narrow audience or to a[n] extensive audience, is part of the good life if you will'. And, by 'reflecting on higher order events', the 'experiences can influence yourself as well as potentially your small circle of friends and, ultimately, the ripple can transcend the oceans'.

The young people studied 'orient their lives' in different ways, but there is a danger that 'you begin to pigeonhole kids', but 'that's not the goal'. The goal, Sink continued, 'is to inform, and also to use in a counselling setting'. He gave an example of his work in a US high school with 'pretty high functioning kids'. 'They're all really interested in meaning of life', so 'they took the instrument, they got their scores back and then they compared them, and they said "oh that makes sense to me – yeah I really am more optimistic and you're really kind of not really optimistic – why is that?", and so, you can use that as a tool to build rapport and further conversation within the therapeutic context'. There is a tension between creating statistically-validated research tools that can be used by professionals and by young people, without also creating the means by which people label and separate. So the young people in his example are given these 'tools', 'but I'm not giving them tools to structure and differentiate, and to label'. The same goes for professionals.

> I really dislike interacting with bureaucrats who don't really care about research and are only wanting to know what's in it for them: in other words, are you going to fund a new programme or are you going to bring grant money into our district. Research for the sake of research and knowing kids and knowing teachers and knowing things is often times not of value to them, and so we have a clash: they're pragmatic and they are 'instant gratification', and if you can't do anything for them immediately, they oftentimes forsake. As one of the districts I recently contacted said there were not enough outcomes that they would value, [not enough] 'deliverables'. And I didn't even know what that meant, to be honest with you.

Understandably, 'it's a disappointment and a discouragement to see schools shutting their doors and not recognising the value of quality research'. Although 'I understand they're so overburdened by the state mandates', but, 'on the other hand, aren't you supposed to be lifelong learners?' The problems of labelling and of being driven by 'mandates' is not only relevant to those studying and working in schools. They also relate to research in higher education itself. Amongst the list of virtues developed by Peterson (taken from Csikszentmihalyi and Csikszentmihalyi, 2006: 45), Sink listed a number that were relevant to his research, one of which was 'intimacy'. I was interested in this idea, particularly with respect to counselling research, because counselling itself is typically a very intimate process. How was this virtue exemplified in Sink's work?

> I think the intimacy comes with the work they have to do with the teachers, the administrators, to build the rapport. I spend a lot of preparatory time in the schools. Once the school district has given me the okay, or even if before, I may meet with heads and administrators to talk about their studies. So there is a sense of social intimacy that you have to establish, and trust, which is an intimate [quality], and honesty, and transparency, which I think are all parts of intimacy.

The issue of gaining the trust of teachers or principals helps them feel confident with the materials that they're going to use with the young people, and the researchers 'have to convince them that this is safe'. And this is equally important for Sink's graduate students who carry out much of the research in schools: 'You have to create a level of trusting intimacy with those graduate students to be willing to do this work and to be vulnerable, to take the hits they're going to get [when] they go to the school and the teacher's not there, or the kids, half the kids are on a field trip'. He also described the value of trust in the very conversation we were having: 'I know you, and I trust you, but if I was just off the street, and you asked me this question, I think there would be a more hesitant nature of me to express more of my deeper feelings'. 'Spirituality' was another virtue highlighted by Sink, but this is connected to intimacy and the social, relational, aspects of research. 'Meeting people, making relationships, community, building community, are all spiritual acts for me', he said, and 'not in a religious sense but certainly in a broader context of giving meaning'.

These virtues are articulated specifically as *higher education* virtues, although relevant also to other contexts. Sink explained how much he *cares* about what he does. 'I care about what I do, and that's a different word that's not included on [Peterson's original] list of strengths'.

> Just really caring, deeply caring for the kids you're working with, the community you're working with, and the outcomes, and the data itself, and the processes. I really care to do it right, rather than sloppily putting something together. Caring for what you do, caring from yourself, caring for the inanimate nature of research. Those are all indescribable, but they do, they do generate a lot of motivation for me. I care what you think. Now there are researchers I know, and I'm curious to see if you'll find any, who only care about the product and using the product to advance their career, which is

more of an instrumental care, not what I call a virtuous care. I think this is where it gets to this notion of what is a professor. The virtuous professor in my opinion, does research because they care. But there's many people who just say 'I have to tick off that research box, I don't really like researching, but I know I have to get three publications to advance, so I'm going to find a way to do it'. And it drives me crazy, and that to me is not virtuous research.

Later in the conversation, I invited questions from him, and what he asked was a surprise: 'The only question I have was, you're looking at ethical practice, [but] you never ask about ethics, because ethics has a legal and a state dimension that is not covered in this kind of study, which is more imposed, external, [but] what you're talking about is more internal'. The procedural ethical challenges 'are incredibly important challenges', and 'they plague me – I mean trying to work with schools on consent forms – it's absolutely phenomenally taxing'. This does not 'affect my virtuous practice as much as it does my own patience'. What is more, the procedural, legalistic, ethical systems can confuse professionals in schools as well as researchers: 'Our society is extraordinarily litigious, and often times it's hard for teachers to differentiate between what is legal and what is ethical, [so] my concern is that they think that what is ethical is what is legal or vice versa'.

These extracts from a much longer conversation illustrate a number of important points. One is that the purpose of researching is important to Sink, as it is to me. Our research is curiosity-driven, educationally-driven, and more broadly socially-driven, and is not driven simply by the need to achieve externally-set targets. Sink's research – like mine – was in danger of being misused by readers, in Sink's case by young people or their teachers who might label and differentiate people. The processes of research can be personally upsetting and frustrating, either when research is misused or when the research itself is blocked. And there are aspects of trust and intimacy and care that are central to the processes of research themselves as well as – in Sink's case – the subject matter of the research. Sink highlighted the issues of relationships within higher education as central to the process.

Conclusion: personalism is personal

A number of philosophers who have influenced my work are referred to as 'personalist' philosophers, and these include Macmurray and Buber (Long, 2000, Chapter 11). As Fielding and Moss say,

'[P]ersonalism' stands in marked contrast to the now familiar notion of 'personalisation'. Personalism places the individual in an inescapably relational nexus, within which individuality emerges and learning occurs and from which community and all other human forms of engagement derive their vibrancy and legitimacy. Personalisation, by contrast, sees the individual in isolation, the autonomous learner restlessly seeking to become an ever-better entrepreneur of the self. ... [P]ersonalism as a philosophical and political movement is antagonistic to both individualism and collectivism and argues for a deeply relational view of the self. Amongst its best-known twentieth century proponents were Emmanuel Mounier and Jacques Maritain in France and John Macmurray in the UK. Later thinkers with affinities to the movement include Emmanuel Levinas and Paul Ricoeur. (Fielding and Moss, 2011: 48)

In this chapter, I have explored some of the implications of personalism for the processes of research itself, and for the putative 'research virtues' that may be demonstrated by researchers. Personalism is not simply a cognitive stance, a narrowly-conceived 'philosophical system'. It is a way of being in the world, which inevitably has personal consequences. Marx's gravestone quotes him: '[t]he philosophers have only interpreted the world in various ways: the point, however, is to change it' (http://highgatecemetery.org/visit/cemetery/east). His philosophy can hardly be described as personalist, even if some of his earlier writings come closer than might be expected to that position. But his insistence on intellectual work being socially engaged has influenced a great deal of philosophy, and the personalism of Macmurray and Buber are no less politically charged for having personhood itself as central to the most profound of their philosophical insights. What I hope to have demonstrated here is that the personal and the relational are just as central to an understanding of the processes of research as they are to any other social practice.

Personal issues may be difficult to understand from the outside, but research in and on higher education nevertheless raises personal issues that should be understood if the research itself is to be understood. The challenges of positionality, of sincerity, of trust and honesty, the pain and frustration involved in research: all are better admitted and discussed. Ignoring them gives a false sense of research in and on higher education being impersonal and blandly objective. That would also ignore the personal, communal, nature of higher education itself. Seeing higher education as a service industry, a kind of high street banking system that trades in knowledge, misses the point – misses many points. The exploration of the various relationships involved in research in and on higher education reveals, I hope, how important the personal is, and how important, in turn, is personalism.

References

Aristotle (1976) *The Ethics of Aristotle: The Nicomachean Ethics*. London: Penguin.
Barnett, R. (ed.) (2005) *Reshaping the University: New Relationships Between Research, Scholarship and Teaching*. Maidenhead, Berkshire: Open University Press.
Barnett, R. (2011) *Being a University*. London: Routledge.
Boyer, E. L. (1997) *Scholarship Reconsidered: Priorities of the Professoriate*. San Francisco, CA: Jossey-Bass.
Buber, M. (2002) *Between Man and Man*. London: Routledge.

Csikszentmihalyi, M. and Csikszentmihalyi, I. S. (eds) (2006) *A Life Worth Living: Contributions to Positive Psychology.* Oxford: Oxford University Press.

Dalin, P., with Rolff, H-G., in co-operation with Kleekamp, B. (1993) *Changing the School Culture.* London: Cassell.

Dalin, P. and Rust, V. D. (1983) *Can Schools Learn?* Windsor: NFER-Nelson.

Fielding, M. and Moss, P. (2011) *Radical Education and the Common School: A Democratic Approach.* London: Routledge.

Higher Education Funding Council for England (HEFCE), Scottish Funding Council, Higher Education Funding Council for Wales, Department for Employment and Learning (2011) *REF2014: Research Excellence Framework: Assessment Framework and Guidance on Submissions.* Bristol: Hefce.

Lave, J. and Wenger, E. (1991) *Situated Learning: Legitimate Peripheral Participation.* Cambridge: CUP.

Long, E. T. (2000) *Twentieth-Century Western Philosophy of Religion 1900–2000.* Dordrecht, The Netherlands: Kluwer.

Macmurray, J. (1946) 'The Integrity of the Personal', *Joseph Payne Memorial Lectures,* King's College, London, 1 November 1946.

Macmurray, J. (1958/2012) 'Learning to be human', *Oxford Review of Education,* 38 (6): 661–674.

Macmurray, J. (1962/1995) *Reason and Emotion.* London: Faber.

McDonald, J. P. (1989) 'When outsiders try to change schools from the inside', *Phi Delta Kappan,* 71 (3): 206–212.

Newman, J. H. (1858/1907) *The Idea of a University Defined and Illustrated.* London: Longmans.

Noddings, N (1984) *Caring: A Feminine Approach to Ethics and Moral Education.* Berkeley: University of California Press.

Noddings, N. (2012) 'The caring relation in teaching', *Oxford Review of Education,* 38 (6): 771–781.

Serres, M. (1997) *The Troubadour of Knowledge.* Ann Arbor, MI: University of Michigan Press.

Sink, C. (ed.) (2005) *Contemporary School Counseling: Theory, Research, and Practice.* Boston, Massachusetts: Lahaska Press.

Stern, L. J. (2001) *Developing Schools as Learning Communities: Towards a Way of Understanding School Organisation, School Development, and Learning.* PhD Thesis. London: London University Institute of Education.

Stern, L. J. (2002) 'EMU leadership: An egalitarian magnanimous undemocratic way for schools', *International Journal of Children's Spirituality,* 7 (2): 143–158.

Stern, L. J. (2011) 'Dialogues of space, time and practice: supporting research in higher education', *British Educational Research Association Conference,* London, September 2011.

Stern, L. J. (2014) 'Dialogues of space, time and practice: supporting research in higher education', *Other Education: The Journal of Educational Alternatives,* 3 (2): 3–21.

Stern, L. J. (forthcoming, 2016) *Virtuous Educational Research: Conversations on Ethical Practice.* Oxford: Peter Lang.

Stern, L. J. and Backhouse, A. (2011) 'Dialogic feedback for children and teachers: evaluating the "Spirit of Assessment"', *International Journal of Children's Spirituality,* 16 (4): 331–346.

Chapter 5

The emergence of open-logic sense-making

A practitioner-researcher's experience of openness and criticality

Jane Rand

Introduction

This chapter began as a paper presented at the 2014 Value and Virtue in Practice-Based Research conference, whose theme was 'Openness and Criticality: Evaluating and Publishing Our Research'. Turning the paper into a chapter has made me reflect on my own experience of openness and criticality as a practitioner-researcher, and how these have become core values for me.

This exploration into my values became especially significant during my doctoral (EdD) research (Rand, 2011) where I explored the nature of the then-dominant epistemological traditions of initial teacher education within the English post-compulsory education and training sector. It helped me develop my interest in the discourses of what had emerged, in my view, as an unhelpful opposition, or polarity, between knowledge and skills in the sector. Because my research was practice-based – that is, understandings developed both *from* practice and *for* practice – I chose an action-oriented approach. I also wanted to find out how those who were new to teaching in the sector thought about knowledge and knowing. I therefore needed a reflexive methodology that would help me theorise my practice: as a teacher in the sector, a teacher-educator in the sector and a practitioner-researcher. I put constructivist grounded theory and action learning together, and found them to be powerfully overlapping fields of practice (see Rand, 2013).

In this chapter, therefore, I reflect on my research experience and propose that a mutually reciprocal theory-practice research methodology can create a space for a form of sense-making that Soja (1996: 60) calls 'open logic' – that is, a way of thinking that recognises multiple truths; a 'both/and also' alternative to the closed logic of 'either/or'. In my view, this type of theory-practice methodological choice can provide a means through which openness and criticality can become a core aspect of the practitioner-researcher's practice.

First I outline the contexts that informed my doctoral studies.

Contexts

From 2005 to 2013 I worked in a large English general Further Education College with responsibility for Initial Teacher Education. Throughout the course of my EdD programme (2007–2011) I found myself drawn into the discourses of, in my view, an unhelpful polarity between knowledge and skills within the sector, which was also called 'post-compulsory education and training'. Before that, I worked in a large Scottish general Further Education College, and I was aware even then that such a polarised view fosters an academic:vocational divide.

My research concern stemmed from an understanding that, unless the notion of an academic:vocational divide is problematised within the sector, there is a risk that student teachers (amongst others) would both uncritically accept, and actively promote a polarised (or 'binary') view that knowledge comprises separate categories. Tomlinson (1999a: 535) describes this phenomenon as 'experiential residue' – the 'default options' that student teachers bring with them to educa-tion from their own experience of schooling; in this case the residue appeared as a commitment to a binary (knowledge/skill) epistemology. This divisive perspec-tive is contradictory to contemporary expectations that knowledge and skill are being 're-integrated theoretically – as in "thinking skills" or "problem-solving skills"' (Ainley, 2000: 5).

Throughout my doctoral studies, and in contrast to the dominant view of forms of knowledge comprising separate categories, I found myself drawn to an understanding of the relationship(s) between skills and knowledge. I there-fore wished to explore what kind of polarities might contribute to the 'default options' that student teachers bring with them to education. To engage with these issues meant exploring my own positionality as a practitioner-researcher, including my own 'experiential residue' (Tomlinson, 1999a: 535); this became central to my EdD experience and to writing up my thesis. My autobiography therefore inevitably shaped my study, and exploring it helped me to make sense of why I found the concept and experience of polarity so problematic.

Exploring positionality requires a commitment to both openness and critical-ity. My own critical exploration of polarity was typified by 'a persistent effort to examine any belief or supposed form of knowledge in the light of the evidence that supports it and the further conclusions to which it tends' (Glaser, 1941: cited in Thomson, 2009: 3). That exploration led me to the work of Soja (1996) and Anderson (2002). Soja's work explores how people make 'practical and theoreti-cal sense of the world' through 'interpretive dualism' (1996: 5), and engaging with Anderson's (2002: 304) work helped me to appreciate how elements that have once been polarised could be combined 'in positions that are flexible and tentative' rather than fixed, and which enable researchers to 'focus more on the spaces "in between" these binaries' (308–9).

Background

The Organisation for Economic Cooperation and Development identifies education as a knowledge-intensive service sector of a knowledge-based economy (1996: 9). They contend that a knowledge-based economy is 'characterised by the need for continuous learning of both codified information and the competences to use this information' (1996: 13). They challenge government policies to prioritise knowledge-diffusion, promote change, and upgrade human capital through policies which should 'promote access to skills and competences and especially the *capability to learn*' (18–19; my emphasis).

The *Learning and Skills Act 2000* located all post-compulsory education in England and Wales, excluding Higher Education, in the newly named learning and skills sector (Steer et al., 2007). This is a diverse sector, encompassing 16–19 education and training, adult and community learning, workforce development and work-based learning (Edward and Coffield, 2007; Spours et al., 2007).

However, a post-compulsory education system purposively designed to promote learning appears to have been replaced by a learning and skills system dedicated to the 'development of economically useful skills' (Finlay et al., 2007: 140–142). Finlay et al. argue that the discourse of skills has overshadowed learning, where learning is defined as 'significant changes in capability or understanding' (Eraut, 1997: 556). This shift is problematic, especially when a (contemporary) knowledge-based economy demands a theoretical integration of the two (Ainley, 2000). Ainley (2000: 6; my emphasis) argues that the two 'cannot be logically be separated', but recognises within English culture a tendency towards a 'separation and superiority of mental *knowledge* over manual *skills*'. Within the discourses of post-compulsory education and training, this separation and hierarchisation is known as an academic:vocational divide.

In her review of vocational education, and how it can 'ensure progress into higher learning and employment', Alison Wolf (2011: 6) describes how the British government designed and promoted 'non-academic' (2011: 45) alternative routes to General Certificate in Secondary Education (GCSE) and Advanced-level qualifications, yet simultaneously ascribed them equivalent academic value (for example, a Business and Technology Education Council [BTEC] 'First Diploma' is equivalent to four GCSEs A*-C). This now-established conception valorises the academic; consequently, any alternative perspective (in this case a perspective of education as vocational) results in a dichotomy – a division into two mutually exclusive and oppositional parts. Wolf (2011: 23) argues that this separation has arisen from misguided 'quantification incentives' – a term used to denote a calibration of educational 'worth', through the use of comparable indicators such as credit value, as if it were a kind of single currency. This has resulted in a confused discourse; she says:

> There is no formal definition of 'vocational education' in England, and the term is applied to programmes as different as the highly selective, competitive and demanding apprenticeships offered by large engineering companies and the programmes which recruit highly disaffected young people with extremely low academic achievement. Some submissions to the review were concerned that using the term 'vocational' for the latter was wrong, and

damaged the former. Others insisted that low-achievers needed vocational qualifications and argued for their protection.

The many ways in which the term vocational is used reflects the many different purposes which 14–19 education serves and its large and diverse student body. Some qualifications are highly specific, oriented to a particular occupation. Others are more general, and are referred to sometimes as vocationally-related or pre-vocational. Some are very difficult and demanding, others not.

Critique of educational quantification is not new. In 2000, Coffield argued that the dominant culture of Western twenty-first century education is credentialist – geared around the quantification of an individual's abilities and experiences. Others agree, arguing that our contemporary education system is built upon a paradigm that responds to educational challenges of the past (Davidson, 2011), and 'conceived in the intellectual culture of the Enlightenment and in the economic circumstances of the industrial revolution' (Robinson, 2010: 01:59). A production-line mentality, 'modelled on the *interests* of industrialism and in the *image* of it' (Robinson, 2010: 06:44; emphasis in original) is instrumentalist, focussed on the ends rather than means, and on concrete and readily comparable indicators such as learning outcomes and accreditation (Bartlett, 2003). This view is echoed by Hartley (1995: 419; emphasis in original):

> The current quest of the government is to regard education *as if* it had some inert material essence, or *as if* its production process could be readily broken down into a set of fixed, measurable and assessable procedures ... *as if* its output should be predictable, standardisable and quantifiable. But all this ignores the consideration that the means and ends of education in a democracy are in principle varied, diverse and negotiable.

In practice, the sector has become geared towards quantification, driven by a commitment to the commodification of learning, and characterised by a 'parasitic test-taking practice where the exchange value of knowledge increases independently of its use value' (Lave and Wenger, 1994: 112; cited in Ainley, 2000: 8). Such a simplified and mechanistic system of learning and skills maintains a view of separation of mental (knowledge) and manual (skills) throughout the sector. This can prevent the facilitation of change *through* education. Curriculum and pedagogy, driven by policy, become overwhelmed by commodification and separation, and 'experiential residue' (Tomlinson, 1999a: 535) is underpinned by student teachers' (closed) perceptions of knowledge. Teachers' capacity to act as agents of change is therefore compromised.

This experience is not exclusive to Further Education. Barnett (2009: 439) suggests that there has also been 'nothing less than a largely unnoticed revolution in higher education, [which] can be understood as the exchange of one dogma for another: from knowledge to skills'. This modern realisation of Ritzer's (1993) view of 'McDonaldization' (emphasising the dimensions of efficiency, calculability, predictability and control) satisfies political requirements for commodification and comparability (Hartley, 1995; Lomas, 2004). But it reduces the experience of education to one of inspection, appraisal and measures of compliance (Burgess, 2004) at the expense of 'creativity, innovation and criticality' and assumes a 'fixed, bounded, unambiguous and unproblematic' conceptualisation of knowledge (Lomas, 2004: 177–8).

Significantly, at the time my research took place, the policy document *The Further Education Teachers' Qualifications (England) Regulations 2007* required all new teachers appointed from 1 September 2007, and in a role that 'requires the teacher to demonstrate an extensive range of knowledge, understanding and application of curriculum development, curriculum innovation or curriculum development strategies' (2007: 1–2) to hold or acquire a professional qualification at a level equivalent to (or higher than) a university second year undergraduate programme, and to gain Qualified Teacher Learning and Skills (QTLS) status. So the student teachers whose education (of curriculum and pedagogy) I was committed to were situated within a complex context: positioned simultaneously as further education student *teachers* and higher education *learners*, and caught (up) within the epistemological assumptions of each system.

My research

I now consider the importance of the idea of researcher positionality.

Reflecting on researcher positionality

As an 'insider' interpretive researcher (Sikes and Potts, 2008), it was essential to explore my positionality in my research. I recognised in myself a personal dissatisfaction with the concept of an academic:vocational divide in post-compulsory education, which I will outline here. I have had the privilege of working with many who have embarked on 'post-school', other than university-based, learning, ranging in age, experience, confidence, qualifications, ambition and self-belief. Almost all would have described themselves as 'not academic'. As a learner myself, I first entered higher education as a mature student, having chosen a post-school route which included both full-time further education and, later, a combination of work and part-time study in further education. Later still, I left the world of work to study in higher education full-time. I returned to work, now in a second career, as a teacher in the post-compulsory education and training sector. During the time of my own higher education experience, my learning 'diet' included both subject-specific and pedagogical studies. In contrast to those learners I have worked with in post-school settings, I did not consider myself as either 'academic', 'not academic' or 'vocational'.

I have since then continued my education through part-time post-graduate study, whilst working in education, at both masters and doctoral level. As my teaching career developed into one to do with post-school initial teacher education I have had the privilege of working with a new group of learners, commonly termed 'dual professionals' in the discourses of Further Education and Higher Education: that is, both subject-specific experts and also educational professionals (see also Institute for Learning, 2012 and Peel, 2005). Despite the sector-specific expectations of dual professionalism, what I found was that many post-school student teachers did not view themselves as educational researchers or scholars. They too would describe themselves as 'not academic', having come from the world of work into post-compulsory education and training in order to teach. Specifically they appeared to believe that they were 'not academic' because they considered their subject-specialism(s) to be 'vocational' rather than 'academic' (Rand, 2011).

This raises the issue of identity. Sen (2007: 19) offers a view that I describe as open-logic; he argues that human beings are multi-identitied and 'each identity brings both a richness and warmth and also constraints and freedoms'. In exploring my own positionality and identity, as a researcher and doctoral student, I recognised some key characteristics that had developed through my post-graduate study, including a focus on:

- understanding meaning/s, processes and contexts
- identifying unanticipated phenomena and generating results and theories that are understandable
- 'particularistic' research (Maxwell, 2005: 22).

These intellectual and practical goals were consistent with a qualitative approach, one which I had comfortably adopted in my masters research (Rand, 2006). But, in preparing the initial framework for my doctoral research, the greater challenge was the examination of my epistemological, ontological and axiological assumptions, and their potential impact on my research practice. What I particularly learned about myself was that (perhaps in contrast to some of my colleagues in the sector) my research and scholarly activity was closely linked to a desire to satisfy an internal(ised) concern about the validity of my occupying a professional role in education. In Further Education, lecturers are typically appointed on the basis of their 'vocational' experience, whilst in Higher Education, qualifications that indicate subject expertise are normally required. I felt confused as a Higher Education lecturer based in a Further Education College and working in a relatively new context known as 'HE in FE'; I was grappling with, or attending critically to, my developing identity as an initial teacher educator. As a doctoral student, I came across Maxwell's work on interactive approaches to the design of qualitative research and this helped me explore my developing identity. Maxwell (2005: 27) recommends writing a researcher identity memo to:

> examine your goals, experiences, assumptions, feelings, and values as they relate to your research, and to discover what resources and potential concerns your identity and experience may create.

Writing a researcher identity memo helped me to realise that my insecurity was related to a personal concern with credibility – I had 'vocational' experience of being a teacher in further education but I had concerns about how 'academically' experienced I was. Memoing enabled me to explore a personal transition from an early focus on quantifiable academic achievement (suggesting my own experiential residue was highly influenced by quantification/credentialism) to a distinct qualitative underpinning of my scholarship and practice. As a result, I became aware of my own reflective and reflexive approach to developing myself as a researcher. Memoing revealed the deep-seated nature of the value I place on retaining, and promoting, high quality scholarship within further education, and within the initial teacher education of those who wish to teach in the sector. Without it, further education (and the initial teacher education of those who join the sector to teach) risks becoming 'dumbed down'. I saw my complementary role as a teacher-educator and active scholar as pivotal in championing the scholarship and professionalism associated with teaching in the sector, regardless of whether a subject-specialism might typically be considered as 'academic' or 'vocational'.

I now work in a University Education department; I would still not consider myself as *being* academic, although I recognise that I might be considered as *an* academic since my work (my vocation) is located within the academy.

Making one's own epistemic, ontological and axiological identity explicit is important for practitioner-researchers. This process has been described by Luca as *embodied bracketing*: placing 'assumptions and preconceptions in parenthesis ... constantly accessible for reflection' (2009: 13). I adopt an interpretivist approach; this means others' perceptions and values are significant to me and, as a practitioner-researcher I am more interested in *process(es)* rather than *product(s)*. My broad ontological assumptions are of voluntary agency and subjective meaning, and that social reality is a product of individual consciousness (Burrell and Morgan, 1979). These assumptions fit with methodological approaches that might be described as *particularistic* – that is, approaches that set out to discover deep(er) levels of meaning (Burns, 2000: 11). The approach I chose in my EdD research made my identity explicit through a process of iterative reflexivity – a process of consciously subjecting my beliefs, values and ideology to critique (Johnson, 1999; Krimerman, 2001: 72; Payne and Payne, 2004). My research approach was directed towards both openness and criticality.

I found the duality of my own tutor/researcher role and my contextual pre-understanding (Smyth and Holian, 2008) of the post-compulsory education and training sector advantageous to me as a doctoral student, but I was able to use these to legitimise my research only because of my choice to articulate what Coghlan and Pedler (2006) call an *experienced problem*. My experienced problem was the lived nature of a knowledge/skills (academic/vocational) polarity within post-compulsory education and training. As a practitioner with the opportunity to work with colleagues new both to teaching and to post-compulsory education and training, this problem was 'within my influence and not capable of easy solution' (Coghlan and Pedler, 2006: 129), and therefore one which was suited to exploration through action learning.

Reflecting on methodology

Action learning is differentiated from action research, because research is not its primary aim (Kember, 2000: 35). Both are concerned with social practice, are cyclical, systematic, participative, contexualised, improvement-oriented and underpinned by critical reflection (Kember, 2000). Action-oriented strategies link the targets of inquiry to their context; they are geared towards improvement and underpinned by a collaborative and reflexive development of understanding, and the principle that humans actively construct their own meaning (new knowledge) (Pedler et al., 2005: 52; Plauborg, 2009; Rand, 2013). The focus in action learning is *learning* which, sometimes, may not extend beyond personal observation and reflection. Definitions of action learning vary; my own understanding of it is:

> Development-oriented learning through collaborative engagement with real problems, based on questioning insight and critically reflective thinking. (Rand, 2011: 42)

Action learning, whose roots are in management education, is a process of *critical colleagueship* (Lord, 1994). It typically involves a group of professionals coming together on a regular basis to form an Action Learning Set. Set meetings are geared towards helping individuals better understand their experienced problems, and to develop and implement responsive strategies and/or actions.

Action learning *research* has built a presence more widely within the academy over the last two decades, largely in business, management, health and education. Research by Pedler, Burgoyne and Brook investigated the range and effectiveness of action learning in business and management teaching; in this they describe part of their own process of researching action learning as involvement in '"sense-making" conversations' among themselves (Pedler et al., 2005: 53). For me, this is the essence of action learning – a space in which practitioners can examine their experienced problems through reflection and conversations that are geared towards 'sense-making'.

I had explored the issue of an academic:vocational (knowledge:skill) divide in the first part of my EdD programme and developed an argument against polarity. I then presented a new argument, which I will show here in three parts:

1   that knowledge relates to understanding on a continuum between practical (or 'applied') and theoretical (or 'pure');
2   that an individual's power or capacity to engage with and/or employ knowledge is referred to as their *skill*;

3 that the process we call *learning* involves gaining 'knowledge of or skill in' something by 'study, experience or being taught' (Thompson, 1996: 564).

And so, I developed an argument for complementarity – for *knowledge of* and *skills in* to be considered as interconnected, dynamic, mutually sustaining and developmental (Rand, 2011). As a result I developed a conceptual model, *Dimensions of knowing* (Rand, 2011), designed to promote an alternative to a binary knowledge/skill conceptualisation. *Dimensions of knowing* is based on three dimensions of generality (width), complexity (depth) and materiality. This conceptual model developed from my exploration of accounts of knowledge reported by others (Ainley, 2000; Albino et al., 2001; Ancori et al., 2000; OECD, 1996; Vermunt, 1996). Although it is explored in detail elsewhere (Rand, 2015a), the key features are relevant to this reflective account:

- *knowledge of* can be considered through the two dimensions of generality (width) and complexity (depth)
- *skills in* can be considered through the dimension of *materiality* – as outputs, or knowledge states on a continuum between material (physical) and immaterial (mental)
- the interconnected, dynamic and mutually sustaining relationship(s) between the three dimensions of generality, complexity and materiality can be conceptualised as a *portrait of knowing* (considered by one student teacher to be "like the lava in a lava lamp").

In Part II of my EdD programme, I set out to operationalise the model in a real context and explore its potential. Through the critical colleagueship of action learning, I asked student teachers to discuss their own *experienced problems* within an Action Learning Set environment, and I also presented my experienced problem to them as Set members (see Rand, 2013 and 2015a). I wanted to objectify how student teachers in the post-compulsory education and training sector thought about knowledge and knowing; it was important to me to represent, and re-present, their particular understanding about knowledge and knowing so that it could 'enter the experience of others and so become common property' (Blumer, 1969: 158). Constructivist grounded theory enabled me to do this through the processes of abstraction and theory-development and, significantly, it also enabled me to accommodate the collaboration, active agency and reflectivity of action learning.

Constructivist grounded theory 'sees knowledge as socially produced ... takes a reflexive stance ... [and] assumes that we produce knowledge by grappling with empirical problems' (Charmaz, 2009: 129–30). It is an investigative, iterative, constant comparative process through which data are *fractured, selected, related* and *integrated*, typically into a substantive (explanatory) theoretical framework (Charmaz, 2006: 6; Luca, 2009; Rand, 2015b). The explicit link between action approaches and constructivist grounded theory is the agency of those who are grappling with empirical problems (Rand, 2013), including both researchers and those who participate with us in research.

Reflecting on sense-making

What I found in my research was that student teachers' engagement with my model *was* dominated by dualism. I found that the experiential residue of those who participated in my study was underpinned by polarised conceptions of knowledge and knowing; the substantive grounded theory framework which represented their particular understanding(s) objectified this (see Rand, 2015a). However, the substantive grounded theory framework also illustrated that student teachers could successfully conceptualise *knowledge of* and *skills in* as interconnected, dynamic, mutually sustaining and developmental when the *Dimensions of knowing* model was used to support an interruption of their habituated views (Martin, 1997).

My study demonstrated 'the way in which the teaching and learning process (in contemporary post-compulsory education and training) is dominated by 'particular ways of "knowing", about the teacher, the learner and educational practices' (Malcolm and Zukas, 2001: 34). This was interesting, because the majority of the practitioners within my study were new teachers. For me, it raised the question of why polarity might be integral to the 'default options' (Tomlinson, 1999a: 535) of student teachers in the twenty-first century. An exploration of the literature suggested that polarity has in fact been the subject of scholarly critique for well over a century as explained in Dewey's seminal text *How We Think* (1910: 135–6):

> The maxim enjoined upon teachers, 'to proceed from the concrete to the abstract,' is perhaps familiar rather than comprehended. Few who read and hear it gain a clear conception of the starting-point, the concrete; of the nature of the goal, the abstract; and of the exact nature of the path to be traversed in going from one to the other. At times the injunction is positively misunderstood, being taken to mean that education should advance from things to thought – as if any dealing with things in which thinking is not involved could possibly be educative. So understood, the maxim encourages mechanical routine or sensuous excitation at one end of the educational scale – the lower – and academic and unapplied learning at the upper end.
>
> Actually, all dealing with things, even the child's, is immersed in inferences; things are clothed by the suggestions they arouse, and are significant as challenges to interpretation or as evidences to substantiate a belief. Nothing could be more unnatural than instruction in things without thought; in sense-perceptions without judgments based upon them. And if the abstract

to which we are to proceed denotes thought apart from things, the goal recommended is formal and empty, for effective thought always refers, more or less directly, to things.

I believe that a conceptualisation of education based on commodification and quantification has become normalised through familiarity, rather than through (critical) comprehension. This is problematic because the educational model has changed, from one based only on a conceptualising pedagogy, with roots in the Enlightenment and where intellectualism was valued (Bloomer and Hodkinson, 2000; Davidson, 2011; Eneroth, 2008; Robinson, 2010), to one which also includes what Eneroth (2008) calls 'handiwork', or circumstantial pedagogy – where ways of thinking *and* practising are valued. The result of this 'action in practice', and the attempts to quantify and validate it, is a 'growing academisation of practical work' (Eneroth, 2008: 233). The custom and practice of maintaining and 'serially re-designing' (Wolf, 2011) an education system in the familiar image of industrialism – in Robinson's (2010) terms from a production-line mentality – has resulted in education being conceptualised as academic and vocational product(s). But the *product* of an education system is knowledge.

Absolute binaries, or 'sharp dichotomies' (Coffield, 2000) can hide the *practice* of learning (Whitchurch, 2010). A constructivist epistemology does not view knowledge as absolute; instead it views knowledge as the creation of new 'rules and resources' derived from various 'originary' spaces (Whitchurch, 2010: 633). Through a constructivist lens, knowledge is 'dynamic and uncertain and the truth remains provisional' (Ramsden, 1988: 18).

As an alternative to the kind of dichotomies presented throughout this text, Young et al. (1997: 532) propose a unified education system based on 'connectivity'; they argue for the development of 'new relationships between theory and practice', which gives less emphasis to separating learning (and learners) through 'distinguishing types of qualifications which stress either theoretical or practical learning'. This echoes Hartley's (1995) view of a negotiable, varied and diverse output from an education system.

If dichotomies can hide the practice(s) of learning, then promoting a connective alternative is advantageous. A connective paradigm promotes theory:practice complementarity; it supports a richer conceptualisation than is possible through conceptualising two elements in contrast, which Anderson (2002) calls a 'bicameral confinement'. Relying on a dichotomy to conceptualise knowing separates knowledge-generation from its use, and knowledge from the knower (Cochran-Smith and Lytle, 1999). As an alternative, complementarity supports the notion of collocation, that skill development is co-dependent on certain knowing and that practice is not atheoretical (Cochran-Smith and Lytle, 1999; Moje et al., 2004; Tomlinson, 1999b). Complementarity supports a constructivist view that learning prioritises sense-making over acquisition (Bloomer and Hodkinson, 2000) and promotes dynamic interrelationships between knowledge and skills.

The real danger in dichotomies is that they disguise differences *within* dualisms, and permit one side to be valued over the other (Pile, 1994). Rather than 'sharp dichotomies' (Coffield, 2000) and absolute binaries, Soja (1996: 5) offers an argument that people make 'practical and theoretical sense of the world' through 'interpretive dualism', which is a method for describing perceptual limits, or the points beyond which something does not continue (Mezirow, 1981: 16). Soja explores this through the work of Lefebvre and encourages a 'dialectically open logic of both/and also' as an alternative to the compacted meaning of a 'categorical and closed logic of either/or' (1996: 60). Dialectics is the art of investigating the truth of opinions. Within an open logic, I believe there exists an opportunity for reconceptualisation, for 'new combinations of once dualized elements' and for 'entangling the once exclusive' (Anderson, 2002: 304, 316).

Tomlinson's notion of 'experiential residue' (1999a: 535) however, suggests that such a reconceptualisation would be problematic for today's student teachers, because of their own experiences of a commodified, production-line, education system. Zeichner (2010: 89, 92) therefore encourages a 'paradigm shift in the epistemology of teacher education' to facilitate an 'equal and more dialectical relationship between academic knowledge and practical knowledge'. I agree. I also argue that this paradigm shift is relevant to twenty-first century research practice; my experience as a practitioner-researcher is of an equal and dialectical relationship between theory and practice, between constructivist grounded theory and action learning.

Conclusions: open-logic sense-making

The focus of the fourth International Value and Virtue conference in 2014 was openness and criticality. My research embodied this combination. It enabled me both to look *out,* to literature and policy, and also to look *in,* to [and *into*] practice. Charmaz (2006: 181) argues that '[T]he sense we make of the journey takes form in our completed work'. In my research, the sense-making was *both* of student teachers' practices *and also* of my 'experienced problem' (Coghlan and Pedler, 2006). As such, in writing up my research I *both* objectified the particular *and also* explored my positionality through a rich description. Each element powerfully improved the other.

As practitioner-researchers we must remember that the reader is active in interpretive research. We therefore have a responsibility to communicate and (re-) present the information generated from our research in a way that enables the readers (including those who participate with us in research) to verify *both* the findings *and also* the research process(es). This *re-*presentation also needs to be accountable to the quality criteria of interpretive research: credibility, dependability, transferability, typicality, relatability and translatability (Burton et al., 2008; Lincoln and Guba, 1985; Popay et al., 1998).

To achieve this accountability, Silverman (2000) champions a 'natural history' style of reporting qualitative research, one which promotes a technique of telling a 'structured story' of our research. But in order to avoid an unnecessarily confessional approach (Hammersley, 2000) we must combine openness *with* criticality, that is '[F]aithful, reportorial depiction' *with* critically 'analytical probing' (Blumer, 1954: 10), in order to share the 'distinctive impression' of our research (Blumer, 1954: 8). This means our beliefs, values and ideologies must be both explored reflexively and also subjected to the intellectual rigour of critical subjectivity (Johnson, 1999; Krimerman, 2001; Luca, 2009; Payne and Payne, 2004). For me, this was enabled through combining the 'productive disequilibrium' of action learning (Males, 2009: 930) and the constant comparative abstraction of constructivist grounded theory.

This combination of constructivist grounded theory and action learning is one reciprocal 'theory-practice' approach. The interconnection of theory and practice is called praxis; Coghlan and Pedler (2006: 132) would probably call my methodological combination 'praxeological' – it unites knowing and doing. My experience is that a praxeological research approach can create 'originary' spaces (Whitchurch, 2010), *within* which practitioner-research can embody both openness and also criticality, and *from* which a new, open-logic sense-making can emerge.

References

Ainley, P. (2000) *Teaching in a Learning Society, the Acquisition of Professional Skills.* ESRC Teaching and Learning First Programme Conference. Held February 2000 at the University of Leicester, England [online], available from <www.tlrp.org/acadpub/Ainley2000.pdf> [8 August 2008]

Albino, V., Garavelli, A.C., and Schiuma, G. (2001) 'A metric for measuring knowledge codification in organisation learning', *Technovation* 21 (7): 413–422.

Ancori, B., Bureth, A., and Cohendet, P. (2000) 'The economics of knowledge: the debate about codification and tacit knowledge', *Industrial and Corporate Change* 9 (2): 255–287.

Anderson, J. (2002) 'Researching environmental resistance: working through Secondspace and Thirdspace approaches', *Qualitative Research* 2 (3): 301–321.

Barnett, R. (2009) 'Knowing and becoming in the higher education curriculum', *Studies in Higher Education* 34 (4): 429–440.

Bartlett, S. (2003) 'Education for lifelong learning', in S. Bartlett and D. Burton (eds) *Education Studies – Essential Issues* (pp. 190–211). London: Sage.

Bloomer, M., and Hodkinson, P. (2000) 'Learning careers: continuity and change in young people's dispositions to learning', *British Educational Research Journal* 26 (5): 583–597.

Blumer, H. (1954) 'What is wrong with social theory'? *American Sociological Association* 19 (1): 3–10.

Blumer, H. (1969) *Symbolic Interactionism. Perspective and Method.* California: University of California Press.

Burgess, T. (2004) 'What are the key debates in education?' in D. Hayes (ed.) *The Routledge Guide to Key Debates in Education* (pp. 217–221). Abingdon: Routledge.

Burns, R. (2000) *Introduction to Research Methods* (4th edn.) London: Sage.

Burrell, G., and Morgan, G. (1979) *Sociological Paradigms and Organisational Analysis: Elements of the Sociology of Corporate Life.* London: Heinemann Educational Books.

Burton, N., Brundrett, M. and Jones, M. (2008) *Doing Your Education Research Project.* London: Sage.

Charmaz, K. (2006) *Constructing Grounded Theory: A Practical Guide Through Qualitative Analysis.* London: Sage.

Charmaz, K. (2009) 'Shifting the grounds: constructivist grounded theory methods', in J. Morse (ed.) *Developing Grounded Theory The Second Generation* (pp. 127–193). Walnut Creek: Left Coast Press.

Cochran-Smith, M. and Lytle, S.L. (1999) 'Chapter 8: relationships of knowledge and practice: teacher learning in communities'. *Review of Research in Education* 24 (1): 249–305.

Coffield, F. (ed.) (2000) *The Necessity of Informal Learning.* Bristol: The Policy Press.

Coghlan, D., and Pedler, M. (2006) 'Action learning dissertations: structure, supervision and examination', *Action Learning Research and Practice* 3 (2): 127–139.

Davidson, C. (2011) '*So* last century'. *Times Higher Education* 28 April: 32–36.

Dewey, J. (1910) *How We Think.* Boston: D.C. Health & Co Publishers.

Edward, S., and Coffield, F. (2007) 'Policy and practice in the learning and skills sector: setting the scene', *Journal of Vocational Education & Training* 59 (2): 121–135.

Eneroth, B. (2008) 'Knowledge, sentience and receptivity: a paradigm of lifelong learning', *European Journal of Education* 43 (2), 229–240.

Eraut, M. (1997) 'Perspectives on defining "The Learning Society"', *Journal of Education Policy* 12 (6): 551–558.

Finlay, I., Spours, K., Steer, R., Coffield, F., Gregson, M., and Hodgson, A. (2007) '"The heart of what we do": policies on teaching, learning and assessment in the learning and skills sector', *Journal of Vocational Education & Training* 59 (2): 137–153.

Hammersley, M. (2000) *Taking Sides in Social Research: Essays on Partisanship and Bias.* London: Routledge.

Hartley, D. (1995) 'The 'McDonaldisation' of higher education: food for thought?' *Oxford Review of Education* 21 (4): 409–423.

Institute for Learning (IfL) (2012) *Professionalism: Education and Training Practitioners across Further Education and Skills* [online], available from <www.ifl.ac.uk/media/110497/2012_10-IfL-professionalism-paper.pdf> [28 February 2015].

Johnson, M. (1999) 'Observations on positivism and pseudoscience in qualitative nursing research', *Journal of Advanced Nursing* 30 (1): 67–73.

Kember, D. (2000) *Action Learning and Action Research: Improving the Quality of Teaching and Learning.* London: Kogan Page.

Krimerman, L. (2001) 'Participatory action research – should social inquiry be conducted democratically?', *Philosophy of the Social Sciences* 31 (1): 60–82.

Learning and Skills Act (2000, c.21) London: The Stationery Office.

Lincoln, Y. and Guba, E. (1985) *Naturalistic Inquiry.* London: Sage.

Lomas, L. (2004) 'The McDonaldisation of lecturer training', in D. Hayes (ed.) *The Routledge Guide to Key Debates in Education* (pp. 175–179). Abingdon: Routledge, 175–179.

Lord, B. (1994) 'Teachers' professional development: critical colleagueship and the role of professional communities', in N. Cobb (ed.) *The Future of Education: Perspectives on National Standards in Education* (pp. 175–204). New York: College Board.

Luca, M. (2009) *'Embodied Research and Grounded Theory'* [online], available from: <regents.ac.uk/media/611246/Article-for-Research-Centre1-Doctor-M-Luca-2009.pdf> [12 March 2016].

Malcolm, J. and Zukas, M. (2001) 'Bridging pedagogic gaps: conceptual discontinuities in higher education', *Teaching in Higher Education* 6 (1): 33–42.

Males, L.M. (2009) *Confronting Practice: Critical Colleagueship in a Mathematics Teacher Study Group.* Paper presented at the Annual Conference of the North American Chapter of the International Group for the Psychology of Mathematics Education. 2009. Atlanta: GA, September [online], available from: <http://michiganstate.academia.edu/LorraineMales/Papers/412689/Confronting_Practice_Critical_Colleagueship_In_a_Mathematics_Teacher_Study_Group> [12 December 2009].

Martin, J. (1997) 'Mindfulness: a proposed common factor', *Journal of Psychotherapy Integration* 7 (4): 291–312.

Maxwell, J.A. (2005) *Qualitative Research Design: An Interactive Approach* (2nd edn). London: Sage.

Mezirow, J. (1981) 'A critical theory of adult learning and education', *Adult Education* 32 (1): 3–24.

Moje, E.B., Ciechanowski, K.M., Kramer, K., Ellis, L., Carrillo, R. and Collazo, T. (2004) 'Working toward third space in content area literacy: an examination of everyday funds of knowledge and discourse', *Reading Research Quarterly* 39 (1): 38–70.

Organisation for Economic Cooperation and Development (1996) *The Knowledge-Based Economy.* Paris: OECD.

Payne, G. and Payne, J. (2004) *Key Concepts in Social Research.* London: Sage.

Pedler, M., Burgoyne, J. and Brook, C. (2005) 'What has action learning learned to become?', *Action Learning: Research and Practice* 2 (1): 49–68.

Peel, D. (2005) 'Dual professionalism: facing the challenges of continuing professional development in the workplace?', *Reflective Practice: International and Multi-Disciplinary Perspectives* 6 (1): 123–140.

Pile, S. (1994) 'Masculinism, the use of dualistic epistemologies and third spaces', *Antipode* 26 (3): 355–277.

Plauborg, H. (2009) 'Opportunities and limitations for learning within teachers' collaboration in teams: perspectives from action learning', *Action Learning: Research and Practice* 6 (1): 25–34.

Popay, J., Rogers, A. and Williams, G. (1998) 'Rationale and standards for the systematic review of qualitative literature in health services research', *Qualitative Health Research* 8 (3): 341–351.

Ramsden, P. (1988) 'Studying learning: improving teaching', in P. Ramsden (ed.) *Improving Learning: New Perspectives* (pp. 13–31). London: Kogan Page.

Rand, J. (2015a) 'Dimensions of knowing: a conceptual alternative to an unhelpful polarity between knowledge and skill', *Research in Post-compulsory Education* 20 (2): 140–158.

Rand, J. (2015b) 'Navigating a safe route through the turbulent waters of grounded theory research: a diagrammatic framework', *The Qualitative Review* (Under Review).

Rand, J. (2013) 'Action learning and constructivist grounded theory: powerfully overlapping fields of practice', *Action Learning: Research and Practice* 10 (3): 230–243.

Rand, J. (2011) *Dimensions of Knowing: A Constructivist Exploration of a Conceptual Model in a Real Context*. Sheffield: EdD dissertation, University of Sheffield.

Rand, J. (2006) 'Mini-ethnography: a multi-method approach in an ESOL IT class', *Reflecting Education* 2 (1), 85–102 [online], available from http://reflectingeducation.net.

Ritzer, G. (1993) *The McDonaldization of Society*. London: Pine Forge Press.

Robinson, K. (2010) *Changing Paradigms*. Animate adaptation of talk by Ken Robinson, in receipt of the RSA's Benjamin Franklin Award [video], available from <www.youtube.com/watch?v=zDZFcDGpL4U> [24 November 2010].

Sen, A. (2007) *Identity and Violence: The Illusion of Destiny*. London: Penguin.

Sikes, P. and Potts, A. (eds) (2008) *Researching Education from the Inside: Investigations from Within*. Abingdon: Routledge.

Silverman, D. (2000) *Doing Qualitative Research: A Practical Handbook*. London: Sage.

Smyth, A., and Holian, R. (2008) 'Credibility issues in research from within organisations', in P. Sikes and A. Potts (eds) *Researching Education from the Inside* (pp. 33–47). Abingdon: RoutledgeFalmer.

Soja, E.W. (1996) *Thirdspace*. Oxford: Blackwell Publishing.

Spours, K., Coffield, F. and Gregson, M. (2007) 'Mediation, translation and local ecologies: understanding the impact of policy levers on FE colleges', *Journal of Vocational Education & Training* 59 (2): 193–211.

Steer, R., Spours, K., Hodgson, A., Finlay, I., Coffield, F., Edward, S. and Gregson, M. (2007) '"Modernisation" and the role of policy levers in the learning and skills sector', *Journal of Vocational Education & Training* 59 (2): 175–192.

The Further Education Teachers' Qualifications (England) Regulations (2007) SI 2007/2264. London: The Stationery Office.

Thompson, D. (ed.) (1996) *The Oxford Compact English Dictionary*. Oxford: Oxford University Press.

Thomson, S. (2009) *Critical Reasoning: A Practical Introduction* (3rd edn) Abingdon: Routledge.

Tomlinson, P. (1999a) 'Conscious reflection and implicit learning in teacher preparation. Part II: implications for a balanced approach', *Oxford Review of Education* 25 (4): 533–544.

Tomlinson, P. (1999b) 'Conscious reflection and implicit learning in teacher preparation. Part I: recent light on an old issue', *Oxford Review of Education* 25 (3): 405–424.

Vermunt, J.D. (1996) 'Metacognitive, cognitive and affective aspects of learning styles and strategies: a phenomenographic analysis'. *Higher Education* 31 (1), 25–50

Whitchurch, C. (2010) 'Some implications of "public/private" space for professional identities in higher education', *Higher Education* 60 (1): 627–640.

Wolf, A. (2011) *Review of Vocational Education – The Wolf Report* [online], available from <www.education.gov.uk/16to19/qualificationsandlearning/a0074953/review-of-vocational-education-the-wolf-report> [4 March 2011].

Young, M., Spours, K., Howieson, C. and Raffe, D. (1997) 'Unifying academic and vocational learning and the idea of a learning society', *Journal of Education Policy* 12 (6): 527–537.

Zeichner, K. (2010) 'Rethinking the connections between campus courses and field experiences in college- and university-based teacher education', *Journal of Teacher Education* 61 (1–2): 61–89.

Chapter 6

Perspectives on criticality and openness in educational research in the context of Latvia

Linda Pavītola, Lāsma Latsone and Dina Bethere

Introduction

Conducting research and publishing its results are core elements of being an academic (Hyland, 2007; Murray, 2012), so criticality in the analysis and interpretation of results, together with openness for the exchange of knowledge and ideas take on the utmost significance. However, while we can learn in principle about different philosophies and approaches to research processes, the most significant form of learning probably comes from the personal experience of social and cultural contexts. Such experience can have direct influence on our scientific activities, interpretation of results and elaborated models, and can determine the meaning we attribute to the experience itself (Brookfield, 1995; Merriam, 2009).

These ideas have special relevance for us three authors in writing this chapter. We are research-active academics working at Liepāja University, Latvia, all committed to the idea of personal self-evaluation for institutional and cultural development. We believe passionately in the idea that universities should be guided by a strong values base in relation to intellectual and social accountability, and that academics should demonstrate how they hold themselves responsible for their practices. It is therefore a matter of concern for us that we are continually faced with the problematic of the lack of criticality and openness in educational research in our workplaces in the context of Latvia, our home country. This situation represents a real challenge for us, given that openness and criticality are two of the main values that inspire our own practices as lecturers and professional educators in Latvia and in other international contexts. Consequently, we welcomed the opportunity to take part in discussions about improving the quality of practice-based research, the focus of the Value and Virtue series of conferences at York St John University. These discussions have helped us to reflect on and critically evaluate our own research experiences, consider what might count as successful aspects and identify some of the main challenges facing us as educational researchers.

It has to be remembered that Latvia has only recently emerged from Soviet rule and a learned culture of silence. While there is generally an attitude of openness towards a more cosmopolitan stance and a willingness to engage with the other, established attitudes are not so easily unlearned. It takes time and patience for attitudes and practices to change, and a major part of cultural change can often come from respected figures and institutions who set new behavioural and attitudinal patterns. In this, the university can act as an institution with potential for setting new directions for the future. Part of this change involves academics learning to transform a tendency towards intellectual conformity and to develop attitudes of openness and criticality that will eventually influence the culture.

Therefore, in order to understand why values such as openness and criticality are not given appropriate priority in Latvia, and to find ways of possibly redressing the situation, we undertook a qualitative study in several Latvian universities, bearing in mind the social and cultural aspects of traditional academic contexts. This chapter communicates our understanding of the extent to which openness and criticality are (or are not) considered core aspects of research in Latvia, based on an analysis of theoretical findings and research resources in Latvia. We also aim to share our findings and offer possible solutions to identified problems in the field, emphasising those aspects that may help or hinder the research process in the Latvian context. The results of the study emphasise the ways in which conceptual frameworks can be used openly and critically to evaluate both how educators work and conduct research, and also to consider how their work can be relevant and helpful to others.

We would therefore like to outline the opportunities available in Latvia for building research capacity for academics and researchers. We also consider how academics and researchers can extend the impact of their work locally and nationally by introducing a model we have developed that aims to promote and encourage openness and criticality in educational research practices (see Figure 6.1 later in the chapter).

First we explain why openness and criticality are such important concepts in and for educational research.

Openness and criticality

An exploration of the theoretical context reveals current trends in educational research that highlight the significance of and mutual interconnectivity between the concepts of openness and criticality. Our understanding of these concepts stems from engagement with the works of, among others, Andreozzi et al. (2014), Brookfield (1995), Korol (1981), Merriam (2009), Niehaves and Stahl (2006), Solso (1997), and RIN/NESTA (2010). All these sources indicate that *openness* involves the achievement of an appropriate level of transparency reached by exchanging ideas through collaboration and teamwork, in order to promote trust and credibility in the research community. New research questions emerge that can show the potential of the research for increased economic and social impact. Also, the European Commission (2013) emphasises the need for accessibility through discussion to a broad range of research findings as the main vehicle for improving the circulation and exchange of knowledge, achieving progress and efficiency in scientific understanding, and promoting innovation in the public and private sectors. Their study confirms international movements towards encouraging openness in the communication of research findings, with the conclusion that 50 per cent of published scientific research is now available free of charge.

Therefore, in relation to openness and the availability of research it is important to consider two main questions:

- What kind of materials should be made open and available, and at what stage in the research process?
- Who is the audience to whom the material is made available? (RIN/NESTA, 2010: 10)?

Usually the aim is to disseminate journal articles or book chapters; these are held as the key outcomes of research irrespective of the audience addressed or the research aims. But researchers also produce many other research materials, including bibliographies, protocols and field notes, which could also be usefully published at different stages of the research. Our engagement with the theoretical literatures also identified several other constraints to enabling openness in research and access to research findings (RIN/NESTA, 2010: 4). Among them the most characteristic in the Latvian context are:

- a lack of evidence of the potential benefits and rewards from engaging in research;
- lack of skills, time and resources;
- embedded cultures of independence and competition.

These issues need to be addressed urgently.

As well as the concept and practice of openness, *criticality* can also be viewed as a means of understanding and making meaning from experience. This is a positive philosophy rather than sceptical, and the focus on testing the validity of findings according to particular criteria underpins new ideas and releases creative energy (Korol, 1981). Criticality includes an explicitly articulated intention to change reality: it raises critical research questions and develops questioning attitudes (Niehaves and Stahl, 2006). It also raises considerations of strategies for ensuring that research activities, including their analysis and interpretation, are meaningful. These include:

- evaluating and testing knowledge with regard to demonstrating reliability;
- stimulating the search for new ideas;
- introducing a corrective function that sets limits to a search area;
- building in a predictive function of possible results (Korol, 1981).

The process of developing criticality mirrors the phases involved in any creative process: preparation, incubation, illumination and testing (Solso, 1997). Externally created spaces permit initiative to flourish, while, at the same time, the availability of ideas developed by the person themselves ensures that the incubation period is more effective. The mutual interaction between external, socially-created and internal, personally-created spaces encourages understanding. Thus, these external and internal factors influence the development of criticality as well as openness, and both are equally significant in that the availability of external spaces does not necessarily mean that a person would have to rely only on their inner motivation for their research to go ahead.

It is vital to be critically reflective throughout this process, to be able to reflect on and perceive practices in new ways. Brookfield (1995) identifies four further steps that, in our opinion, contribute also to openness and must be taken into consideration if we are to become critically reflective researchers. These are:

- investigating autobiographies as researchers: personal self-reflection has to be seen as the starting point for the development of criticality;
- inviting scrutiny by students: this helps to confirm or challenge findings and check how students understand and make meaning out of our practices;
- draw on the experiences of colleagues: to get different perspectives on aspects of practice;
- draw on theoretical literatures: this enables the articulation of experiences in different ways by providing multiple interpretations of familiar situations (Brookfield, 1995: 29–30).

Therefore, doing research implies that one begins with one's self and only then seeks conversations with colleagues, books and practices to challenge the assumptions and beliefs we might develop. It is also important to identify and avoid the situation where, in order to be reflective, we seek out only those people who share our assumptions and read the authors we already agree with (Brookfield, 1995: 29). Not challenging our assumptions and beliefs results in the situation where, as also indicated by international experts in their report on the research situation in Latvia (Arnold et al., 2014), a self-referential unproductive loop can be created.

Thus, providing a space for openness and creating an attitude towards criticality could serve as the grounds for improving the quality of research in relation to the following dimensions:

- a theoretical and methodological dimension: this provides for the trustworthiness of research and its contribution to knowledge;
- a value dimension, characterised by purposefulness and responsiveness to needs;
- a capacity dimension, built by collaboration, reflection, criticism and personal growth;
- an economic dimension, characterised by marketability, competitiveness and value-efficiency (Furlong and Oancea, 2005: 15).

These theoretical frameworks form the context of our study.

Design of the study

We are claiming in this chapter that the exercise of criticality and openness can enhance the quality of a research process. The aim of our research study therefore was to reflect on and critically evaluate, in broad terms, new and experienced researchers' educational research experience in the context of Latvia. We used a qualitative research methodology, based on a social constructivist paradigm and interpretive phenomenology approach. This enabled immediate access to the voices of participants as they reflected on their research experience. Our intention was both to understand the experience of higher education researchers in Latvia and show the interconnections between political and subjective factors, and also to present our vision of how it may be possible to engage with possible challenges and present potential solutions.

Our research questions were the following:

- How have openness and criticality been practised in higher education educational research practices in Latvia?
- What can be done to improve these practices?

Our research methods involved the analysis of sources and structured interviews.

Our research sample comprised 23 respondents: 12 academics and 11 doctoral students from Latvian universities and scientific research institutions, selected by purposeful random sampling.

Context of the study

As part of creating the framework for this research, legislative documents such as *On the Priority Directions in Science for 2014–2017* (2013), *Law on Scientific Activity* (2013), *Strategies of Scientific Activity 2010–2016 of Liepāja University* (2009), *Latvia University* (2009) and *Rezekne Higher Education Institution* (2011) were analysed in order to flag existing problems in the field of educational research in Latvia, and find possible solutions, with a focus on those aspects that may help or hinder the implementation of any potential solutions.

The *Strategies of Scientific Activity* (see above) identify scientific research and creative activities as main conditions for the sustainable development of Latvia as a fully-fledged partner within the education arena of Europe. Aspects of openness in research are emphasised, including the need to strengthen the development of scientific institutes that are open to international collaboration, publish research results at an international level, integrate the latest research findings from study programmes across all levels, and support and encourage students' participation in research. It is the responsibility of scientists to inform society about their research results, especially if the research is funded out of the state budget, and to provide consultancy and expert advice according to the level of one's competence (*Law on Scientific Activity*, 2013).

Unfortunately, the analysis of the theoretical sources we accessed reveals that education is not among Latvia's research priorities (*On the Priority Directions in Science*, 2013). This is contrary to the published opinion of international experts who state that educational and pedagogical research is one of the strongest areas of social science in Latvia, and there is a considerable amount of evidence to show that it has a social and economic impact in Latvia (Arnold et al., 2014). In his study on educational research conducted in Latvia, Grīviņš (2011) summarises the most important research topics and theoretical perspectives and identifies those difficulties that must be taken into consideration if we are to develop research as a meaningful activity based on the principles of criticality and openness. According to Grīviņš (2011), the major drawbacks to realising this aim are as follows:

- a clear description of the theoretical positions of researchers is missing and too many statements are expressed descriptively and uncritically, and only from the perspective of approved policy without offering alternative solutions;
- there is lack of continuity among different studies, which hinders the integration of acquired knowledge into educational policy development;
- decisions about which interests researchers pursue often depend on availability of funding; sometimes they have to specialise in a particular aspect not of their choosing, which, in turn, can limit the quality of discussion and criticality.

These factors, combined with the existing evaluation system, which appears to be more quantitative than qualitative, significantly reduce the social impact of educational research so that research results rarely get cited in scientific publications (Arnold et al., 2014: 64–66). This often leads to the conclusion that, in real-life Latvian educational research contexts there is a lack of reflection, critical analysis, discussion about research findings, and purposefully-directed progress towards achieving the research goals that show the potential realisation of the Strategies of Scientific Activity of higher education institutions.

Analysis of the interviews

The interviews were conducted in academic contexts, and the data analysis communicates the opinions of the two groups of respondents: new researchers (doctoral students) and experienced researchers (academics). The data obtained from the interviews were analysed and interpreted according to the following categories:

- openness and criticality and their expression in the research process;
- access and availability of research findings, realisation of openness and criticality in the research process;
- the potential social and economic impact of the research in question.

In what follows, we give the questions and topics posed to interviewees, and summarise their responses.

Question: Please describe the support available for new and experienced researchers to encourage openness and criticality

In relation to the realisation of the values of openness and criticality, respondents were asked to describe the support provided for new and experienced researchers, as well as about the activities that can promote openness and criticality in scientific institutions and higher education establishments. Many respondents emphasised the value of financial support, saying that European financial funds as well as funds for national level research projects are available for their research, in relation to the access of data, dissemination and international assessment.

Some new researchers acknowledged the support of their mentors or supervisors while developing their research focus, or while accessing information about other similar research studies and conducting literature searches. Other factors identified as supporting and promoting openness and criticality included the provision of winter or summer schools for doctoral students, open thesis defences, guest lectures, scientific inter-university seminars, international, national and regional conferences and free access to theses on public and private websites. Only relatively rarely did the respondents describe what efforts they made to get financial support. One respondent stated that 'Support for new scientists is sufficient provided they define the aim of their research and data collection clearly. The more precise the description, the greater the support'.

Some cases produced different opinions and perspectives. One doctoral student said that in a specific higher educational institution,

> doctoral students do not receive any individual support. The institution operates as an administrator, putting on record what a doctoral student should be able to do by him/herself, and students who are not able to gather the required information by themselves, who are unable to respond quickly to incomplete or incorrect information or are unable to adapt to programme requirements are removed from the programme.

Experienced scientists also tended to be somewhat pessimistic, commenting on the lack of the kind of support that would promote scientific growth and would allow for an extended continuation of their research studies. The need for discussion with peers or advisers about research findings was also mentioned:

> Research findings are not discussed. The paper gets published – great. We can add a new line to our CV and say in our reports that we have published a paper. But there are no scientific advisors. I have to say that there is a considerable lack of scientific advice.

Question: Please describe the process of choosing a research topic and methodology. Does it include different kinds of cooperative practices?

Respondents were also asked to analyse their preferred procedures for choosing their research topics and methodology, which implies that there were opportunities for collaboration and engaged discussion. Doctoral students indicated that the selection of research topic and methodology usually takes place cooperatively during individual supervision sessions with their supervisors. In some cases the choice of research topic is based on their successful Master's level study with the aim of developing it further, adding that 'the support offered tends to depend on the Professor's personal interest in the topic or methodology'. But in some institutions the selection of research topic and methodology takes place during academic discussions with a group of peer researchers. Academic discussions are usually scheduled throughout the study programme or are part of the action plans for projects.

Regarding the question of how often various cooperative practices took place, a relatively typical answer was that 'activities take place often enough, but not regularly. Discussions and activities occur according to need or when the opportunity arises. By "opportunities" I mean seminars, meetings and conferences, where people participate in order to find and/or establish new contacts and prospects'. Comparatively seldom was it mentioned that the choice of research topic and methodology was the work of each individual researcher, indicating that 'being on such a road implies several difficulties. For example, the doctoral student gathers information and plans their methodology according to how they understand it'. The supervisor helps only when something is already completed, adding from his/her experience, but decisions might not always be endorsed by the Promotion Board of a particular educational institution.

Many of the experienced researchers we interviewed did not comment much on how they came to choose their research topics. Their responses can be summarised in this observation: 'the topic of a new research study in humanitarian sciences usually conforms to the research priorities identified by the Latvian government or to calls for tendering on particular topical issues'. Commenting on the extent of collaboration and frequency of meetings when they are engaged in a common project, the experienced scientists noted that it depends on the length of the study and its anticipated results: for example, 'if a book is being written collaboratively, the number of meetings, both in person and virtually, will be determined by the length of the text and the number of researchers involved'.

Question: In which phase of the research process do you usually make your research data/results publicly available?

With regard to access to and availability of research findings and the degree of openness and criticality in research processes, one of the questions was related to the point of time in the research process when research data and results are published. Responses from both new and experienced scientists virtually unanimously confirmed the tendency to publish research results at all points of the process:

> Even if the emphasis is on the theoretical grounding in the initial preparatory phase, initial examples are always required that illustrate the research orientation, and to predict and outline possible trends. In other phases the presentation and evaluation of results is inevitable, because the analysis of the results has been a main goal.

However, in this respect concerns were also expressed about issues of scientific ethics: 'The research data may be published as early as the preparatory phase, but then there is a potential risk that ideas can be "borrowed" by other researchers'.

Question: Please describe any positive aspects and difficulties that may arise through the publication of results

Reflecting on the positive aspects and difficulties involved in the publication of results, both groups of respondents were positive about the potential opportunities for strengthening their academic capacity, developing a research language, formulating issues to be investigated, engaging in intellectual and creative processes in order to be seen and heard, and participating in rethinking methodological orientations. Some doctoral students identified more positive aspects such as feedback from external readers that 'allows an analysis of the research from the point of view of a person who is not directly engaged in the research', commenting that the 'evaluation of external experts of my work reinforced my decision to continue in my existing direction'.

In relation to the main difficulties of doing research, representatives from both groups of respondents mentioned lack of time and finance. A requirement to publish articles in English was also described as an inhibiting factor, given that some researchers' knowledge of a foreign language is limited, as well as the need to comply with the formal criteria of style and the structure of academic writing. The following statement is symptomatic of this reluctance: 'I do not want to spend so much time and attention focusing on the size of letters, fonts, the requirements of different referencing styles or formatting. Sometimes it seems that form is more important than content'. Other critical views identified specific structural difficulties, including an 'incompetent science management bureaucracy, which has no understanding of or knowledge about publication processes, or the nature of science and the dissemination of findings'.

Question: What provides evidence of improvement in the quality of your research? How do you evaluate the availability of topical issues in your research field?

Questioned about evidence of claims to improvement in quality, both groups identified mainly external indicators, including approval for publication ('articles are accepted at the first or second go'), as well as the quantity and nature of the remarks and recommendations of anonymous peer reviewers. In some cases experienced researchers referred to quality indicators such as number of citations of publications and/or the adoption of the publication for study courses or as compulsory or recommended reading. Subjective self-reflection as a quality indicator was mentioned comparably rarely, as well as the condition that 'publication must not just reproduce the theory but produce tangible research results, providing suggestions for resolving potentially inherent contradictions'.

In relation to questions regarding the availability of research findings and new knowledge deriving from research studies, a typical response was that 'in our e-age, the age of the global Internet and technologies, everything is possible and can be found, so a lot depends on the technological skills of the researcher'. As an obstacle to access, the lack of financial resources was often mentioned: 'Lack of funds does not allow all scientific institutions to subscribe to the most important electronic databases, so researchers are not always able to participate in scientific conferences that report on contemporary work in the field'.

Question: Please give some examples of the potential social and economic impact of your research

In relation to the potential social and economic impact of one's research, specifically in the sharing of examples that would test the social and/or economic significance of research findings, the respondents from the doctoral students' group gave general comments: 'The research generated specific recommendations'; 'Models were developed with potential for solving a particular social or economic problem'; 'Study results were applied in practice'. A typical response was the assertion that the research results could take the form of sociological surveys, studies that describe existing challenges and the provision of potential solutions. As a result of a research study an innovative approach may be made available to the business or sales sectors. But some experienced scientists considered the research process itself an achievement, because in this way 'qualitative research traditions are being developed and issues with high relevance for society are being promoted' or:

> Research results always have social and/or economic meaning! The main thing is that the results should not only stay 'on the shelf', but should be published, presented, made available to other interested parties to be used

in practice, starting with their acceptance in the public domain and subsequent approval for the continuation of work, with possible relevance for other areas.

Reflecting on the criteria of social and economic effectiveness, respondents from both groups rarely mentioned or analysed the findings of their own personal research. Only one doctoral student gave a specific example, stating that 'throughout the case study, slowly but gradually, both the basics of the organisation of the work and the methodological aspects of speech therapy changed. Public perceptions changed too about pre-school children's language development in education and teachers' professional careers'. Experienced researchers also seldom named specific effectiveness indicators for the research, and then only in a few cases: 'The research results in the field of national culture, literature and art can be used in the tourism industry, in museums or for organising exhibitions or guided tours' or 'Research studies about the Latvian language and its forms of development can be used for producing school text books, handbooks and dictionaries and can be made available to all interested parties'.

Question: In your opinion, what is needed to encourage and achieve openness and criticality in research processes?

Regarding future prospects, the interviews implied that questions were being raised about the possibilities of achieving openness and criticality in everyday research processes. Both groups of respondents gave similar responses, typically that 'it basically depends on the person in charge of the research process, the personal characteristics of each researcher, and the institutional research traditions'. In our opinion, the most comprehensive recommendation was given by a doctoral student who described an optimum condition as:

> availability of specific research instruments, access to research databases and scientific journals in the field, scholarships and state guaranteed financial resources, as well as remuneration for conducting research, to support the presentation of research findings at international conferences and publication of the findings in internationally recognised scientific journals. Science cannot be based solely on a researcher's enthusiasm and the continuous implementation of projects, which requires a lot of 'bureaucratic' work in addition to direct research work.

Discussion

The analysis of these findings points to the importance of the establishment and acceptance of openness and criticality in research processes. Both principles are viewed more like subjective categories. However, according to established regulations regarding scientific activities, there is no clearly stated demand for openness and criticality, though it is the responsibility of the researcher to inform the wider community about the research results. The positive aspect is that in a democratic society every researcher can feel free to select a topic of their own choosing and research it. The only exception is projects funded by European Structural Funds, where the priorities of the European Union and Latvia coincide and there is 'an obligatory requirement to ensure openness and criticality'. However, the development of scientific activities at national level is not seen as a priority; thus no systemic developmental strategy has been developed in this field. In other words, in Latvia a lot of excellent research outcomes are published that could help 'to make the world a better place to live in', but these results are not systematically implemented in practice because of the lack of a commonly-agreed research strategy at national level. Therefore, considering the socio-economic conditions of Latvia, there is need for different kinds of support from the state, including the development of appropriate infrastructures, financial support and political decisions regarding a systemic development strategy. Ensuring the implementation of original ideas in practice arising from research outputs might be a very efficient form of support.

When analysing the initial phase of the research process such as in the selection of a research topic, an unfortunate tendency is evident. One of our respondents commented: 'Usually the starting point for a new research project in the humanities is defined by state priorities or invitations to tender for projects'. Consequently, although such priorities can be inappropriate, it is only in these cases that researchers can count on real support. This can be frustrating for researchers who often find that the national priorities are not in line with their own individual priorities.

These kinds of practices can have a strong influence on new researchers. The interviews revealed that the selection of a research topic is based on collaboration with the doctoral supervisor. This raises questions about how criticality can be initiated and supported by a colleague whose understanding is constrained by their own experience of limited scientific freedom. Thus, to a certain extent both new and experienced researchers are confronted with limited opportunities for the development of their own capacity for criticality from the very start of their research.

In this context greater support is available for new researchers to develop openness, as their experience of study offers opportunities for discussion and consultation about the research topic. However, experienced researchers are in less favourable conditions: they can have financial support and the support of research group members only if they are involved in already agreed research projects.

Respondents in our study agreed that opportunities were available for publishing their research results; the majority of them believed that publicity is a positive driver of criticality, since it helps promote the analysis of one's own research and provides feedback from experts and peers. Our respondents did not see the availability of published research findings as a problem, but some did mention a fear of other people 'stealing' their ideas and findings. It could be said that those who wish to make research findings visible and share them with others are more the donors rather than the recipients of openness.

This issue provokes reflection about the criteria that interviewees identified for judging the quality of research. Their view was that the quality of their scientific activity was judged mainly in terms of the evaluation of external experts and the publication of their research results in English in 'reputable journals' or 'valid databases'; thus publication came to be understood as 'the fulfilment of external demands'. This can lead quickly to an imbalance between the internal and external evaluation of research activities and their outcomes. However, relying only on external experts' assessment can easily diminish the significance of the research itself; moreover, publishing only in English runs the risk of the results of these studies not being seen as relevant for local contexts and simply serving the fulfilment of external demands. Consequently, at national level there is a gap between the conduct of scientific research and real life.

This supports the findings of the national critical evaluation of educational research and policy in Latvia (Grīviņš, 2011), which points to the lack of researchers' criticality and their unwillingness to express and support any opinions that differ from generally accepted beliefs. Possibly it is rooted in Latvian culture and stems from our 'cultural heritage' from the Soviet regime: people are not used to expressing opinions, or may even be afraid to do so. Therefore, as academics we need to learn how to collaborate, listen to other voices, share information and critically evaluate our own research findings and those of other professionals.

Because of the situation described here, there is also a lack of insight regarding the potential social and economic influence of research. Comparatively seldom are specific data or facts cited and there is a general lack of systemic strategy. In this regard, the opinion expressed by a respondent that 'any research is valuable in itself' makes sense.

A model for promoting openness and criticality in educational research

Resulting from the findings of our study, we have created a model that shows the relationships between openness and criticality and suggests possible steps towards the establishment of these principles in wider research practices (see Figure 6.1).

We authors consider *openness* and *criticality* as key aspects of any research process. We say this because, in order to reach the intended research goal of demonstrating social and economic impact, including articulating how the quality of theoretical knowledge should be judged in terms of its value for use and capacity building (Furlong and Oancea, 2005), the question 'How to achieve it?' becomes urgent and significant.

Disseminating and receiving feedback

Collaborating, networking, sharing
locally, nationally and internationally

Being aware of the goal and
the audience

How to ensure

Listening to and sharing experiences
with students and colleagues locally,
nationally and internationally

Analysing theoretical literature that
challenges different points of view

Personal self-reflection

How to ensure

Figure 6.1 Model for promoting openness and criticality.

All three of us hold a strong commitment to the idea that a researcher needs to be critically reflective (Brookfield, 1995). Although personal self-reflection is a starting point in the process of learning to be critical, it should be embedded right through the research process. It is especially important to focus on the meanings and interpretations that people create and share through their interactions (Merriam, 2009). This can be achieved in research seminars by discussing matters of quality with other colleagues, and also by collaboration, networking and sharing ideas and knowledge. These practices nurture the much-needed skill of listening to others' opinions, noticing different perspectives and challenging one's own beliefs.

With regard to *openness*, we want to emphasise the internal and external character of this principle. It is not enough only to provide free access to scientific publications; it is crucial to understand the internal motives that drive people's cognitive interests. Our research showed that important aspects in Latvian academic contexts are the lack of attention to research goals and the identification of the audience who will benefit from the findings. There is a general lack of feedback from society, other colleagues and experts; this does not support or encourage reflection or the critical evaluation and improvement of research results. Although strategies such as international assessment and peer review have been employed, their relevance for further improvement is not always taken into consideration or fully appreciated.

We also share Merriam's (2009) belief that research has to emphasise the importance of experience, understanding and meaning-making. In our opinion, the means of achieving this capacity are cumulative: every single aspect is interconnected with others and becomes stronger and more influential through the process of doing research. We hope our model illustrates how openness and criticality can help to develop the kind of personal competence and awareness that is crucial for conducting valid and internationally recognised research.

Conclusions

We hope we have communicated how, in a Latvian context, internal and external factors can work together to influence the degree of criticality and openness of research processes and reflect the links between individual and national levels: there is great need for a change in attitude and for the introduction and support of a systemic strategy for research activities. A further challenge is how to promote self-reflection and the meaningful use of academic freedom. The solution to such dilemmas is often not available to individual researchers or academics and should involve state politics and legislation.

This study has shown that research is often dominated by political issues, and there is a widespread tendency for quantitative indicators (numbers of publications, conferences and so on) to be seen as superior to qualitative ones (including content analysis and self-reflection). Very little attention is paid to self-reflection, although this is a crucial element for any research study. Researchers must continue to advance in how to understand critique as an opportunity that allows one to grow, reflect, assess and improve one's own work, and how to be open, given that the research results are not only for the researcher themselves, but also for the development of scientific enquiry and for the common good.

Based on our theoretical and empirical study, we believe that our model highlights the need for heightened awareness of the importance of educational research. A continuous articulation of the relationship between criticality and openness has to be provided to show the relevance of their relationship for the research study, the significance of the publication of the research, and for the meaningful dissemination of research results.

The outcomes of our research will, we hope, contribute to extending theoretical and practical knowledge about the power of research to promote positive attitudes towards the principles of criticality and openness, and to establishing a sustainable research culture within and beyond the borders of individual research institutions.

References

Andreozzi, S. et al. (2014) Open Science Commons. From www.egi.eu/news-and-media/publications/OpenScienceCommons_v3.pdf. (Accessed 29 March 2016).

Arnold, E. et al. (2014) *Latvia. Innovation System Review and Research Assessment Exercise: Draft Final Report*. Brighton: Technopolis Group, United Kingdom.

Brookfield, S. D. (1995) *Becoming a Critically Reflective Teacher.* San Francisco: Jossey-Bass Publishers.

Eiropas Komisija (2013. gada 21. Augusts) Zinātnisko publikāciju brīvas pieejamības ziņā sasniegts "kritiskais punkts". Brisele: Eiropas Komisija. Ielādēts no http://europa.eu/rapid/press-release_IP-13-786_lv.htm. (Accessed 29 March 2016).

European Commission (21 August 2013). 'Open access to research publications reaching "tipping point"'. Brussels: Press Release. From http://europa.eu/rapid/press-release_IP-13-786_en.htm. (Accessed 29 March 2016).

Furlong, J., & Oancea, A. (2005) *Assessing Quality in Applied and Practice-Based Educational Research: A Framework for Discussion.* Oxford: Oxford University Department of Educational Studies.

Grīviņš, M. (2011) Izglītības pētījumi un politika Latvijā: kritisks izvērtējums [Education research and policy in Latvia: a critical evaluation], in B. Bela and T. Tisenkopfs (eds), *Latvijas Universitātes raksti [Scientific Papers of University of Latvia].* 769, pp. 102–119. Rīga: Latvijas Universitāte.

Hyland, K. (2007) *Writing in the Academy: Reputation, Education and Knowledge.* University of London: Institute of London Press.

Король, С. А. (1981) К классифиации особенностей критичности мышления. *Вопросы психологии* (4), 108–112. Korol, S. A. (1981). 'Towards the classification of pecularities of critical thinking', *Issues of Psychology* 4: 108–112.

Law on scientific activity (16 December 2010). From http://www.vvc.gov.lv/advantagecms/LV/meklet/meklet_dokumentus.html?query=Law%20on%20scientific%20activity&resultsPerPage=10. (Accessed 29 March 2016).

Merriam, S. B. (2009) *Qualitative Research: A Guide to Design and Implementation.* San Francisco: Jossey-Bass.

Murray, R. E. (2012) 'Developing a community of research practice', *British Educational Research Journal* 38 (5): 783–800.

Niehaves, B., & Stahl, B. C. (2006) Criticality, epistemology, and behaviour vs. design – information systems research across different sets of paradigms. From www.cse.dmu.ac.uk/~bstahl/publications/2006_paradigm_ecis.pdf.

On the priority directions in science for 2014–2017 (20 November 2013). Republic of Latvia, Cabinet Order No. 551.

RIN/NESTA. (2010) *Open for All? Case Studies of Openness in Research.* London: The Research Information Network/The National Endowment for Science.

Strategy of scientific activity of the 'Scientific institution of Liepaja University' for 2010–2015 (26 October 2009). Liepaja University, approved by the Senate of Liepaja University, protocol No. 3. [Zinātniskās institūcijas 'Liepājas Universitāte' zinātniskās darbības stratēģija 2010–2015 (2009. gada 26. oktobris). Apstiprināts Liepājas Universitātes Senāta sēdē, protokols Nr. 3.]

Strategy of scientific activity of the 'Regional scientific institution of Rezekne Higher Education Institution' for 2011–2016 (01 November 2011). Rezekne Higher Education Institution, approved by the Senate of Rezekne Higher Education Institution, protocol No. 7. [Zinātniskās institūcijas 'Rēzeknes Augstskolas Reģionālistikas zinātniskā institūta' darbības stratēģija 2011–2015 (2011. gada 1. novembris). Apstiprināts Rēzeknes Augstskolas Senāta sēdē, protokols Nr. 7.]

Strategy of scientific activity of the state scientific institution Latvia University for 2010–2016 (16 November 2009). Latvia University, approved by the regulation No.1/295. [Valsts zinātniskās institūcijas Latvijas Universitātes darbības stratēģija 2010–2016. gadam. Latvijas Universitāte, apstiprināts ar rīkojumu Nr. 1/295.]

Solso, R. L. (1997). *Cognitive Psychology.* Boston: Allyn and Bacon.

Chapter 7

The 'questionableness' of things

Opening up the conversation

Jon Nixon, Alison Buckley, Andy Cheng, Sue Dymoke, Jane Spiro and Jonathan Vincent

This chapter developed from a number of conversations that took place at the Fourth International Conference on Value and Virtue in Practice-Based Research, the twin themes of which were 'openness' and 'criticality'. These chance and often fleeting conversations focused on ideas explored in the keynote address that Jon delivered at the conference, but spanned out into a wider discussion of the relevance of those ideas within different arenas of professional practice.

After the conference we agreed via email that Alison, Andy, Jane, Jonathan and Sue would respond – from their different perspectives and value orientations – to the ideas explored in Jon's keynote. How might these ideas translate into professional practice? How might embedded practice speak back to the generality of these ideas? How do the ideas relate to our core values as educators involved in practice-based research?

These were our starting points. They have resulted in the following edited version of Jon's original address interlaced with questions and interjections from the co-authors of this chapter. We are not claiming that what follows is dialogical, but it does attempt to open up a conversation on the nature of understanding and what it means to be someone who seeks to understand.

Jon began his address with a quotation from the philosopher Hans-Georg Gadamer: **And what is hermeneutical imagination? It is a sense of the questionableness of something and what this requires of us** *(Gadamer, 2004: 41–42).*

I'd like to approach the twin themes of openness and criticality through a consideration of what I call the interpretive tradition: the tradition, that is, of philosophical hermeneutics. Hermes was the son of Zeus and the god of transitions and boundaries. He acted as the messenger and emissary of Zeus, traversing the space between the mortal and divine, the human world and Mount Olympus. It is in this *in-between* space – the transitional space where meaning is made and boundaries transgressed – that philosophical hermeneutics is located.

> **Jane:** *In-between* space is what interests me as an educator and communicator. In Dante's *Purgatorio* there is a limbo-land which is a reverse image of the terraces of heaven. For him it was a kind of hell to be in an 'in between' place without the capacity to travel to or from, to be caught

without movement between two conditions. I interpret this for myself, as an educator, as a metaphor for creative opportunity. If the space between people is seen as the chance to travel between, we have so much to learn from one another; if it is seen as a 'gap' we are separated from one another in lonely and threatening limbo-lands. When I arrived as a new teacher in a country where I knew neither the language nor anyone in my new community, I wrote a sequence of poems I called *Exile*:

> I am a changeling, plucked
> and wrongly placed, my history
> mute, a failure to know
> where I am going, to remember where from.

I empathise here with the experience of physically entering these 'in-between' spaces, as an exile, refugee, traveller, plucked from a first language and culture. The need to cross emotional, linguistic and physical space is urgent. As a teacher of second culture students I have always considered it my responsibility to recognise this 'in-between' space and to ensure it is a journey towards transformation, rather than a place in which to be lost.

To interpret is to seek meaning. We human beings have always searched for meaning. We have looked to the stars to divine our destinies. We have looked at the footprints in the sand to see who passed this way before us. We have noted in the flight of birds the passing of the seasons. But alongside this primary practice of interpretation has evolved the secondary practice of understanding what it is we are doing when we interpret. Rabbis have asked: 'What are we doing when we interpret the Talmud and the Torah?' Philosophers of law have asked: 'What are we doing when we interpret the Law?' Humanist scholars have asked: 'What are we doing when we interpret the Text?'

Jane: The image of the footprints in the sand evokes for me a Joshua Indian creation myth. The Creator/First Mover in the story creates the earth through rings of smoke, and brings land out of the water. But to his horror, as the sand lifts from the sea, there is a line of footprints clearly imprinted. No matter how many times he washes the sand with sea, each time it re-emerges with the footprints. Even the First Mover, believing himself to be the originator of all, has a predecessor. Behind each of our movements, is another; it is simply that we are still unaware. I see hermeneutics as the process of becoming aware, returning to those footsteps again and again to realise they are in fact ours, as well as those of our known and hidden ancestors.

The interpretive tradition

Two insights in particular form the basis of what I am terming the interpretive tradition. The first insight is that *in any attempt at interpretation we are interpreting that which has already been interpreted*. The object of our interpretation is a construct that we inherit from the historical layering of countless prior interpretations and re-interpretations. There is no blank page of history upon which we can inscribe our entirely original understandings. History is a palimpsest of layered inscriptions and layered commentaries. The second insight follows from the first. If all understanding is always already interpretation, then *the interpreter is always already part of what is being interpreted*. The subject that interprets is implicit in the object of interpretation. Notions of 'objectivity' and 'neutrality' as the privileged criteria of rationality become increasingly difficult to justify in the light of this second insight.

A third insight follows from the first two and was developed in particular by Hans-Georg Gadamer. If all understanding is always already interpretation and the interpreter always already part of what is being interpreted, then *all understanding necessarily involves an element of self-understanding*. Gadamer elaborated this insight with reference to the notion of 'application', which he understood as being implicit in all understanding from the moment of its inception. It is not that understanding is achieved and then applied, but that the application is intrinsic to the process of understanding: 'in all understanding an application occurs, such that the person who is understanding is himself or herself *right there* in the understood meaning. He or she *belongs to* the subject-matter that he or she is understanding. ... Everyone who understands something understands himself or herself in it' (original emphasis) (Gadamer, 2001: 47–48). The hermeneutical task, as Gadamer defines it, is to locate oneself within one's own field – or, as he would put it, 'tradition' – of understanding.

Jane: This insight that 'he or she *belongs to* the subject-matter' represents for me the very essence of action research. Being given permission to belong to the subject-matter liberates the practitioner-researcher. As a teacher, what has meaning is what we can translate into real change in our professional lives. As an early teacher-researcher I was fascinated by the imagination; I was directed by supervisors to the testimonies of writers, philosophers, poets, biologists, artists, and their accounts of imagination. Yet the more I read, the less satisfying seemed to be my task. I withdrew from the PhD programme after two years instead of three, with a worthy dissertation that included several thousand references to others, but had no further value beyond the MPhil I was awarded. Years later I discovered action research: in other words, I was given the permission to 'belong to my subject-matter'. I researched what imagination meant to me as a writer and teacher, how it impacted on my students and colleagues, how it could impact even more, in what ways it represented positive change, where there were conflicts and what to do about this. It became my life work. Belonging to our subject-matter is critical: without this we are indeed lost in the in-between spaces, talking to ourselves; but with it, we are making connections in the world.

The idea of 'tradition' is central to hermeneutics as developed by Gadamer: 'we stand in traditions, whether we know these traditions or not; that is, whether we are conscious of these or are so arrogant as to think we can begin without presuppositions – none of this changes the way traditions are working on us and in our understanding' (Gadamer, 2001: 45). Traditions pose questions in response to which we define ourselves and our own sense of purpose. The coherence of any tradition, as understood by Gadamer, can only be defined with reference to its intrinsic plurality and potential for innovation. Traditions are constantly evolving as new generations interpret and re-interpret them and, by so doing, modify and elaborate them. Traditions may initially present themselves to us as assertions, but, as Gadamer (1977: 11–13) insists, 'no assertion is possible that cannot be understood as an answer to a question, and assertions can only be understood in this way. ... The real power of hermeneutical consciousness is our ability to see what is questionable'.

Central to the argument of Gadamer's (2004) *Truth and Method* is what he calls 'the hermeneutic priority of the question' (pp. 356–371). 'Understanding begins', as he puts it, 'when something addresses us. This is the first condition of hermeneutics' (p. 298). In becoming receptive to that which addresses us we are opening ourselves to the question it asks of us: 'the essence of the *question* is to open up possibilities and keep them open' (p. 298) (original emphasis). Interpretation is the process whereby we receive the object of interpretation as a question. In clarifying and addressing that question the interpreter makes plain its meaning. Gadamer's major contribution to the interpretive tradition is his insight into the dialogical nature of all interpretive acts. The inherent structure of that tradition, he argues, is that of question and answer.

Andy: From my perspective as a researcher/activist seeking to intervene in the executive function of community development through co-production, I recognise that the interpretive tradition has some well-founded benefits and much to say about a hope for living together with difference. However, the operation of inquiry runs counter to the operation of tradition. And faith, the antithesis of enquiry, is the cornerstone of how tradition delivers the compliance to attitude and behaviour that

(continued)

is the advantage bred into it over eons of human/cultural evolution. This is perhaps at odds with Gadamer's insistence that traditions are mutable. Reflecting on Gadamer's statement that 'the real power of hermeneutical consciousness is our ability to see what is questionable', ought we not to ask: could it be that the real power of tradition is its capacity to blind us to that which is questionable? In considering what the interpretive tradition 'requires of us' is there not an onus on us to invite the faithful to enter into the conversation about what is question-able without challenging their faith in the unquestionable and what they see as the benefit that devotion brings?

Horizon, prejudice and method

Tradition as understood and developed by Gadamer is not a bounded and impermeable system. On the contrary, it is a dynamic process that is both open-ended and unpredictable. It is a kind of ongoing conversation. Indeed, conver-sation was, for Gadamer, not just a metaphor for the interpretive tradition as he understood it, but its very substance: the means by which ideas are sustained and transformed across generations. It is in the *in-between* of conversation that we make meaning, share understanding, and reconcile the strange and the familiar. Gadamer spent his life as a philosopher trying to make sense of this *in-between* space of human interchange. In doing so, he explored three major themes in particular: the fusion of horizons, the power of prejudice and the problem of method.

The fusion of horizons

Gadamer's notion of 'horizon' relates directly to the importance he places in tradition as the legacy of the past to the future and the corresponding debt owed by the present to the past. In *Truth and Method*, Gadamer provides a general explanation of how and why he is using the concept: 'The concept of "horizon" suggests itself because it expresses the superior breadth of vision that the person who is trying to understand must have. To acquire a horizon means that one learns to look beyond what is close at hand – not in order to look away from it but to see it better, within a larger whole and in true proportion' (Gadamer, 2004: 304). The concept as applied by Gadamer invariably relates to our understand-ing of the past and of how we interpret the past with reference to the sources available to us. Gadamer's central point on this matter is that our horizons of understanding are never static: 'Every historian and philologist must reckon with the fundamental non-definitiveness of the horizon in which his understanding moves. Historical tradition can be understood only as something always in the process of being defined by the course of events' (ibid.: 366).

The meaning to be derived from any act of interpretation is always *in-between*: between the interpreted and the interpreter, between the object of interpretation and the interpreter as subject, between different historical positions and perspectives. This means that the object of interpretation does not simply surrender its meaning as a form of divine revelation or authorial intention. Notwithstanding its historical roots in biblical exegesis, hermeneutics is in this respect both secular and humanist in its assumption that neither divine authority nor authorial intention provides the final arbiter in any interpretive act. There can be no appeal to a divine purpose that lies outside the historical course of events or to a human will that is immune to the consequences of those events.

The *in-between* nature of human understanding also means that interpretation is not simply imposed – as imported theory or pre-specified criteria – by the interpreter on the object of interpretation. Although the world is always already interpreted, every act of interpretation is a new beginning occasioning a necessary shift in the interpreter's self-understanding; or, as Joseph Dunne (1997: 121) puts it, 'the interpreter's horizon is already being stretched beyond itself, so that it is no longer the same horizon that it was independently of this encounter'. Because both interpreter and interpreted are located in the process of history – *in medias res* – the horizon of interpretation can never achieve permanent fixity. It changes constantly, just as our visual horizon varies with each step we take: 'horizons are not rigid but mobile; they are in motion because our prejudgements are constantly put to the test' (Gadamer, 2001: 48). Consequently, each interpretation is both unique and open to reinterpretation. Plurality is a defining feature of the interpretive field.

The power of 'prejudice'

What the interpreter brings to the process of interpretation is vitally important. We understand the world in relation to what we bring to it by way of prior assumptions, preconceptions, and prejudices. We understand the world in and through our experience of the world. This perspective, as Gadamer (2004: 271) puts it, 'involves neither "neutrality" with respect to content nor the extinction of one's self, but the foregrounding and appropriation of one's own fore-meanings and prejudices'. If we are an integral part of the world that we are seeking to understand, then we can 'formulate the fundamental epistemological question for a truly historical hermeneutics as follows: what is the ground of the legitimacy of prejudices? What distinguishes legitimate prejudices from the countless others which it is the undeniable task of critical reason to overcome?' (p. 278). Prejudice – our historicity – is where interpretation begins: 'the concept of "prejudice" is where we can start' (p. 273). We bring with us to any attempt at interpretation prior values and assumptions that shape what and how we interpret.

Gadamer insists that this importing of ourselves into the process of understanding is a necessary component of that understanding. However, he also insists that we must be aware of what we are importing. Some of our prejudices may assist understanding, while others may distort or deny understanding. A large part of the hermeneutical task involves self-examination through the sifting of prejudices. To have trust in an interpretation is to trust that the interpreter has undergone this process of self-examination in respect of the values and assumptions that have shaped that interpretation. Similarly, to trust in one's own interpretive capacity is not to have blind faith in one's own convictions, but to trust in one's own commitment to questioning those convictions. Trust is a necessary condition of understanding and understanding is a necessary condition of our being in the world. If we trusted nothing in this world of ours, then it would be a world beyond our understanding – and a world beyond our understanding is no longer *our* world.

Gadamer is not arguing on behalf of relativism: an ethics of 'anything goes'. Rather, he is arguing for an ethics of deliberation. He is arguing on behalf of mutuality and reciprocity as the conditions necessary for whatever shared understanding is necessary for being together. Understanding implies – and requires as a necessary condition – recognition of both selfhood and difference and of the necessary relation between the two. To seek to understand is to adopt an ethical stance – not a moralistic or moralising stance, but a stance which affirms the central importance of personhood (of the other and of the self). If our world is shaped by our understanding of it, and if that understanding is conditional upon our meeting of minds, then understanding is nothing if not ethical. The originality of *Truth and Method* lies in its injunction to overcome what Gadamer sees as the alienation implicit in the ideal of 'prejudiceless' objectivity: acknowledge the presence of yourself in your own understanding; recognise the other person's understanding as central to your own understanding; develop your understanding as you would a dialogue. Above all, Gadamer insists, do not assume that human understanding can be reduced to method. That is not how human understanding works.

Beyond method

At the time when Gadamer was writing, 'method' was in the ascendancy. The idea of 'method' was particularly associated with scientific enquiry, but the idea of there being a pre-ordained methodology of enquiry across disciplines and fields of study held sway. For enquiry to be taken seriously – whether within the natural, human, or social sciences – it had to be conducted systematically and in accordance with pre-specified methodological procedures. In its most extreme form this scientific positivism – buttressed by the philosophical presuppositions of logical positivism or logical empiricism as it is sometimes termed – claimed that observational evidence is indispensable for knowledge of the world and that only when supported by such evidence could a belief that such and such is the case actually be the case (i.e. be 'true'). A methodical approach to the selection, gathering and analysis of empirical 'data' – and to the inferential process whereby 'findings' were derived from this approach – was and to a large extent still is the means by which scientific enquiry gained legitimacy and public recognition. 'Method' would enable one to gather and analyse 'data' which would then provide knowledge in the form of 'findings'. This became the dominant paradigm of scientific enquiry and exerted a strong influence on the social sciences generally and on social psychology in particular where it was supported by the presuppositions of behaviourism.

Gadamer's starting point in *Truth and Method* is the 'problem of method' as he terms it (Gadamer, 2004: 3–8). Understanding, he maintains, cannot be reduced to a method, although interpretive methods may contribute to our understanding. Gadamer does not deny that there are methods, but denies that such methods are constitutive of human understanding: 'as tools, methods are always good to have'. But, he insists, we must understand where they can be fruitfully used if we are to avoid what he terms 'methodical sterility': [I]t is not their mastery of methods but their hermeneutical imagination that distinguishes truly productive researchers. And what is hermeneutical imagination? It is a sense of the questionableness of something and what this requires of us' (Gadamer, 2001: 41–42).

Jonathan: Gadamer's hermeneutical imagination resonates strongly with the philosophy that underpins the Stratus Writers Project, a participatory action research project working with university students on the autistic spectrum. Our project used autoethnographic narratives as a means of identifying unique insider knowledge about autism and experiences of higher education. Our research process aimed to be fully participatory, where data were collected, analysed and disseminated by the students themselves.

Gadamer's invitation to meaningful conversation with traditions, phenomena and others has much import for participatory action research *with* students on the autistic spectrum whose 'conditions' and 'disorders' have often resulted in their being silenced. Jim Sinclair (1989) puts this well in his personal narrative 'Bridging the Gaps': 'My credibility is suspect. My understanding of myself is not considered to be valid, and my perceptions of events are not considered to be based in reality. My rationality is questioned because, regardless of intellect, I still appear odd'.

Sinclair's critique reflects the historical reality, where discussing autism was the exclusive prerogative of clinicians and researchers and where autistic people were the *objects* of medical examination, rather than *active participants* in the creation of knowledge relating to their own experiences (Milton and Bracher, 2013). However, building on Gadamer's challenge to 'see what is questionable' – in this case about autism – the Stratus Writers Project asserted that the autistic students themselves are authoritative and carry revealing wisdom about their own lives. By emphasising the participatory nature of the research process, 'in-between' spaces were identified

(continued)

and indeed celebrated; the lines between researcher and researched were blurred and the students' collective experiences were explored as 'first person plural accounts' (Couser, 2000: 306).

The analysis of the qualitative data by the students themselves might, in research terms, be considered the transgression of a boundary for some, yet for us it represented an opportunity to construct new and valid meanings in a humanising way. Megan, one of the participants, summed it up in her evaluation when she said, 'The greatest success from my point of view was having a voice. We weren't treated like research subjects but research partners in the process ... right from the beginning through to presenting at conferences'.

Implicit in Gadamer's critique of method is the idea that understanding involves self-formation and human flourishing that is open-ended in the extent and scope of its proliferation. The application of method, on the other hand, assumes a notion of rationality that seeks closure and predictability. Human understanding, argues Gadamer, must be true to the nature of humanity: a humanity that is necessarily fragile and vulnerable by virtue of its complex interconnectivities and its uncertain relation to the future. Gadamer saw this as a struggle between the human and natural sciences, with the latter imposing an inappropriate methodology on the latter. But his analysis was such as to reframe the terms of the debate in ideological rather than methodological terms: the scientific method when inappropriately applied to the human world insists upon a particular version of humanity. Moreover, since the natural world is always already an interpreted world, the methodology derived from the natural sciences may be severely limited even when applied within its own traditional domain.

Alison: Using narrative inquiry, I am interested in understanding the lived experience of delirium following a neurological event, from both the patient's and carer's perspective. My position both as a nurse and a researcher with a clinical background and an empirical 'view' of the research subject poses a methodological challenge. Whilst this priori experience was formative in shaping my initial research interests, I am conscious as to how I 'situate' myself in the research trajectory such that my personal constructs and assumptions as a nurse do not unduly influence both the researcher–participant relationship and the emerging dialogue. I need to remain respectful of the primacy and immediacy of the participant's narrative and whilst acknowledging that participant–researcher dynamics will exist, the utterances, descriptions and dialogue of the participants need to remain dominant and authentic. This methodological challenge between the relative merits of research methodologies and the pursuit of rigour and objectivity has been debated at length. However, Michael Crotty (1998: 17) rightly acknowledges that throughout the research journey, there is an inevitability that the assumption and 'situatedness' of the researcher will shape 'for us the meaning of research questions and the purposiveness of research methodologies'. Indeed, as discussed by Christine Stephens (2011: 67) the interviewer is 'not a neutral bystander and their direct contributions to shaping the narrative, as well as their representation of a broader social world in which the narrative is orientated, cannot be minimised or ignored'.

To remove the very essence of my practice experiences in an attempt to strengthen rigour and objectivity and lose a perspective of self appears not only naïve but unattainable. As Gadamer posits we already 'belong to the tradition'; we already have a relationship with the case. My 'situatedness' and relationship not only with patients but with the 'life-world' of nursing, the culture and tradition to which I belong, should be viewed as an important contribution to the research and a valuable guide to enquiry, not a distraction or encumbrance.

For Gadamer, the position of the researcher is paramount; he is always located in a *situation,* and because we are inevitably influenced by a historical position, then the interpreter must adopt, as Jon examines, a 'historical horizon' whereby there is a conscious intention and acknowledgement of bias which may influence the interpretation. Gadamer refers to this as 'consciousness of being affected by history'. An acknowledgement of these prejudices is necessary so that as Kitt Austgard (2012: 830) posits, 'the text, as another's meaning, can be isolated and valued on its own'. Jon suggests that the very essence of the researcher is a powerful tool for interpretation – indeed, that we 'understand the world in and through our experience of the world ...'.

The iterative process within the hermeneutic process, defined by Douglas Ezzy (2002: 24) as 'the art & science of interpretation' actively engages the researcher in the interpretive process and recognises that an awareness of the researcher's 'starting position' as a sense-maker inevitably contributes to the research ends. It is not that the a priori position influences the interpretation but rather that a new meaning arises from the data analysis which may shift the overall understanding.

Reflexivity involves the realisation of an honest examination of the values and interests of the researcher that may impinge upon research work (Primeau, 2003). Constance T. Fischer's (2009: 584) position is possibly more enviable in that in challenging the notion of objectivity she recognises that 'it is not possible to view without viewing from somewhere'. Indeed it could be argued that the prejudices of the researcher are in themselves

(continued)

a 'view' which inevitably bestows meaning and is the very source of our repertoire of knowledge. I believe the negative attribution of researcher 'prejudice' should be redefined and seen rather as a positive influence on the explication of meaning derived in the interpretive paradigm. As a nurse I will inevitably bring knowledge and my own reality to this interpretive work, which I propose will undoubtedly shape the research questions and the very purpose of my work.

'... what this requires of us'

If we are to follow Gadamer's metaphorical lead, we need to see humanistic enquiry as an ongoing conversation: a continuous process of question and answer. Among our interlocutors are both the living and the dead: the dead who still speak to us through the record of their words and deeds, the living who share our object of interest and enquiry. It is a conversation that may be conducted in company, but that is equally valid and worthwhile when conducted in solitude – what Hannah Arendt (1978), in her last great work on thinking, called 'the two-in-one' of thought (pp. 179–193). All thought, she argued, is dialogical in nature, which is why the experience of solitude is radically different from the experience of loneliness. 'Thinking', she maintained, 'is a solitary but not a lonely business; solitude is the human situation in which I keep myself company. Loneliness comes about when I am alone without being able to split up into the two in one, without being able to keep myself company' (p. 185).

Andy: From a background of two decades of community development and activism, I find Gadamer's metaphorical lead, 'to see humanistic enquiry as an ongoing conversation', inspirational. And, indeed, my own work – seeking co-production between the users of social care and community services and the practitioners who design, manage and deliver them – has been committed to facilitating a '... living together with difference'. Crucial in this is, of course, what we (all) mean by 'living'. And in the field I work in there is a clear difference between the motivations, operations and aspirations for outcome as enacted – even if not fully articulated – by different participants. In my world these are groups of participants we designate as service users and practitioners, who in turn are both tacitly and explicitly negotiating with managers, funders, regulators and, truth be known, me. What strikes me most about the challenge of forging '... the firm commitment to live together with difference' is my perception of a gap between what it is to *inquire* and what it is to apply the inquiry in our *living*. Perhaps this is an insurmountable gap – the tackling of which presents us with a Sisyphean challenge.

So, what *is* required of us on first entering the conversation? First, we require the *courage* and *patience* to listen to the other. Listening requires courage because so often it involves hearing what we don't want to hear or what is difficult to wrap our heads round. It requires patience because listening – and reading with a listening mind – can be a long and hard slog. Reading, in particular, is crucial: being attentive to the words on the page and/or screen; persevering with what on first and even subsequent readings may appear difficult and unfamiliar; reading in such a way as to understand the text from its own historical perspective; reading inter-textually so as to understand the text in context; and, finally, interpreting the text with reference to our own contemporary concerns.

The crucial requirement in entering the conversation is to be attentive to what is being and has been uttered in both the written and spoken word. It is only by listening in on the ongoing conversation – the conversation 'out there' in the collective experience of thinking together *and* in the 'two-in-one' of solitary thought – that we can begin to understand what questions we want to pose, what questions we are being asked to address, and the terms and conventions within which those questions need to be framed. We can't simply blunder into the conversation. We have to take stock of it – understand its parameters and emergent themes – and, crucially, identify our own interests within it: identify, that is, the particular question that the conversation asks of us, and that we might want to ask of it. That question is our point of entry.

Let us suppose, then, that we have identified that question, that we have a sense of our starting point, that we have identified the origins of our enquiry. What now is required of us? I suggest that we require the *determination* and *imagination* to stay with the question, to refine and focus it, to sharpen it and apply it. Refining the question requires determination because it is a process rather than a single act or event. It requires imagination because it precedes though inference, guesswork and intuition. It is an ongoing process of question and answer. Only by refining the question can we understand the nature of the problem that is the object of our enquiry – an object that is only gradually revealed through this process of progressive focussing. The endpoint of this process of question and answer is not a definitive answer, but a defining question: a question so refined as to imply the parameters if not the substance of any response to it.

> **Sue**: What strikes me is the extent to which questions are at the root of experience and how much of my life as educator, researcher and poet is bound up with questioning. Education is all about developing curiosity and, with that, the means to learn through discovery. If we give our students endless answers, we diminish their power to take an active role in their own learning – both in school and in their adult lives. Through my work in education, first as a secondary school English teacher and latterly as a teacher educator and researcher, I have constantly encouraged young

(continued)

people and those at the beginning of their teaching careers to question, listen and reflect on their developing classroom practices as learners and teachers. I want them to take time and make space for these processes. They should be enabled to frame new questions through creative risk taking, through asking themselves, their peers and/or their students: how would it be if I tried out this activity or if I wrote this line this way or if I read the text from that point of view?

I think they must learn to seize and twist the question kaleidoscope for themselves, to see new and endlessly reflecting patterns, to interrogate why a person has arrived at such an interpretation, whether it is better than theirs or just different and if it could help them to arrive at a new understanding. This breaking down of questions into smaller fragments is a fine art that many doctoral students are challenged by. On beginning their research they often appear adamant that they know what they want to investigate and refuse to be distracted by other ideas. Nevertheless, only by redefining, refocusing and sharpening their questions will they productively engage in original research.

As Jon says, the interpreter is within the world in which they are questioning. However, the nature of an individual's questions (and thus their horizon) changes as the student, beginning teacher or researcher becomes further embedded within a particular world. As they grow in confidence they can begin to look beyond the obvious colour-pattern variations in order to explore the intricate traceries of light and shade in the far distance.

In writing poetry and researching the act of poetry writing, I am constantly questioning the nature of things around me in order to reinterpret what others have interpreted in a way that, I hope, will shed new light. For example, currently I am seeking to explore why poets feel constrained by the demands of academic writing; how other passengers might react when someone invades their personal space; and why a blackbird sings in a particular way at twilight in winter. In some of my poems, such as 'Mass Observation', I have experimented with a form that solely consists of questions. In doing so, I am not trying to be cantankerous: I am simply trying to get closer to an understanding of how others might experience, and question, the world.

> What's in your head?
> What dreams are you dreaming?
> What does night rain on the window feel like
> while your boy's away at war?
>
> (Dymoke, 2012, 1)

The process of question and answer is endless – 'in reality', as (Gadamer, 2001: 60) puts it, 'the last word does not exist'. But there does, of course, come a point when we decide to give an account of ourselves – when, that is, we contribute publicly to the debate through some form of publication or public address. What is required of us in giving such an account? The prime requirements are, to my mind, *openness* and *magnanimity*: openness in acknowledging that no one – least of all one's self – ever has the last word, and magnanimity in recognising the value of alternative and possibly critical viewpoints and counter-arguments. These qualities suggest a style of reporting that focuses on provisional insights rather than proofs, dilemmas and concerns rather than resolutions, and frameworks for further thinking rather than definitive statements. The point of a conversation is not to win with a view to achieving closure, but to forestall closure with a view to achieving increased understanding. We must always – *always* – argue beyond the point of seemingly irreconcilable difference.

> **Jonathan:** Although challenging historical hegemony can be subversive and creative, it should be acknowledged that the essential 'questionableness' of things also urges us to act with humility. We participants of the Stratus Writers Project must recognise that our voices are only some among many and so we must also relinquish our claims to certainty in accepting the essential openness of our findings. Thus, it is through honest and reciprocal dialogue such as this that our knowledge about autism and what can make university better for autistic students can be reimagined and more ethical understandings made possible.

That is not to say that difference can be transcended or overcome in the interests of some overarching unity – whether defined in spiritual, essentialist or absolutist terms. Difference is real and must be recognised. It is only through the recognition of difference that we can live together. We live together in difference or not at all. That is why we must seek to understand that which we choose to criticise. We can only criticise with honesty what we have fully received; the quality of our criticism depends upon the quality of our receptivity. To criticise without first opening ourselves to that which we are criticising is a particularly pernicious – and increasingly prevalent – form of philistinism. When we 'go public' we very often position ourselves critically in relation to others and, in turn, receive criticism from those against whom we have positioned ourselves. That is how the conversation works. But it only works well insofar as we genuinely seek to understand prior to engaging in critique.

Hermes – the go-between in our world of *in-between* – is having a particularly hard time at the moment. Dashing between Hebron and Jerusalem, Damascus and Homs, the Ukraine and Crimea, our god of transitions and boundaries is undoubtedly under considerable strain. He is witnessing us mortals kill and maim ourselves with wilful abandon. Hermes also has to contend with the superpowers and their internal wrangling – for example, the 'tea party' squabbling in the US and the coalition tiffs in the UK. Ours is an incontrovertibly agonistic world. *Nothing now is more important than the understanding of difference and the firm commitment to living together with difference.* The interpretive tradition – as I have tried to elaborate it – is much more than a scholarly outpost of Western philosophy. It is our only hope of living together. It is the only space left. The interpretive tradition has much to teach us.

> **Jane**: I am in warm agreement with Jon that *Nothing now is more important than the understanding of difference and the firm commitment to living together with difference.* The Old Testament has a notion that human beings themselves create the conditions for a Golden Age: it is not a place, but a state, and not freely 'given' but earned by each of us. To navigate in-between spaces with an open heart is our challenge. In 1973 the reform rabbi Jonathan Magonet opened a symposium that brought Jews, Christians and Muslims together into open dialogue. This symposium, intended as a one-snapshot event, at the time of writing now enters its 42nd year. He writes: 'The complexity of modern civilization is a daily lesson in the necessity of not pressing any claim too far, of understanding opposing points of view, of seeking to reconcile them, of conducting matters so that there is some kind of harmony in a plural society' (Magonet, 2003: 16). Why this paper of Jon's is so deeply resonant for me is that it has dared to connect what we do as writers, researchers and thinkers with what we do in the wider world, and with the belief and hope that this connection can make a positive difference.

References

Arendt, H. (1978) *The Life of the Mind: One/Thinking.* New York and London: Harcourt Brace Jovanovich.

Austgard, K. (2012) 'Doing it the Gadamerian way – using philosophical hermeneutics as a methodological approach in nursing science', *Scandinavian Journal of Caring Sciences,* 26 (4): 829–834.

Couser, G. (2000) 'The empire of the "normal": a forum on disability and self-representation: introduction', *American Quarterly,* 52 (2): 305–310.

Crotty, M. (1998) *The Foundations of Social Research: Meaning and Perspective in the Research Process.* Thousand Oaks, CA: Sage.

Dunne, J (1997) *Back to the Rough Ground: Practical Judgment and the Lure of Technique.* Notre Dame, IN: University of Notre Dame Press.

Dymoke, S. (2012) *Moon at the Park and Ride.* Nottingham: Shoestring Press.

Ezzy, D. (2002) *Qualitative Analysis: Practice and Innovation.* Crows Nest, Australia: Allen and Unwin.

Fischer, C.T. (2009) 'Bracketing in qualitative research: conceptual and practical matters', *Quantitative and Qualitative Methods for Psychotherapy Research*, 19 (4–5): 583–590.

Gadamer, H.-G. (2004) *Truth and Method* (trans. J. Weinsheimer and D.G. Marshall) (2nd revised edn). London and New York: Continuum.

Gadamer, H.-G. (2001) *Gadamer in Conversation: Reflections and Commentary* (ed. and trans. R.E. Palmer). New Haven and London: Yale University Press.

Gadamer, H.-G. (1977) *Philosophical Hermeneutics* (ed. and trans. D.E. Ling). Berkeley, Los Angeles and London: University of California Press.

Magonet, J. (2003) *Talking to the Other*. London: I.B. Tauris and Co. Ltd.

Milton, D. and Bracher, M. (2013) 'Autistics speak but are they heard?', *Medical Sociology Online*. 7 (2): 61–69.

Primeau, L.A. (2003) 'Reflections on self in qualitative research: stories of family', *American Journal of Occupational Therapy*, 57: 9–16.

Sinclair, J. (1989) *Bridging the Gaps*, available at http://jisincla.mysite.syr.edu/ (accessed 9/3/14).

Stephens, C. (2011) 'Narrative analysis in health psychology research: personal, dialogical and social stories of health', *Health Psychology Review*, 15 (1): 62–78.

Chapter 8

Sharing the learning from community action research

Josephine Bleach

This paper examines how the Early Learning Initiative (ELI), a community-based educational project in the National College of Ireland (NCI), shares the learning from its action research–based process with local, national and international audiences. We, at ELI, believe that, if our work, and action research as a methodological approach to organisational and community development, are to influence wider practices, policy and theory, the learning from the process needs to be shared with others. A core element of this is to show how we learned to realise our underpinning values as living practices. Such sharing requires the development of thoughtful and targeted dissemination strategies (Patton and Horton, 2009) if it is to influence thinking in the public sphere (McNiff, 2010). These strategies include the regular production of evidence of outcomes and an account of their impact in order to keep stakeholders, policy makers and funders interested, informed and involved.

This kind of communication and the form of language we use matter because what we call what we do affects what we do and how we do it (Patton, 1994). It also impacts on how others perceive us and decide on their relationship with us. However, articulating our theories and practice in ways that make sense to others can be difficult, and can require a high level of political sophistication (McNiff and Whitehead, 2006).

In this paper, as Director, I describe how ELI, in partnership with the local community, shares the learning from its programmes. I first outline our aims in sharing our learning with others, and then explain the action research process used to develop our programmes. I go on to describe how our evaluation processes are used to provide evidence for our learning and practices, which can then be shared through a variety of media and forums with a range of audiences. ELI's key messages are then described, together with the audiences for those messages, and an outline of the range of dissemination strategies used to share our learning with others. Finally I offer my reflections on the benefits and challenges of sharing our learning with others.

First, to contextualise the paper and the research, here is some information about the NCI and ELI.

About the National College of Ireland and the Early Learning Initiative

The National College of Ireland (NCI) is an Irish third level learning, teaching and research institution. Since its inception in 1951, NCI has a long-standing commitment to widening participation in higher education (Bleach, 2013a). As a third level provider, it has a unique relationship with its local community in the Dublin Docklands and believes that early intervention is critical if educationally disadvantaged young people and their families from the area are to access third level education.

The Early Learning Initiative (ELI) is an integral part of NCI's mission to 'change lives through education' (ELI, 2011). As a third level institution, NCI is a potent symbol in its local community, providing pre-school, primary and second level students and their families with a visual reminder that they have a right to third level education and that with support it is within their reach (ELI, 2011; Bleach, 2013a). Through ELI, NCI supports children and their families as they progress into and through the education system and on to third level.

Operating as a partnership between NCI, local parents, early years services, schools, health services, community organisations and neighbouring corporate leaders, ELI was established in 2006 to address the specific problem of educational disadvantage. Recognising the need to generate solutions *with*, not *for*, parents and others in the community (Bleach, 2013a), action research, with its emphasis on building cross-organisational learning communities (Senge and Scharmer, 2001; Bleach 2013b), was chosen as the research methodology for the initiative. Over the past nine years, innovative programmes have been developed, which have raised educational aspirations and supported children and young people in progressing through the education system and on to third level (Bleach, 2013a).

Some of ELI's programmes are funded by the Irish Government in collaboration with Atlantic Philanthropies. Learning communities are important elements of these programmes. They bring together the government agencies responsible for programme governance and implementation, representatives from each project involved in the programme and the programme evaluation team to share and disseminate learning from project implementation with the aim of collectively influencing policy (Pobal, 2014). They also provide opportunities for participating projects, like ELI, to share their practice and experience with the other projects.

At national and international level, ELI engages with others who share our values and goals. Priority is given to individuals, organisations and networks that focus on action research, early childhood development, educational disadvantage and support for parents. Networking with other practitioners, researchers and policy makers enables us to challenge our assumptions and provides us with fresh insights into our theories, practice and the communities in which we work.

Further, continually engaging with others is important for ELI to secure funding and influence thinking in the public sphere. As different audiences require different information, a variety of communication methods are used to share our learning with others.

Aims of sharing our learning

Action researchers, Sommer (2009) has argued, have certain obligations in dissemination if they are to achieve the three goals proposed by Lewin (1946) for action research. These are to progress knowledge, improve a concrete situation and advance methodology. Sharing our learning with others is at the heart of ELI's action research process and mission of 'Working in partnership with local communities to support educational journeys and achievements' (ELI, 2013: 6). It is an important element of our learning community of parents, children and staff from local statutory, community and corporate organisations. The commitment from all our stakeholders to share their knowledge and practice is critical to nurturing and sustaining a knowledge-creating system, based on valuing each other equally (Senge and Scharmer, 2001: 240). Without it, our long-term vision of leading 'the way in providing first class educational support programmes within local communities, thereby enabling children, young people and their families to develop the dispositions, skills and knowledge needed to achieve their educational, career and life goals' (ELI 2013: 6) will not be achieved.

Successful change requires an emergent, evolutionary and educational process of engagement that needs to be sustained for significant periods of time (Herr and Anderson, 2005). This can be done only through the systematic sharing of learning through what Schön (1983) calls 'dynamic conversations'. Sharing our practice, theories and learning through action research develops our reflective, relational and representational knowledge (Park, 1999, 2001), which, in turn, increases our capacity, individually and collectively, to manage change and produce results we truly care about (Senge and Scharmer, 2001).

Over the past seven years, the action research process used by ELI has evolved from a simplistic 'plan, do, review' model (Lewin, 1946) to a more complex annual cycle of communication, evaluation, planning and implementation (Figure 8.1) through which we, as a community of learners, investigate and evaluate our own practices and programmes (McNiff and Whitehead, 2006). It has grown into a developmental process of incremental change, informed by data and judgement that has led to the significant cumulative evolution of our theory, practice and programmes (Patton, 1994). These changes were the result of a multitude of 'dynamic conversations' at each stage of the process. As a result, effective and innovative communication and dissemination strategies have been developed and included in the process to enable all involved to share their knowledge and experience in a variety of ways.

Figure 8.1 Community action research cycle.

Action research process

Beginning in 2005, community action research (Figure 8.1), with its emphasis on building inclusive learning communities, was used to develop ELI's programmes. Acknowledging, respecting and utilising the expertise and experience within the local families and communities is at the heart of the cyclical process that revolves around participants when they come together to share their learning. Each cycle begins with a network meeting, where previous action plans are reviewed and new ones developed. At these meetings, facilitated by the ELI team, participants have the opportunity to discuss evaluation findings, address implementation difficulties and integrate new learning and innovative ideas into the plans. Bringing the action plans back to their colleagues and engaging them in further discussion on how the plan might be implemented in their service is an essential element in the process. Regular visits by the ELI team to each member of the network provide opportunities to discuss the action plan and its implementation in more detail. It enables participants to share their experience and highlight any issues that might have implications for their service. These visits also support individual practitioners to develop the language and confidence need to engage in dialogue with others (Bleach, 2013b) at network events.

Organisational and evaluation structures have been developed to implement, monitor and amend our plans and programmes in a systematic, inclusive and collaborative way (Senge and Scharmer, 2001). Each service takes responsibility for implementing the action plan, with ELI providing support as required. Following implementation, all participants are encouraged to reflect on and evaluate their experience. Key questions we ask ourselves are: What worked? What did not work? What have we learned? What impact did the programme have on the children, parents and staff involved? What do we need to change? What improvements can we make? Engaging with these kinds of questions has enabled us to build the systematic evaluation 'of' and 'for' learning into the process and provide evidence of its impact in our own and other colleagues' learning.

Chelimsky and Shadish's (1997) three perspectives on evaluation – evaluation for development, knowledge building and accountability – have been incorporated into our evaluation procedures and communication strategy. They are also intrinsically linked to Lewin's (1946) three action research goals of advancing methodology, progressing knowledge and improving a concrete situation. Evaluation for development provides us with the information needed to improve existing programmes and develop new ones. It also improves our reflective knowledge (Park, 1999) and our deeper understanding of our action research methodology. Evaluation for knowledge-building develops our understanding of the theories underlying our programmes and practice and enhances our ability to make our theories and practice explicit. Evaluation for accountability supplies us with the evidence needed to convince funders and third parties of the authenticity of our claims (McNiff, 2010). It enables us to open the process to public scrutiny and debate (Chevalier and Buckles, 2013) and assess whether we have achieved our goals.

Quarterly reviews are scheduled to review existing plans and develop new ones. They enable us to discuss our evaluation findings, address implementation difficulties and integrate new learning and innovative ideas into our action plans and programmes. The reviews also provide us with 'safe', yet challenging, opportunities to develop our personal 'voices' (McNiff and Whitehead, 2009) and articulate our theory and practice in ways that make sense to others (Park, 1999). Following the reviews, our findings are summarised and communicated through a variety of media and forums to a range of audiences.

Audiences

Sharing learning is at the heart of ELI's development. Over the past nine years, a gradual snowball or phased approach was used to develop our programmes and communication structures. Proximal processes, i.e. systematic exchanges with others of progressively more complex reciprocal interactions (Bronfenbrenner and Morris, 1998), are used to communicate with our stakeholders. This takes place through four interrelated levels (Figure 8.2) with ELI often acting as bridge (Elliott, 2010) between the different levels.

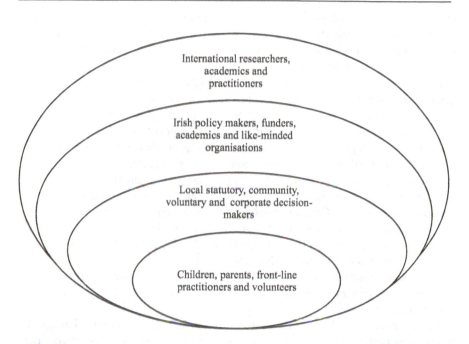

Figure 8.2 ELI's network levels.

Partnership is a key value for ELI. Priority is given to relationships, which are free, open and sincere, unhampered by oppressive power relations, hidden agendas and bad faith (Park, 1999). The disposition and skills of our stakeholders to engage in an open dialogue of equals is critical as is their willingness to share their knowledge and practice. While each participant at each level may have a different role and level of expertise, each is considered by ELI as equal in personal and professional value. Our primary concern is their willingness to work with us to improve outcomes for children and their families.

Level 1 involves parents, volunteers and front-line professionals working together to deliver programmes that support children's learning. Multiple methods of communication are used at this level, including visits, meetings, e-mails, texts, programme materials, newsletters and Facebook. This helps to ensure that everyone is actively involved in the process and has the opportunity to contribute to the development of the programme. It also supports the implementation of the action plans.

Level 2 addresses the overall direction and development of ELI as well as key local issues. It involves regular meetings between decision-makers in local statutory, community, voluntary and corporate organisations to discuss and plan programmes, which, it is anticipated, will improve outcomes for children and their families. As with level 1, a range of communication tools are used to keep everyone informed and involved in the process. Each individual organisation's commitment to implementing the agreed action plans is critical as is the willingness of their staff to feed back their experience of and learning from implementation to the wider learning community.

Leadership is a key feature at this level. Programmes appear to be most successful and have the most significant impact on the children's learning, parental involvement, the learning environment and teamwork within the setting in those organisations where the management proactively support the implementation of the action plan. Supporting these leaders of change (Fullan et al., 2005) through site visits and other exchanges is a key role for the ELI team.

At level 3, we focus on influencing policy and practice in Ireland by sharing our theories, practice and evaluations with policy makers, funders and other similar organisations. Getting involved in public consultations allows us to explain what works for us and its significance for the wider policy context. It has, in the past, enabled us to contribute to the national literacy, numeracy and early years strategies (DES, 2011; DYCA, 2014). Being members of the learning communities associated with the Irish Government and Atlantic Philanthropies programmes allows us to share our practice and experience with other similar projects.

Learning from tried and tested international theory and practice has always been important to ELI's learning network. Level 4 enables us to reflect critically on global hypotheses and to consider ELI's position in relation to international theories and practice. It involves engaging with and learning from researchers, academics and practitioners in other countries. International conferences provide a safe, neutral venue for us to discuss and explore our action research practices. Academic journals and other literature give us access to the thoughts and perspectives of other action researchers around the world. They also provide us with a language, theory and evidence-base to describe and discuss our work. Sharing our knowledge and experience in this way enables us to contribute to the flow of knowledge and learning between multiple local communities about the processes of effective change (Somekh and Zeichner, 2009: 18).

The four levels consist of complex networks and movements that mesh and intersect in many different ways. It is best represented by Chevalier and Buckles's (2013: 32) description that 'Multitudes of nodes, flows and connecting lines give rise to rhizomatic growth rather than clearly delineated systems'. As a result, ELI could get distracted and caught up in interactions and issues that do little to support the children and the families we work with. We have to remind ourselves continuously of our core vision and check whether we are doing the right things at the right time with the right people for the right end and in the right way (Bleach, 2015). If not, we have to redirect our energies towards activities and people that support us in 'enabling children, young people and their families to develop the dispositions, skills and knowledge needed to achieve their educational, career and life goals' (ELI, 2013: 6).

Messages that communicate our values

While we may communicate differently with different audiences we perceive sincerity as a paradigmatic value for creating virtuous relationships (Habermas, 1981). Therefore, our messages are always linked to ELI's mission, vision and key values. They have evolved from our theories, experiences and practices and are grounded in our action research processes. Up-to-date data, obtained during each action research cycle, is analysed and the results compared with previous findings. It is then summarised into information briefs, stories, theories and policy measures and communicated to participants, funders, policy makers and other interested parties as appropriate. In this way, there is consistency in the messages being communicated, despite variation in the content, language and medium as appropriate for the audience. This section highlights ELI's three key messages that communicate our values.

Early learning is the foundation for all subsequent learning

At three years of age, there are already big differences in language and mathematical development between children from rich and poor backgrounds (ELI, 2012). This gap continues to widen unless it is addressed before children start pre-school. ELI works with children from as young as 18 months of age so that these children will enter the educational system equipped with the reading and numeracy skills appropriate for their age.

It takes a village to raise a child

Children's learning is a product of the learning environments they experience in the homes, services and the community in which they live. Since 2005, ELI has been collaborating with parents, public health nurses, early years services, schools and statutory, community and corporate organisations to address educational disadvantage (Bleach, 2013b) and enable children, their families and the community to acquire the skills and self-confidence needed to benefit fully from the educational system. All of our partners understand the challenges faced by the local community and are genuinely committed to making a real, measurable and positive difference to the lives and learning successes of children and young people. Together we are improving outcomes for children, families and the community (Share et al., 2011; ELI, 2013; Lalor, 2013, McKeown et al., 2014) by thinking, acting and relating to one another differently around how we support and extend learning for children and adults alike (Kemmis, 2009).

Real change is not a once-off isolated event

Successful change is a complex, analytical, political and cultural process of challenging and changing, as appropriate, the core beliefs, structure and strategy of a community (Pettigrew, 1987). In today's economic climate, with an increased emphasis on 'evidence' and 'outcomes', there is a preference for 'big bang' answers (Blamey and Mackenzie, 2007) to social issues through independent scientific evaluations and/or evidenced-based programmes. A key message from ELI is that while independent evaluations are useful in providing baseline data, endorsing the work of the project and highlighting future directions, they do not provide the process or ongoing data required for continuous improvement and community building (Bleach, 2013c). Generating indicative evidence (Veerman and van Yperen, 2007) using multiple research methods over repeated action research cycles is far more effective. In addition, designing 'bespoke' programmes rather than using 'off-the-shelf' prescriptive programmes allows new language, theory and practice to develop incrementally, thereby enhancing our capacity to improve outcomes for children. This cumulative approach to knowledge generation (Blamey and Mackenzie, 2007) provides systematic evidence of outcomes and impact, which can be presented to our partners, policy makers and funders at regular intervals to keep them informed, interested and involved in ELI (Bleach, 2013c).

Dissemination strategies

Learning, as Park (1999) suggested, is a social activity. It begins and ends with interactions. ELI combines multiple methods of dissemination in order to share our learning with others. For us, the most successful are those methods that engage others in our action research process and deliver information that is relevant to their own theories and practice. As enabling positive educational change is a key goal for ELI, we hope that the learning from our programmes will be used to improve the quality of services provided to children and their families.

The first step in ELI's dissemination strategy is to reflect on why we need to communicate with others. Before any decision is made about communication methods, we discuss the following questions:

- How will communicating with others support ELI's action research process to be more effective at improving outcomes for children and families? Who do we need to target? What are the most effective ways of doing this?
- What communication structures do we need so that the expertise, practice and experience of our stakeholders can directly influence the dialogue, process and content of our programmes?
- How do we, in ELI, share our learning and influence policy and research in the public sphere? Who are our audiences, at local, national and international level?

Having engaged with these questions, we can then move on to deciding the messages, audiences and methods of communication. However, a dissemination strategy will only be effective if viewed as an evolving and constantly developing process (Harmsworth et al., 2000). This is why 'Communicate Findings' was included as a stage in our action research process (Figure 8.1). Like other elements of the process, our dissemination strategy is reviewed regularly to ensure that it is meeting our aims and conveying our vision, mission and values.

The next stage of our dissemination strategy is to identify and understand our various audiences (Figure 8.2). This requires us to reflect on their organisational, professional and personal learning needs, interests and goals. We have to see our theories, practice and learning through the recipients' eyes and consider carefully what aspects would be most relevant to them. Having considered the array of multiple and potentially divergent perspectives (Gregory et al., 2011), our learning is translated into useful and understandable information, stories and policy measures that the recipients can relate to. We communicate with others through informal conversations, meetings, visits, programme materials, newsletters, e-mails, phone calls, text messages, Facebook, Twitter, journal articles and presentations.

Communicating with others is constant and enriching, but also time-consuming and intense (Bruce et al., 2011). Managing the quality and quantity of our communications can be challenging. Too much can result in overload, particularly for our partners, who are all busy people. Too little and their engagement in the action research process and interest in ELI drops. To achieve the greatest impact, we have to be selective (Harmsworth et al., 2000) in how much information we provide and how often we communicate it. Nowadays, with everyone being constantly bombarded with information from multiple sources, it is critical that ELI's messages stand out and are heard. This requires us to present our learning in as interesting, accessible, timely and brief a way as possible. Regular communication undertaken relatively consistently throughout the year reduces the risk of our partners becoming disengaged by the passage of time or other pressures (Bruce et al., 2011). It also allows us to highlight progress, adjust strategies and brainstorm possible future actions.

While written and online communication is important, we have found face-to-face meetings to be the building blocks of relationships. The reassurance and encouragement of real-time non-verbal cues such as nodding, smiling, eye contact and laughter (Thang et al., 2011) makes the formation of trust and social bonding easier. They also allow us to discuss in depth our findings and their implications for practice and policy. These can range from one-to-one conversations, training sessions and working group meetings to networking events and conferences. One-to-one contact with people, despite being a heavy drain on resources, is useful for targeting key people (Harmsworth et al., 2000) who will enhance our action research process and enable us to achieve our goals. Small group discussions, on the other hand, provide safe yet challenging spaces, where theory, research findings and lived experiences can be discussed. All these interactions with others are valued as they support us, as individuals and collectively, to share our learning with others. They also help us to understand the perspectives of others more and enable them to contribute to the debate and decision-making processes of our programmes.

Systematically gathering evaluation data, both quantitative and qualitative, is a key element of our communication strategy. It enables the participants in all our programmes to contribute to the action research process and the development of a collaborative approach to children's learning, where everyone's expertise and experience is acknowledged, respected and used. It also encourages and supports the participants to reflect on and improve their own practice. At the end of each action research cycle, there is a review of ELI's programmes and the evaluation findings for that period. This data is summarised and used to inform our programme materials, reports, newsletters, e-mails and social media. It also provides us with material for group reflection, discussion and decision-making. In addition, it can be very useful in making funders and policy makers aware of the implications of their decisions on children, families and local communities. The findings also inform and add credibility to our presentations, academic papers and journal articles.

Reflection

Communicating with others is an integral part of the part of ELI's action research process. It has enabled our reflective, relational and representational knowledge (Park, 1999, 2001) to develop simultaneously. In this section, I, as Director of ELI, reflect on the benefits and challenges of sharing our learning with others.

The more action research cycles we engaged in, the more opportunities there were to discuss our theories, values and practices. This has made it easier for us to conceptualise and articulate our learning. However, sharing our learning with others still requires us, at times, to labour through a range of tensions, challenges and conflicts (Montoya and Kent, 2011). Participants belong to diverse and complex organisations with different systems and priorities (Gregory et al., 2011). Their different experiences, expertise, expectations, priorities and perspectives have to be acknowledged, respected and managed. This requires the careful negotiation and establishment of trusted relationships (Herr and Anderson, 2005) as well as a range of communication strategies. It also requires, as Nooteboom (2004) suggested, sufficient cognitive distance between participants for new insights to emerge but enough similarity for dialogue to be possible and constructive.

While our understanding has improved of how people with different mindsets and political interests experience working together (Coghlan and Brannick, 2001), articulating our theories and practices in ways that make sense to others continues to be challenging. While we understand what we are trying to achieve, it can be difficult to convey this to others in a way that they can understand it too. Simplicity appears to be the key with the theories needing to be simple, yet robust, for people to understand and accept in a short space of time. Too much detail obscures the main points and confuses the audience. There needs to be the right mix between narrative, graphs and images with a clear explanation of how what we do makes a difference to the educational outcomes of the children and young people we work with.

Translating practice into theory can also be difficult, especially as emerging theory has to be weighed against established theory and national policy. Everyone has to think abstractly and objectively about what has been learned and what needs to be done next (Strauss and Corbin, 1990). Some of our participants find the language and concepts used problematic and feel that they have not the 'words' or language to express their opinions. Others need to develop the confidence to speak about their practice in front of others. Empowering participants to speak 'multiple languages' (McNiff and Whitehead, 2009), including academic and official technical-rational discourses, across a range of cultures and spheres enables us to share our learning with wider audiences.

A cumulative approach to knowledge generation (Blamey and Mackenzie, 2007) and programme development has been a critical element of our action research process. It allows learning to accumulate slowly within and across action research cycles rather than delivering 'big bang' answers to questions of programme effectiveness. We have found, as Harmsworth et al. (2000) suggested, that providing people with advance notice of what is planned and inviting them to participate strengthens our partnerships and networks. There has been enormous value in not feeling that we have to deliver a finished product or all the answers. Engaging a diverse network through brainstorming and critical questioning of ideas adds to the quality of our programmes and action plans. It releases our creativity and enables us to work smarter together rather than harder alone (NCSL, 2002). In addition, the more active the involvement of a range of stakeholders in the development of a programme, the more likely it will be implemented and attain its goals.

Continually defining and understanding our values and the policy context in which we operate is crucial to our ability to engage successfully with a diverse audience (Bleach, 2013c) and improve outcomes for children. By discussing our work with others, we have acquired insider knowledge (Park, 1999), which we try, if relevant, to incorporate into our programmes. This has enabled us to develop and test the ideas of professional and political elites (Park, 1999) through our action research processes, thereby generating regular and systematic evidence for what does and does not work. In this way, we retain intellectual and moral control over our practice (Kemmis, 2009) and ensure that we do not become dependent on the expertise of outside professionals.

Conclusion

Sharing learning is at the heart of ELI's action research process and mission. As the 'bridge' between different interest groups (Elliott, 2010), ELI engages in a disciplined and structured way with a range of local, national and international stakeholders on issues of mutual interest. These opportunities enable all involved to create and share knowledge, learn from one another's experience and to find solutions to common problems (NCSL, 2002). Analysing and reflecting on what we have learned through action research develops our reflective, relational and representational knowledge (Park, 1999, 2001), which, in turn, enables us to generate new knowledge and contribute to the growing knowledge base that informs policy and practices in Ireland.

References

Blamey, A. and Mackenzie, M. (2007) 'Theories of change and realistic evaluation: peas in a pod or apples and oranges?' *Evaluation* Vol 13 (4): 439–455.

Bleach, J. (2013a) 'From 18 months to 18 years – Supporting access to third level education'. Paper published as part of 2013 HEA Conference on *Equality of Access to Higher Education in Ireland*, Dublin, 7 November.

Bleach, J. (2013b) 'Improving educational aspirations and outcomes through community action research', *Educational Action Research Journal*, 21 (2): 253–266.

Bleach, J. (2013c) 'Community action research: providing evidence of value and virtue', in J. McNiff (ed.) *Value and Virtue in Practice-Based Research*. Poole: September Books.

Bleach, J. (2015) 'Improving numeracy outcomes for children through community action research', *Educational Action Research*, 23 (1): 22–35.

Bronfenbrenner, U. and Morris, P. A. (1998) 'The ecology of developmental processes', in W. Damon and R.M. Lerner (eds) (1998) *Handbook of Child Psychology, Vol.1: Theoretical Models of Human Development* (5th edn) (pp. 993–1028). New York: Wiley.

Bruce, C.D., Flynn, T. and Stagg-Peterson, S. (2011) 'Examining what we mean by collaboration in collaborative action research: a cross-case analysis, *Educational Action Research Journal*, 19 (4): 433–452.

Chelimsky, E. and Shadish, W.R. (1997) *Evaluation for the Twenty-first Century: A Resource Book*. London: Sage.

Chevalier, J.M. and Buckles, D.M. (2013) *Participatory Action Research: Theory and Methods for Engaged Inquiry*. Abingdon: Routledge.

Coghlan, D. and Brannick, T. (2001) *Doing Action Research in Your Own Organisation*. London: Sage

Department of Education and Science (DES) (2011) *Literacy and Numeracy for Learning and Life: The National Strategy to Improve Literacy and Numeracy among Children and People 2011–2020*. Dublin: Stationery Office.

Department of Children and Youth Affairs (DYCA) (2014) *Better Outcomes, Brighter Futures: The National Policy Framework for Children & Young People 2014–2020*. Dublin: DYCA.

Early Learning Initiative (ELI) (2012) *Submission to the Joint Committee on Jobs, Social Protection and Education on Educational Disadvantage*. Dublin: National College of Ireland.

Early Learning Initiative (ELI) (2013) *Annual Report 2013–14*. Dublin: National College of Ireland (unpublished).

Elliott, J. (2010) 'Building social capital for educational action research: the contribution of Bridget Somekh', *Educational Action Research*, 18 (1): 19–28.

Fullan, M., Cuttress, C. And Kilcher, A. (2005) '8 forces for leaders of change', *Educational Leadership*, 26 (4): 54–58.

Gregory, S., Poland, F., Spalding, N.J., McCulloch, J. and Vicary, P. (2011) 'Multidimensional collaboration: reflections on action research in a clinical context', *Educational Action Research Journal*, 19 (3): 363–378.

Habermas, J. (1981) *The Theory of Communicative Action. Vol. 1: Reason and the Rationalization of Society*. Boston, MA: Beacon Press.

Harmsworth, S., Turpin, S. and TQEF National Co-ordination Team (2000) *Creating an Effective Dissemination Strategy: An Expanded Interactive Workbook for Educational Development Projects* [online], available from <www.innovations. ac.uk/btg/resources/publications/dissemination.pdf> [29 March 2015].

Herr, K. and Anderson, L. (2005) *The Action Research Dissertation: A Guide for Students and Faculty*. London: Sage.

Kemmis, S. (2009) 'Action research as a practice-based practice', *Educational Action Research*, 17 (3): 463–474.

Lalor, T. (2013) NEYAI Numeracy Assessment Research Findings [online], available from <www.pobal.ie/Beneficiaries/neyai/Pages/default.aspx> [20 October 2014].

Lewin, K. (1946) 'Action research and minority problems', *Journal of Social Issues* 2 (4): 35–66.

McKeown, K., Haase, T. and Pratschke, J. (2014) *Evaluation of the National Early Years Access Initiative and Síolta Quality Assurance Programme: A Study of Child Outcomes in Pre-School*. Dublin: Pobal.

McNiff, J. (2010) *Action Research for Professional Development: Concise Advice for New and Experienced Action Researchers*. Poole: September Books

McNiff, J. and Whitehead, J. (2006) *All You Need to Know about Action Research* (2nd edn). London: Sage Publications.

McNiff, J. and Whitehead, J. (2009) *Doing and Writing Action Research*. London: Sage Publications.

Montoya, M.J. and Kent, E.E. (2011) 'Dialogic action: moving from community-based to community-driven participatory research', *Qualitative Health Research*, 21 (7): 1000–1011.

National College for School Leadership (NCSL) (2002) *Why Networked Learning Communities?* Nottingham: National College for School Leadership.

Nooteboom, B. (2004) *Inter-firm Collaboration, Networks and Strategy: An Integrated Approach* (1st edn). New York: Routledge.

Park, P. (1999) 'People, knowledge and change in participatory research', *Management Learning*, 30 (2): 141–157.

Park, P. (2001) 'Knowledge and participatory research', in P. Reason and H. Bradbury (eds) (2001) *Handbook of Action Research, Participative Inquiry and Practice* (pp. 81–90). London: Sage.

Patton, M.Q. (1994) 'Developmental evaluation', *Evaluation Practice*, 15 (3): 311–319.

Patton, M.Q. and Horton, D. (2009) Utilization-Focused Evaluation for Agricultural Innovation. Institute of Learning and Change (ILAC) Brief No. 22. ILAC, Rome.

Pettigrew, A. M. (1987) 'Context and action in the transformation of the firm', *Journal of Management Sciences*, 24 (6): 649–670.

Pobal (2014) *Update on the NEYAI Evaluation and Dissemination Plans Spring 2014*. Dublin: Pobal.

Schön, D. (1983) *The Reflective Practitioner: How Professionals Think in Action*. London: Temple Smith.

Senge, P. and Scharmer, O. (2001) 'Community action research: learning as a community of practitioners, consultants and researchers', in P. Reason and H. Bradbury (eds) (2001) *Handbook of Action Research, Participative Inquiry and Practice* (pp. 238–249). London: Sage.

Share, M., McCarthy, S. and Greene, S. (2011) *Baseline Evaluation of the Early Learning Initiative: Final Report*. Dublin: National College of Ireland.

Somekh, B. and Zeichner, K. (2009) 'Action research for educational reform: remodelling action research theories and practices in local contexts', *Educational Action Research Journal*, 17 (1): 5–21.

Sommer, R. (2009) 'Dissemination in action research', *Action Research*, 7 (2): 227–236.

Strauss, A. and Corbin, J. (1990) *Basics of Qualitative Research: Grounded Theory Procedures and Techniques*. London: Sage.

Thang, S.M., Hall, C., Murugaiah, P. and Azman, H. (2011) 'Creating and maintaining online communities of practice in Malaysian Smart Schools: challenging realities', *Educational Action Research Journal*, 19 (1): 87–105.

Veerman, J.W. and van Yperen, T.A. (2007) 'Degrees of freedom and degrees of certainty: a developmental model for the establishment of evidence-based youth care', *Evaluation and Program Planning* 30 (2007): 212–221.

Chapter 9

Constructing Comenian third spaces for action research in graduate teacher education

Joseph M. Shosh

Each morning as I make my away across the Moravian College campus to my Education Department office housed in a sleek, modern – some might say corporate – academic complex, I pause in admiration before the statue of Jon Amos Comenius, gift of Charles University in Prague, as he stands guard outside the 1892 neo-gothic hall that bears his name. What do I really know about this seventeenth-century man, generally regarded as the father of modern education, and do our graduate education candidates and I share his values and turn them into virtues? I do know that Comenius was so important to the Czech people that Vaclav Havel, the first democratically elected president of his nation in 41 years, rededicated this statue on his very first visit to the United States after the fall of communism while en route to deliver an address to the United Nations.

The master works of Comenius, including the *Great Didactic* (1632) and *Orbus Pictus* (1658) demonstrate clearly that he was significantly ahead of his time in promoting values that included universal education for all – women and men, rich and poor, noble and commoner – and doing so through methods that include what we might today call 'developmentally appropriate pedagogy'. Jean Piaget (1993: 179) notes, 'as a teacher, he [Comenius] is fully aware of the harm done by that enduring curse of education – verbalism or pseudo-knowledge (*flatus vocis*) associated with mere words, as distinct from the real knowledge created by the action of the pupil upon the objects of his study'. Comenius would himself likely perceive these values as virtuous only insofar as one becomes educated to, as he says, know oneself, rule oneself, and direct oneself to God. Declining the first presidency of Harvard College in 1636, he instead moved from his native Moravia to Sweden, where he was persecuted for his religious beliefs, while his home, manuscripts and printing press were burned by those who espoused a different path to salvation.

In offering these observations on the legacy of Comenius I set the scene for this chapter, in which I outline how our contemporary multi-cultural Western society has largely replaced these religious Comenian values, potentially contentious for their time, with secular neoliberalism. The result is that values are now considered virtues largely in terms of marketplace success. In the American public school system in which most of Moravian's graduate education candidates serve as practitioners or practitioners in preparation, the United States federal *No Child Left Behind* (2001–2015) regulations supported technical rational activities such as frequent testing, school choice, and educational privatization. Students therefore became valued in terms of their potentials as future workers and consumers, not for their contributions as thoughtful, self-actualized participants in a democratic society (Hursh, 2007). In this system of what could be seen as educational Darwinism, test scores became the currency through which the fittest (and often wealthiest) achieved success; the curriculum was narrowed to teach only those sub-skills that could be directly tested; and teachers faced tremendous pressures to boost scores through the technical-rational application of so-called research-based 'best practices'. Further, accountability policy measures to reward and penalize teachers, based upon student performance on standardized tests, also failed to improve teaching practice or student performance (Polikoff and Porter, 2014). Within a context such as this, it is imperative that, as Director of Moravian College's Graduate Education program, I make public how I consistently evaluate my own pedagogical practices and model them for the young people and colleagues I work with. I do this to ensure that I am living in the direction of the Comenian values I so much admire and that act as guiding principles for our College and for myself. This chapter therefore contains an account of my own research into how I support the educational action enquiries of graduate students in education at Moravian College.

First, let me provide a brief overview of the Moravian College graduate education program.

Moravian College's graduate education program

Moravian College's Master of Education program in curriculum and instruction is designed to engage practitioners in action research inquiries. The aim is to develop a conversation between the key Comenian value of universal education and individual teacher beliefs, and the dominant neoliberal worldview outlined above, as practitioners seek to improve their professional practice in order to create a knowledge base of teaching and learning for teachers and learners. Developing this conversation requires the construction of the higher education equivalent of what Moje and her colleagues (2004) call a *third space*: this is formed by a synthesis of three contemporary views in the literature that refer to places where students can:

1   build bridges between often-marginalised indigenous ways of knowing and speaking and conventional academic discourses;
2   have opportunities to code-switch to achieve success in multiple discourse communities;
3   develop dialogical relationships between competing paradigms.

Moje adds, 'More research, using a variety of methods, needs to be conducted on third space as a space wherein everyday and academic knowledges and Discourses are challenged and new knowledges are generated' (p. 44). Through focusing on a consideration of the inquiry-based values that guide my professional practice as Director of Moravian College's graduate education program, I aim to create such third spaces for action research in graduate teacher education. This third space merges the first space of professionals' personal beliefs and tacit knowledge with the second space of the officially authorised authoritative voices that often guide their work.

In my view, the learning of teachers (and their students) happens not through the memorization of external knowledge – what the Russian literary theorist Mikhail Bakhtin (1981) might call *authoritative discourse*; rather it happens in the space that is created when that *authoritative discourse* engages dialogically with the individual's *internally persuasive discourse*: that is, the values, beliefs, and knowledge they already hold. For me, action research provides the best medium through which a teacher might examine his or her current professional practice; it represents a third space where a teacher can see the links between his or her own practice and the practice of other professionals, professional associations, published research studies, Common Core standards, and school district curriculum. Within this framework, teachers can construct new knowledge about their professional practice through their own inquiries into teaching and learning. The challenge for managers and leaders like myself, of course, is to encourage our students, and ourselves, to strengthen our internally persuasive discourse without feeling overwhelmed or silenced by the authoritative discourses that surround us. At the same time, we also need to be willing to change our beliefs and remain open to further change as the dialogue unfolds.

The candidates with whom I work are practitioners pursuing the Master of Education degree – often together with advanced Pennsylvania certification, which has its own additional state-mandated competencies – or those seeking initial licensure and earning a Master of Arts in Teaching degree. All candidates complete three 'Foundations of Action Research' courses, focusing, in turn, on classroom inquiry, teacher action research, and methods of assessment and evaluation. All degree candidates go on to conduct a final capstone action research project, building on earlier individual courses that have focused on:

- designing an action research study;
- gaining necessary ethics approval through human subjects internal review boards;
- writing a literature review;
- gathering and analyzing action research data;
- composing and going public with the final study.

(For a more detailed examination of the Moravian graduate education curriculum, see Shosh and Zales, 2007; Shosh 2013, 2016.)

Whether I am mentoring graduate students who are conducting action research for the very first time or conducting action research for their capstone project, I attempt to construct with them these kinds of third spaces in the classroom and online that mediate our *internally persuasive* and *authoritative* discourses in support of the Comenian value of universal public education. In Aristotelian terms, we attempt to examine the impact of our *praxis,* or critically reflective actions guided by our values, as we develop the *phronesis,* or practical wisdom needed to determine which, of many possible actions, is best suited to a particular teaching and learning situation. As Carr and Kemmis (2005: 352) proffer:

> [A]ction research can only be adequately construed as a species of Aristotelian 'practical philosophy': that classical mode of reflective inquiry that enables proficient and experienced practitioners to examine the presuppositions implicit in their pre-reflective practical knowledge and experience in order that they may, in confronting a particular problematic educational situation, reflectively construct their understanding of how the 'goods' intrinsic to this practice may be most appropriately realized and achieved.

The Aristotelian notions of *techne* and *episteme* are inescapable, of course, because they are deeply embedded, both intentionally and unintentionally, within our internally persuasive and authoritative discourses. Often, the *techne,* or, in the context of this chapter, the craft of teaching, remains part of our unexamined belief system; on the other hand, the *episteme,* or so-called scientific knowledge, has too often been delivered as ready-made *a priori* knowledge to be applied to practice, rather than as hypotheses to be tested, as appropriate, through our *praxis.* John Elliott (2015), too, sees teaching as an ethical practice that transcends the notion of *techne,* a notion that, unfortunately, pervades traditional models of teacher education. Elliott explains:

> A critical feature of an ethical practice (*praxis*) from an Aristotelian point of view is that the actions of which it consists are seen by the agent as an expression of the values to which they are committed, in contrast to the skills and techniques that make up a making activity. (p. 6)

Our action inquiries engage us in a mindful and transactional process in which we are all called upon to make conscious ontological and epistemological choices through dialogue with one another and with a wide array of texts. As we write to learn, we create our own authentic, critical and sometimes multimodal responses through what I intend to be educative experiences that help us come to know in important new ways. In summary, I define inquiry through my values as a process that must be mindful, transactional, transcendent, ontological, and epistemological in nature as we engage together in our respective dialogical inquiries.

Together, students and I have identified the following areas as important for supporting action research and writing development:

- developing new mindsets;
- conducting aesthetic transactions with texts;
- exploring critical pedagogies through reflective writing;
- constructing new knowledge about teaching and learning;
- creating hypotheses to guide future inquires.

Developing new mindsets

Harvard psychologist Ellen Langer (1997) points out in *The Power of Mindful Learning* that as students, we have all likely adopted at least some mindsets that interfere with the very learning we desire. In alignment with Langer's view, I want students to create new categories as their understandings grow; remain open to new ideas; and develop new awareness through a multiplicity of perspectives.

The inquiry that students and I conduct collaboratively through action research addresses directly the seven pervasive myths Langer identifies that may undermine the learning process. We do this as follows. Instead of starting with basics in the foundations courses, we dig right in, recording observations of our teaching and learning and reflecting on who will benefit most, and in what ways, from changes we might make to our professional practice. Rather than asking graduate students to begin by paying careful attention to transmitted and approved knowledge, both *techne* and *episteme*, I want us all to follow anthropologist Clifford Geertz's (1973) advice to 'make the familiar strange' and come to see our daily practice in new ways as we begin to compile an action research field log. To do this, we initially conduct a series of shadow log and participant observations, which allows us to see our professional practice through the eyes of our students. We then embark immediately upon experiential learning in our own professional workplaces. Organizing ourselves as teacher inquiry teams, we use immediately available resources to determine how best to collect interview, survey, and artifact data to add to the log, while serving as critical friends for one another to ensure researcher trustworthiness. Forgetting is not a problem since nothing need be memorized; what is most memorable or questionable methodologically will soon be shared on the class digital learning commons website for our individual and collective critique, and we will eventually go public with our findings, first with one another in class, and, when we are ready, with the larger campus and wider research communities. What we learn and come to know is not simply telling back something someone has told us but rather a matter of making our own connections and constructing our own new understandings through writing about and discussing together our accounts of our professional practice. Practitioners often comment upon how the collection of data in field logs for their action research projects is indeed a mindful process that often differs markedly from the routinized testing and too often mindless collection of data required in their schools.

From our first class, we engage in non-participant observation in a public place on campus, reflect upon how the campus spaces meet or fail to meet the needs of users, and explore what we believe are the limits of research that can be conducted in semi-public spaces without gaining additional consent from those who become our informants. Because they tend to bring largely positivist notions of research with them as part of their background knowledge, teachers are often surprised when I explain why I find it unethical to have a control group when our action research efforts show us that a method is indeed working. Many initially question the notion of gaining consent from students or bringing them on board as co-researchers, noting that the students will then 'act differently', thus potentially invalidating research results. We talk through how making action research a regular facet of professional practice privileges the tacit knowledge of the learner and encourages the learner to engage in reflection and metacognition. We also consider whether these processes would actually occur were the teacher not also working as researcher.

Conducting aesthetic transactions with texts

As we conduct our respective inquiries, we use our third space as a safe place within which to engage in transactions with a multiplicity of texts, especially those that bring into dialogue our indigenous ways of knowing and often tacit professional teacher knowledge with the voices of others who might extend our thinking and understanding of the action research process. We read Paley (1992), who refers to herself as a teacher who writes books, and we ponder together why she teaches as she does, how she documents her practice, and why she does not identify herself as a researcher. We watch the Nichols production of elementary school teacher and Pulitzer prize-winning playwright Margaret Edson's play *Wit* (1999/2001); and we deconstruct, among others, some common dualities of researcher/researched, teacher/student, and academic/practitioner, within the context of ensuring ethical professional practice. Gee (2014) helps us to understand how the language we use constructs and helps us enact, often unconsciously, our identities in what he refers to as 'figured worlds'. McNiff (2013) helps us to identify who has influenced our thinking as we attempt to demonstrate the impact of our action research. I eventually share what turn out to be quite comparable but also contrasting views by Newman (1998) and me (2013) of our work with practicing teachers. This acts as a clear reminder that teacher educators should also be engaged in the process of better understanding and refining their own professional practice. I choose the word *transaction* with texts as opposed to *interaction* quite consciously here, borrowing English educator and reader response proponent Louise Rosenblatt's (1995) notion that a literary work comes into being only when the reader has an aesthetic transaction with the text. Meaning resides not in the text alone but rather in the transaction the reader has with the words on the page. Rosenblatt adds:

> Criticism should make the aesthetic transaction the starting point of a further transactional relationship between reader/critic and text – or between reader/historian and text, or reader/semiotician and text. Thus the transactional theory deals not only with the initial reading process, but also with such problems as criteria of validity of interpretation, questions relating to texts from different periods or cultures, and criteria of evaluation. (p. 103)

Graduate students and I place transactional theory into practice, reading to learn as (1) reader/critics, (2) reader/historians, and (3) reader/semioticians. Hendricks (2013) helps us to position action research as an insider's alternative to external quantitative and qualitative studies. Saban (2006) examines how metaphor has historically functioned in teaching and teacher education. Cazden (2001) asks us to examine our classroom discourse practices and ensure that those practices are commensurable with our own instructional purposes.

I remind graduate students that active engagement is at the core of transactional theory and share the personal story of what I believe may have been Rosenblatt's final impromptu speech when I was seated with her at the Conference on English Education luncheon at the American National Council of Teachers of English Conference in Baltimore, Maryland in November 2001. In the immediate aftermath of both the September 11 attacks and the *No Child Left Behind* authorization, she stood and said what I recall as, 'Those of us seated in this room have a responsibility to stand up and stop the endless and mindless testing. The children depend on us to speak when they cannot or will not otherwise be heard' (Shosh in Mayher et al., 2008: 290). Of course, reader response theory itself is currently under attack through a set of Common Core state standards that too often seek to support one best right answer rather than promote a multiplicity of perspectives.

Exploring critical pedagogies through reflective writing

To inquire within graduate education third spaces, we must also examine our existing worldviews and previously held beliefs through an exploration of critical pedagogies that challenge the dominant neoliberal view implicit in American (and much international) education policy. Teachers, whose evaluations are based on their pupils' performance (even though it is well documented that wealthier pupils consistently outscore poorer pupils) tend to view themselves as an oppressed class when reading Paulo Freire's (1970) *Pedagogy of the Oppressed*. They are often initially less responsive to considering themselves as state oppressors of poor, working class, and minority-group children. They tend to question the systemic perpetuation of a banking model only when they explore ways in which only they as professionals may work to end what they perceive as the state-sponsored oppression of teachers. Lisa Delpit, in *Multiplication is For White People* (2012), has the effect of pushing us as mostly white middle-class female teachers out of our comfort zones by forcing us all to examine the perpetuation of inequality for poor and minority children. Such critical engagement usually results in our re-examination of often taken-for-granted traditional classroom practices that may, in fact, marginalize learners along gender, socio-economic, and racial lines. Lev Vygotsky (1978) helps us to determine whether or not the instruction we are providing is actually within our learners' respective zones of proximal development. Bringing these kinds of critical understandings to our action research inquiries helps us to take new action to ensure that we are indeed within their respective zones when we see that the pre-packaged school-sanctioned curricula do not do so. Together Freire, Delpit, and Vygotsky help us to ensure an expanded *phronesis* as we take new action within the *praxis* of our action research studies.

Interestingly, as we engage in dialogue about their own secondary school experiences, most of the teachers identify *No Child Left Behind* instructional practices for test preparation that remind me an awful lot of what writing pedagogy historians and researchers refer to as current traditional modes of writing instruction (see Shosh and Zales, 2005). Mott College English Professor and Writing Center director Gregory Shafer (2012) sums up this point of view as deeply embedded in notions of positivism and the concomitant idea that truth is discovered through rational activities and a system of precision that makes the writer passive, dispassionate and objective. Teachers who engage in this kind of pedagogy, he says, tend to see students as spectators or as novices, who must learn the routine given to them by the instructor. Most of those teachers who have themselves experienced some form of writing as process report whole-class lockstep instruction in pre-writing, drafting and editing. Most don't mention revision or publication and seem largely not to have experienced what Donald Murray (1972/1998) encouraged teachers to do when he exhorted them to teach writing as a process, not a product.

Hence, we engage in reflective practice to determine how best to transcend current traditional modes of writing instruction. While teachers develop their own data collection plans and decide how frequently they want to engage in participant and nonparticipant observation within their own classrooms, we write and discuss within our teacher inquiry support groups a series of analytic memos on classroom discourse (Cazden, 2001; Gee, 2014), figurative language use (Lakoff and Johnson, 1980/2003) and qualitative coding of our data (Saldaña, 2013). A hallmark of my desire that we all examine our professional practice from the point of view of multiple stakeholders is a series of writing to learn opportunities utilizing a variety of narrative forms, including portraits, first person narratives, dramatizations and pastiches (Ely, 2007). Portraits, or brief descriptions of research participants, allow us to examine multiple data points to construct a more complex understanding of an individual learner's perspective than we can generally gain from any single observation or interview alone. Because the third-person portrait can still unintentionally distance the teacher from the student, we transform those third-person portraits into first-person narratives; here the teacher takes on the voice of the student in order to understand better the students' respective worldviews. Sharing key classroom events in dramatized form allows a multiplicity of voices to be heard in the context of teachers' professional practice. Finally, a pastiche, or a quilting together of juxtaposed pieces of data, allows new understandings to emerge as often contradictory or even paradoxical views are clarified and sorted out.

Constructing new knowledge about teaching and learning

Increasingly, our work also transcends the traditional form of texts as we study our teaching and learning in multimodal contexts and explore new ways of reflecting on what we have learned through our semester-long inquiries. We do this by creating multimodal final projects that provide what we hope fellow stakeholders will find compelling evidence of our action inquiries. Literacy educator Robert J. Tierney (2007: 33) explains:

> [B]eing literate is no longer finding the right book or writing a set of papers in a particular genre to specifications. It is not simply learning to master a set of skills such as decoding or comprehension or being able to retrieve certain information about characters and plots of narrative or informational texts. Being literate involves research and development as well as collaboration and community engagement. Being literate requires learners who are designers and public intellectuals.

Ontologically, teachers must develop theories that challenge often taken-for-granted assumptions regarding what exists in the world and what they believe, often uncritically, about the ready-made categories that have often come to them through the culture. For example, we discover that traditional socially constructed roles like *teacher* and *student* need to be re-examined. This often happens most fruitfully when we discuss what we mean by *good teacher* and *good student* and how these are both similar to and different from how the larger society defines these constructs. We engage together in autobiographical inquiry to clarify our own fundamental beliefs about how children learn, and we articulate our personal experiences as students and teachers that have led us to these beliefs. We go on to pen our action researcher stances, sharing our fundamental beliefs after engaging in several cycles of classroom research and reviewing the literature in our respective areas of inquiry in an attempt to position ourselves with the larger schools of thought or '*isms*' that surround us. Concomitantly, we allow ourselves to remain open to new evidence, which may help us to see limitations inherent within our pre-existing worldviews.

Epistemologically, we must provide evidence that logically convinces others that we actually know what we claim we have come to know through our action research studies. This involves engaging in a regular coding of our action research field logs using a constant comparative method based in grounded theory (Saldaña, 2013; Bogdan and Biklen, 2011; Grove, 1988; Lincoln and Guba, 1985; Glaser and Strauss, 1967). What emerges are preliminary theme statements supported by evidence that has been gathered in the field log; these undergo revision until they become the evidence-based findings of the action research study. These findings statements most frequently explore what and how specific teacher actions have led to greater achievement and engagement in the classroom. They also offer new practitioner insights into supporting student collaboration, promoting student ownership, differentiating instruction, and facilitating student metacognition along with challenges faced and largely overcome (Shosh, 2012, 2013). This knowledge production is at the heart of our dialogic process; it sees teacher education as *praxis* in sharp contrast to traditional technical rational views that see teacher training as *techne*.

Creating hypotheses to guide future inquires

Central to the development of our theme statements or preliminary findings from our inquiries is our ongoing and regular reflection on the impact of the actions we take as part of our professional practice. In my attempt to support the education of reflective practitioners who create a knowledge base on teaching and learning for teachers and learners, regular opportunities for meaningful reflection are built into our work together (Schön, 1984, 1987). Importantly here, teachers develop their theme statements as testable hypotheses to guide their future *praxis*. The knowledge they construct is not intended to replace the knowledge base created by those researchers based outside the classroom or to dictate to others what they must do, but rather to indicate what has worked and why this has happened within specific contexts. Elliott (2015: 14) adds:

> The creation of sustainable spaces for virtuous action will need to be supported by the systematic presentation of findings across different action contexts, in the form of practical hypotheses to test, and the use of learning theory to inform the quest for virtuous action through action research.

My analysis of the theme statements from the first 175 action research studies produced by Moravian College graduate students yielded the following meta-thematic statements, or findings, that summarize what we have learned through our studies and may spur our future rounds of inquiry as we examine how best to support student learning:

1   Discourse-rich curricula that include opportunities for accountable talk, conferencing, collaborative problem solving, classroom drama, differentiation, discussion, journaling, metacognition and scaffolding enhance student engagement and achievement.

2   Authentic and purposeful curricula that provide students with multiple
    opportunities for decision-making, choices, independent and collaborative
    inquiry, the use of technological tools and safe risk-taking in the classroom
    promote student ownership of learning.
3   Literacy achievement is enhanced through the development and implemen-
    tation of discourse-rich, authentic and purposeful curricula that include con-
    textualized word study and opportunities to predict, clarify, question and
    summarize, while reading developmentally appropriate texts, both inde-
    pendently and within literature circles or Socratic seminars, and by allowing
    English language learners to use first-language knowledge to support second
    language acquisition as needed.
4   Mathematics achievement is enhanced through the development and imple-
    mentation of discourse-rich, authentic and purposeful curricula that provide
    an array of collaborative, open-ended opportunities to solve challenging
    mathematical problems with opportunities to use graphic organizers, reflec-
    tive writing and student-generated data. (Shosh, 2016)

The abstracts and complete texts of more than 175 action research studies conducted by Moravian College graduate education candidates are available for
perusal and download at http://home.moravian.edu/public/educ/eddept/
mEd/thesis.htm. The studies themselves provide the crucial contexts and teacher
narratives that document their inquiries and provide much of the evidence to
support the meta-themes.

Of course, when studies have been completed and preliminary findings have
been shared publicly, new action research cycles begin. For me, the only effective teacher research mentorship is that which supports professionals to go on
researching their own professional practice in a multiplicity of ways long after the
course and graduate degree program have officially ended. In my professional
practice, I endeavor to develop Deweyan educative experiences, where prior
practitioner learning intersects with current practitioner interests that propel the
inquiry and the learning forward. Conducting my own teacher action research
inquiry into the learning of my Freirean student-teachers is crucial as we inquire
together and become fellow teacher-students. And this returns me to the main
theme of this chapter.

Reflecting on the significance of my own research

Here I reconsider how I create those safe but critical third spaces for colleagues
and students to extend their thinking and practices. In our Moravian College
third space teachers mediate their own internally persuasive discourses with those
authoritative discourses espoused through state law, school district policy and the
expert voices sanctioned by academia to create an inquiry-driven third space in
higher education. Together within this third space, we have indeed built bridges
from teachers' personal ways of knowing to an evidence-based research paradigm

that has allowed us all a crucial role in knowledge production. Our action research inquiries within this third space have helped us to extend our thinking by immersing us in the points of view of multiple stakeholders. Within our third spaces, competing paradigms are continuously in conversation with one another as we pursue answers to the questions that matter most to us, and along the way, learn how to ask what are often even more important questions than those that began our inquiries. Within our collaborative third space, inquiry is a mindful and transactional process that calls upon us as educators to make conscious ontological and epistemological choices through dialogue with one another and with a wide array of texts. This enables us to create our own authentic, critical and often multimodal assignments, intended to be educative experiences, as we support the learning of our students and our own construction of new professional knowledge.

The values-based construction of Comenian third spaces that I have attempted to articulate here is as out of place in the mainstream dialogue of the twenty-first century about improving educational equity through, for example, massive open online courses (MOOCs) as was Jon Amos Comenius's vision of education for all humanity in the seventeenth century. Ultimately, though, Comenius had values that his successors saw as clear virtues. Contemporary efforts to make higher education more affordable for more of the world's population would be laudable were it not for the fact that access to knowledge at the level of *techne* or *episteme* is simply not enough. The learning happens and is documented through the *praxis* and guided by the *phronesis* that develops in Bakhtinian (and Comenian) third spaces. Elites in world society will always have access to a knowledge producing education that encourages *praxis*. It is misguided to think that simply making the course materials of gifted professors freely available on the Internet through MOOCs such as the Harvard/MIT edX will ever be able to do more than provide some technically excellent tutorials.

What is needed most in colleges and universities in support of the Comenian value of universal basic education is not an expansion of the number of prestigious university degrees available through MOOCs, but rather the replacement of a transmission model with action research inquiries. Should they be developed, MOOCs from the Harvard Graduate School of Education or other Ivy League universities are not the answer to educating America's next generation of schoolteachers. MOOCs to date have attempted to educate the masses through a traditional technical rational model in which whatever needs to be known may be transmitted directly from professor to pupil and assessed electronically through a multiple choice exam.

Moravian College, the sixth-oldest institution of higher learning in the United States, the very first to educate women in the American colonies, and today a growing, private liberal arts university, embraces technology that supports inquiry rather than simply knowledge transmission. By doing so, the College provides the knowledge producing education described here to any practitioner willing to engage in an action research process and go public with the results of his or her inquiry. Significantly, the College does so assessing the same or lower tuition than universities in Pennsylvania's public state system of higher education, so the issue here is not one of cost. Will policymakers embrace the Comenian vision of universal education for all – women and men, rich and poor, noble and commoner – by supporting problem-posing action research curricular models focused on *praxis*? Or will they continue to promote the technically rational but ineffective route of continued accountability and deskilling that leads to what Jean Piaget describes as that enduring curse of education—*flatus vocis*? The construction of Comenian third spaces for action research in graduate teacher education offers a clear alternative path toward universal education, while once again politely declining Harvard's offer.

References

Bakhtin, M. M. (1981) *The Dialogic Imagination* (ed. M. Holquist). Austin: University of Texas Press.

Bogdan, R.C. and Biklen, S.K. (2011) *Qualitative Research for Education: An Introduction to Theory and Methods* (5th edn). Boston: Allyn & Bacon.

Carr, S. and Kemmis, S. (2005) 'Staying critical', *Educational Action Research*, 13 (3): 347–359.

Cazden, C.B. (2001) *Classroom Discourse: The Language of Teaching and Learning* (2nd edn). Portsmouth, NH: Heinemann.

Comenius, J.A. (1632/1907) *Great Didactic*. London: A. and C. Black. Available for download from Cornell University Library at https://archive.org/details/cu31924031053709.

Comenius, J.A. (1658/1887) *Orbus Pictus*. Syracuse, NY: C.W. Bardeen. Available for download at www.gutenberg.org/files/28299/28299-h/28299-h.htm.

Delpit, L. (2012) *'Multiplication is for White People': Raising Expectations for Other People's Children*. New York: The New Press.

Dewey, J. (1938) *Experience and Education*. New York: Macmillan.

Edson, M. (1999) *Wit: A Play*. New York: Farber and Farber.

Elliott, J. (2015) 'Educational action research as the quest for virtue in teaching', *Educational Action Research* 23 (1): 4–21.

Ely, M. (2007) 'In-forming representations', in D.J. Clandinin (ed.) *Handbook of Narrative Inquiry: Mapping a Methodology* (pp. 567–598). Thousand Oaks, CA: Sage.

Freire, P. (1970) *Pedagogy of the Oppressed*. New York: Continuum.

Gee, J.P. (2014) *An Introduction to Discourse Analysis: Theory and Method* (4th edn). New York: Routledge.

Geertz, C. (1973) *The Interpretation of Cultures*. New York: Basic Books.

Glaser, B.G. and Strauss A. L. (1967) *The Discovery of Grounded Theory*. Chicago: Aldine.

Grove, R.W. (1988) 'An analysis of the constant comparative method', *International Journal of Qualitative Studies in Education* 1 (3): 273–279.

Hendricks, C. (2013) *Improving Schools through Action Research: A Comprehensive Guide for Educators* (3rd edn). Boston: Pearson Education.

Hursh, D. (2007) 'Assessing No Child Left Behind and the rise of neoliberal education policies', *American Educational Research Journal*, 44 (3): 493–519.

Lakoff, G. and Johnson, M. (2003) *Metaphors We Live By* (2nd edn). Chicago: University of Chicago Press.

Langer, E. (1997) *The Power of Mindful Learning*. Cambridge: Perseus Books.

Lincoln, Y. and Guba E. (1985) *Naturalistic Inquiry*. Beverly Hills, CA: Sage Publications.

Mayher, J.S. (2008) 'The legacy of English education at NYU', *English Education* 40 (4): 277–292.

McNiff, J. (2013). *Action Research: Principles and Practice* (3rd edn). New York: Routledge.

Moje, E.B, Ciechanowski, K.M., Kramer, K., Ellis, L., Carrillo, R. and Collazo, T. (2004) 'Working toward third space in content area literacy: an examination of everyday funds of knowledge and discourse', *Reading Research Quarterly* 39 (1): 38–70.

Murray, D. (1972/1998) 'Teach writing as a process not product', in T. Newkirk and L. Miller (eds) *The Essential Don Murray: Lesson's from America's Greatest Writing* (pp. 1–5). Portsmouth, NH: Heinemann.

Newman, J. (1998) *Tensions of Teaching: Beyond Tips to Critical Reflection.* New York: Teachers College Press.

Paley, V.G. (1992) *You Can't Say You Can't Play.* Cambridge: Harvard University Press.

Piaget, J. (1957/1993) *John Amos Comenius on Education.* Introduction. New York: Teachers College Press. Reprinted in *Prospects* (UNESCO International Bureau of Education) 23 (1–2): 173–96. Available for download at www.ibe.unesco.org/ International/Publications/Thinkers/ThinkersPdf/comeniuse.PDF.

Polikoff, M., and Porter, A. (2014) 'Instructional alignment as a measure of teaching quality', *Educational Evaluation and Policy Analysis*, 20 (10), 1–18.

Rosenblatt, L. (1995) 'Viewpoints: transaction versus interaction – a terminological rescue operation', *Research in the Teaching of English* 19 (1): 96–107.

Saban, A. (2006) 'Functions of metaphor in teaching and teacher education: a review essay', *Teaching Education* 17 (4): 299–315.

Saldaña, J. (2013) *The Coding Manual for Qualitative Researchers* (2nd edn). Thousand Oaks, CA: Sage.

Schön, D. (1984) *The Reflective Practitioner: How Professionals Think in Action.* New York: Basic Books.

Schön, D. (1987) *Educating the Reflective Practitioner: Toward a New Design for Teaching and Learning in the Professions.* San Francisco: Jossey-Bass.

Shafer, G. (2012) 'Living in the post-process writing center', *Teaching English in the Two-Year College,* 39 (3): 293–305.

Shosh, J.M. (2012) 'How teachers define and enact reflective practice: it's all in the action', *Action Researcher in Education* 3 (1): 104–119.

Shosh, J.M. (2013) 'Re-articulating the values and virtues of Moravian action research', in J. McNiff (ed.) *Value and Virtue in Practice-Based Research* (pp. 107–123). Dorset: September Books.

Shosh, J.M. (2016) 'Toward the construction of a knowledge base on teaching and learning by and for teachers and learners', in L.L. Rowell, C.D. Bruce, J.M. Shosh and M.M. Riel (eds), *Palgrave International Handbook of Action Research.* New York: Palgrave Macmillan, in Press.

Shosh, J.M. and Zales, C.R. (2005) 'Daring to teach writing authentically K-12 and beyond', *English Journal* 95 (2): 77–81.

Shosh, J.M. and Zales, C.R. (2007) 'Graduate teacher education as inquiry: a case study of the Moravian M.Ed. model for professional development', *Teaching Education* 18 (3): 257–275.

Tierney, R. J. (2007) 'New literacy learning strategies for new times', in L.S. Rush, A.J. Eakle and A. Berger (eds) *Secondary School Literacy: What Research Reveals for Classroom Practice* (pp. 21–36). Urbana: NCTE Press.

Vygotsky, L. (1978) *Mind in Society: The Development of Higher Psychological Processes.* Cambridge, MA: Harvard University Press.

Chapter 10

Reconceptualising middle leadership in higher education

A transrelational approach

Christopher Branson, Margaret Franken and Dawn Penney

Introduction

Readers who have held a middle leadership position in higher education or another educational context may well regard middle leadership as characterised by tensions associated with constant pressures to manage expectations simultaneously from above and below. It is not surprising, therefore, that the middle leader participants in Marshall's (2012) research described their respective organisational place in terms of 'being caught in between or sandwiched between senior management to whom they were accountable ... and subordinates for whom they had some functional and often moral responsibility' (p. 511). Similarly, Lapp and Carr (2006) identify middle leaders as being synchronistically both master and slave as they enact the complex roles associated with being a subordinate, an equal and a superior. Unfortunately, contemporary theoretical descriptions of leadership seem to provide middle leaders with limited insight about how best to manage these tensions. Hence, this chapter reflects the view that middle leadership remains theoretically and empirically under-explored and that this oversight contributes to the continuance of an unhealthy, unjust and potentially injurious but important organisational role. The chapter, and the research on which it is based, seeks to redress this untenable situation by reconceptualising a more relevant, coherent and virtuous theoretical perspective of middle leadership (Branson et al. 2015).

The chapter is informed by a research study that specifically examined middle leadership as experienced by Chairpersons of Departments (CoDs) within one faculty in a university in Aotearoa, New Zealand. A focus on leadership as, first and foremost, relational provided the frame for our investigation and analysis of the lived reality of middle leadership in higher education. Hence, the analysis presented here emphasises that middle leadership in higher education is best understood as a transrelational phenomenon as its essence is to move others, the organisation and the leader to higher levels of functioning by means of relationships. Moreover, its effectiveness is interdependently related to the organisational culture since the practice of middle leadership in higher education both influences and is influenced by the organisation's culture. The relationships we examine thus encompass middle leaders' interactions with those they are positioned formally to lead, those they are positioned to act as leaders 'for', and those they are positioned alongside as fellow middle leaders. It is in this sense that the focus of our description is on leadership that is transrelational in nature and practice.

To this end, we first outline the middle leadership context that frames this research. We then review research insights about middle leadership and relate these to current leadership theory. This provides the basis for describing our proposed framework and the literature that has informed it. Although this chapter presents a conceptually focused analysis that seeks to contribute to understandings of middle leadership in higher education, these understandings may well apply to other contexts.

Our research context

Our research arose in the context of professional learning conversations between us (three authors), with Margaret and Dawn having recently assumed roles as middle leaders in the faculty as a CoD. As new leaders with an interest in critical pedagogy and practice, they teamed with the first author, Chris Branson, a writer with expertise in contemporary theories of leadership. We wished to go beyond sharing our experiences by simply sharing descriptions of our experiences, to also learn from the process of analysing and theorising them. To that end, we sought ethical approval to embark on a collaborative research endeavour that sought to examine our experiences, discussions and reflections about the nature of middle leadership.

Issues and implications from current leadership research

From a structural perspective, middle leadership roles appear sound and defensible, providing an explicit articulation of 'how the organisation is to function'. Yet the practice of middle leadership itself lacks clarity and precision. A growing body of research literature highlights a range of tensions in middle leadership with regard to the inherent difficulties for the role holder in trying to fulfil varied and often conflicting demands (O'Connor, 2008). By accepting delegated responsibility, the middle leader is set apart structurally from their colleagues, yet is expected to work closely alongside those colleagues as a fellow member of the department or Faculty, with many of the same day-to-day academic responsibilities as their colleagues. Bennett et al. (2007) identified two key tensions in the role of middle leaders. The first is associated with the expectation that they retain loyalty to both the whole-of-faculty as well as to their particular department or area of responsibility. Second, middle leaders are caught between a university culture of line management within a hierarchical framework and the professional need for cooperation and collegiality within their department or area of responsibility.

Hence, Hammersley-Fletcher and Kirkham (2005) highlight three competing expectations inherent in the middle leader's role: collegiality, professionality and authority. The first expectation, collegiality, highlights the need for the middle leader to communicate honestly in order to build a culture of mutual trust and respect. However, the second competing expectation of professionality brings to the fore the delegated responsibilities to ensure adherence to professional standards and to monitor peer performance in relation to those standards. Essentially, building up the professional knowledge and skills of staff based upon collegiality is founded upon trust while the formal monitoring of professional performance has the potential to undermine trust. The third expectation, authority, brings to the fore the matter of why others should do what the middle leader asks of them. As Perloff (2010) observes, authority often engenders compliance. In many instances, a person afforded authority is able to get others to adopt particular beliefs or behaviours not necessarily because they agree with it, but rather because they expect to gain some physical or psychological benefit (Cangemi, 1992; Hersey et al., 2001; Sergiovanni, 1992; Yukl and Becker, 2006). A problem for middle leaders is that they are expected to be able to persuade, influence or direct the beliefs and behaviours of their colleagues, but invariably have little to offer by way of tangible benefits from so doing. Middle leaders' access to discretionary funds, and their capacity significantly to adjust workload or employment conditions and/or alter the workplace environment, are all typically limited.

For Alvesson (1996) and Alvesson and Sveningsson (2003), this seemingly incoherent and conflicted experience of leadership practice highlights the deficiency of contemporary leadership theory to explain its true nature adequately. According to Haslam, Reicher and Platow (2011), this deficiency stems from too great a focus on the leader and not enough attention to leading. Similarly, for quite some time, Evers and Lakomski (2001, 2012) have argued that current educational leadership theory has been overinfluenced by an outdated view of scientific reasoning, one based upon logical, sequential, and empirical rationalisation and devoid of subjective and affective elements, with the result that our theories of leadership do not match our own experiences of it. Lakomski and Evers (2011) propose an alternative approach to the development of leadership theorising whereby explanations and understandings of reality are gained from a wide array of relevant sources of knowledge, especially from beyond the limitations of leadership theory itself.

In response to these challenges to existing leadership theory, this chapter describes some of the theoretical perspectives formed during our study of middle leadership in a New Zealand university. The departure point in our study was the alignment of the lived reality of the participants with understandings of human behaviour gained from philosophy, sociology, psychology and cultural studies. A focus on the practice of middle leadership as a relational phenomenon provided a frame for reconceptualising their lived reality. New understandings are proposed with respect to the nature of a middle leader's role and their sources of power, and how this impacts upon issues associated with the engagement, commitment and responsibility of those being led.

Reconceptualising a theory of leadership

Our starting point for reconceptualising a theory of leadership so that the nature and practice of middle leadership could be conceived as a singularly coherent phenomenon was a critique of how it has been traditionally defined. Although there is no universally accepted definition of leadership, Yukl's (2006) view that leadership is 'the process of influencing others to understand and agree about what needs to be done and how to do it, and the process of facilitating individual and collective efforts to accomplish shared objectives' (p. 8) is commonly applied. We contend that such a definition of leadership directs attention towards the product of leadership rather than its enactment and suggest that leadership theory has concentrated too much on the behavioural characteristics of leadership and has overlooked the more fundamental relational requirements. Simply stated, the person must first be accepted as a leader before they can begin to behave as a leader so as to have the influence described in the above definition. To this end, Haslam et al. (2011) argue that leadership embraces the following four sequential elements: be an 'in group' member; champion the group; shape the group's identity; and align the group's identity to its wider reality. Here, the feature of influence does not come into play until after the leader is authentically established as a member of the group and, as a consequence, can readily and willingly champion, affirm and promote the activities of the group, and its individual members, in various forums. However, to be able to champion the group, or its members, a leader must first be able to understand and appreciate what is happening, which requires the leader to be at one with the group. The basis of leadership is the quality, the interdependency, the intimacy of the relationship between the leader and the group they are intending to lead. Furthermore, we suggest that this same emphasis is as critical in leadership situations that focus on leading an individual as it is in contexts of group leadership.

From this perspective, building relations, and more specifically, building collegiality, cooperation and teamwork, should not be seen as only an aspect of leadership but as its very essence. While not widely acknowledged, this relational perspective of leadership does have theoretical support. Burns's (1978, 2010) seminal leadership theory included the argument that the authentic authority of any leader is manifested through relationships. According to Burns, 'the most powerful influences consist of deeply human relationships in which two or more persons *engage* with one another' (p. 11, original emphasis) and, thus, for a leader, the 'arena of power is no longer the exclusive preserve of a power elite or an establishment or persons clothed with legitimacy. Power is ubiquitous; it permeates human relationships' (p. 15).

However, establishing the right relationship with those they are to lead is only a first step in being an 'in-group' member. The actions of the leader must be seen as maintaining this relationship. Trust is at the heart of all relationships and is built upon predictability, consistency and authenticity (Branson, 2014b). Being trustworthy is about the leader willingly acting openly, honestly and consistently.

It is more than simply telling the truth. Trustworthiness in a leader means that they consistently display total congruence between who they say they are and what they do. In other words, how a leader is able to influence their group members must support and not undermine the relationship that binds them to the group. The leader's influence is by means of, and consistent with, the relationship and not distinct from it. It is in this way that we argue that leadership is transrelational. Extending the individual and collective functionality of group members, the organisation and the leader by means of the relationship between the leader and each member of the group is the essence of how leadership may be understood as transrelational.

Further understandings implicit in transrelational leadership

The formal acknowledgement of a person's public designation as a leader is usually encapsulated in the belief that this person occupies a particularly important and essential role that is distinguishable from the roles of those they are to lead. Moreover, the desired outcomes and expected actions of the role holder are often captured in a role statement to which the leader can be held accountable. Thus, both the establishment of the role and the description of the role promote a detached, line management view of the relationship between the leader and their group members. However, recent advances in sociology question common assumptions associated with the concept of 'roles' and tend to label them as 'positions' (Davies and Harré, 1999; Harré and Moghaddam, 2003; Harré and Slocum, 2003). Leadership as a 'position' acknowledges that the practice and outcomes of leadership evolve largely in response to the effects generated by the interactions between leaders and those they are leading (Harré and Van Langenhove, 1999). Thus the leader is enacting a 'position' rather than performing a 'role'. Positions are seen as socially shaped behaviours around patterns of mutually accepted beliefs, needs and expectations. Roles, on the other hand, are seen as prescribed behaviours that are more explicit, precise, individualistic and practical in formation and nature, and often reflect an ideal rather than reality. To become a leader, the person needs first to negotiate with those they are leading to build a mutually understood and accepted view of what the inherent responsibilities of their position are, and how it may best be performed (Harré and Moghaddam, 2003). As a negotiated position, the ultimate image of leadership is co-constructed through the realisation and consolidation of mutually accepted values, beliefs and expectations. Furthermore, Davies and Harré (1999) posit that the concept of position readily embraces the dynamic aspects of externally structured and imposed human engagements 'in contrast to the way in which the use of "role" serves to highlight static, formal and ritualistic aspects' (p. 32). Seeing leadership as a role gives the impression that the nature of its enactment, and how others experience it, is the prerogative of the role holder and their line managers. In this sense, a role has the potential to be imposed, with the prospect that those being led may then use whatever subtle or explicit means they can to cause the leader to modify their style of leadership to a more acceptable form. In this way, there are no true leadership roles, only negotiated leadership positions.

What all this means is that the nature of leadership is contextual and not generic because it first emerges out of a sincere interpersonal engagement of the leader with those they are leading. As a position, leadership is first and foremost relational. Furthermore, its essence is a relationship that seeks to create a culture based upon the shared values of trust, openness, transparency, honesty, integrity, collegiality and ethicalness (Branson, 2009, 2014a). This is a culture in which all feel a sense of safety and security because they each feel that they can rely on each other in order to achieve their best. The actions of leaders therefore need to be understood as located in and framed by a specific context, while also serving actively to shape that context and the possibilities that it presents for leadership. Hence, power-relations, and the balance between agency and control, are integral and important aspects of leadership. Following Foucault, these power-relations need to be understood as embedded in and expressed through relationships (see Lynch, 1998; Verderber and Verderber, 1992). A Foucauldian conceptualisation of power as always relational posits that, rather than the source of a leader's power emanating from their role, or from their capacity to reward or punish, or from their superior knowledge, it arises out of the outcomes generated by the interactions between the leader and those they lead. In other words, power emanates from the dynamics of the relationship between the leader and their group. Although we frequently assume that a leader's power is derived from their appointment to a particular role, or their inferred level of authority to reward or punish to some degree, or their perceived relevant knowledge, their power is always and strictly relational (Lynch, 1998). Moreover, the essence of relational power is said to be access to truth about the organisation (Widder, 2004). Where a leader is willing and able to create and support relationships with their group that encourage an open, transparent and shared discussion about the organisation, relational power is generated (Abel, 2005).

The power of a leader thus comes from their willingness and capacity to generate knowledge and truth, within the limits of time and place, in a cooperative, relational manner. Hence, such knowledge and truth is co-constructed and not imposed, consistent and not arbitrary, shared and not withheld, and dynamic and not static. Such power automatically binds all involved to a common purpose with loyalty and responsibility, whereas the loss of such power creates suspicion and resistance, and encourages people to limit their involvement to that which is known to be required. Through their interpretation of the myriad discourses experienced within the organisation, each person constructs a belief about the degree of comprehensiveness and completeness of the organisational knowledge presented by the leader and, thereby, the level of truth within the organisation. It is upon this personal judgement that the leader's degree of power is assessed and the measure of required resistance is determined (Abel, 2005).

The framework developed and employed in our analysis of leadership as transrelational is informed by these understandings of power. However, the analysis would remain incomplete if it did not include a description of the practical implications of adopting such a perspective. We therefore conclude our analysis by describing the organisational implications of transrelational leadership on the three key organisational features of group member engagement, commitment and responsibility.

Organisational implications of transrelational leadership

Our examination of the organisational implications discusses how it is possible for the leader to influence others to understand and agree about what needs to be done and how to do it through a transrelational approach rather than through a more traditional line manager approach. To this end, this discussion explores the issues of engagement, commitment and responsibility. Engagement addresses the issue of how those being led come to understand what needs to be done. Commitment attends to the need for those being led accepting what needs to be done, while responsibility focuses on how those being led attend to the agreed tasks.

Engagement

From a line manager perspective, issues associated with motivation and inspiration have been explored as the presumed process by which the leader ensures their group members understand and accept the need to attend to a particular task. Despite literature from the fields of psychology and sociology clearly indicating that intrinsic factors relating to people's search for opportunities to grow and achieve can be more motivational than extrinsic factors associated with pay and conditions, the leadership literature has continued to place the onus upon the leader to be the source of motivation, inspiration and empowerment for their group members. For example, as distinguished social scientist Michel de Certeau (1984) argues, it is self-motivation, the enactment of personal agency in everyday practices that underpins a group member's engagement with a desired outcome. Within a world viewed as globally interdependent, where the financial mistakes of individuals in one country can cause extreme hardship and the loss of personal property across many other countries, individual leaders are seen as possessing very limited power and authority (Clarke and Hennig, 2012). Today, the person's sense of their own personal authority, which arises out of their skill and knowledge, is considered to be far more important than that of their leader. It is the individual's judgement of the level and effectiveness of their own personal skill and knowledge which provides them with a sense of purpose and meaning and, thereby, motivation. From this perspective, group members willingly engage with tasks that provide them with a sense of purpose and meaning (Wheatley, 2006).

From a transrelational position, this understanding of engagement, or self-forming motivation, calls for the leader to be able to create the conditions in which each group member has the freedom to reflect and question their organisational circumstances, to nurture a kind of curiosity in their self within such circumstances, and to seek ways to become more knowledgeable and skilful in successfully attending to these circumstances (May, 2006). Foucault's (1997) perspective argues that the task of the leader is to help 'individuals to effect by their own means a certain number of operations on their own bodies and souls, thoughts, conduct, and way of being, so as to transform themselves' (p. 225). This requires the leader to have nurtured an interdependent relationship with each of their group members. Being in the group in order to learn about each group member and the affordances and constraints they are imposing upon themselves, and what each group member considers to be their personal strengths and aspirations (Haslam et al., 2011), is thus fundamental to relationally based leadership. Through this relationship, the leader is able to discover what is meaningful to each group member as they are engaged in their work. What issues and behaviours get their attention? What topics generate the most energy, positive and negative? In order to answer such questions, the leader must work with each group member, not sit on the side observing behaviour or interviewing individuals. Second, the leader must assume that, in every group, there are as many different interpretations of the current situation as there are people in the group. Thus the leader must assume that they will discover multiple and divergent interpretations, perspectives and meanings for everything that is happening and what needs to happen next.

Hence it is important for the leader to 'try to put ideas and issues on the table as experiments to discover these different meanings, not as a particular person's recommendations for what should be meaningful. [The leader must] try to stay open to the different reactions [they] get, rather than instantly categorizing people as resistors or allies. [They must] expect diverse responses; and, gradually, even learn to welcome them' (Wheatley, 2006: 148). When group members feel that their experiences, opinions, views and suggestions are listened to and taken seriously, they sense they are personally contributing to the future viability and success of the organisation. They feel more productive, and their work becomes more meaningful. Hence, it is suggested that under these conditions, group member engagement does not have to be externally induced since it becomes natural and automatic.

Commitment

For much of the twentieth century the expectation was that a key responsibility of a leader was to implement principles and processes that foster group member discipline, punctuality, efficiency, rationality and order (Hamel, 2007). This line manager perspective directed the leader's attention to administration and coordination activities. Hamel adds that such a line manager approach is 'very good at aggregating efforts, at coordinating the activities of many people with widely varying roles. But [it is] not very good at mobilizing effort, at inspiring people to go above and beyond' (p. 62). In contrast, he advocates for a relational, 'community' form of leadership. In a line-managed organisation,

> the basis for exchange is contractual – you get paid for doing what is assigned to you. In a community, exchange is voluntary – you give your labor in return for the chance to make a difference, or exercise your talents. In a [line-managed organization], you are a factor of production. In a community, you are a partner in a cause. In a community, dedication and commitment are based on one's affiliation with the group's aims and goals. When it comes to supervision and control, [line-managed organizations] rely on multiple layers of management and a web of policies and rules. Communities, by contrast, depend on norms, values, and the gentle prodding of one's peers. (p. 62)

Similarly, contemporary sociologists (see for example, Bauman, 1992, 1999; Castells, 2000) highlight the tendency of people to seek to network with particular others. As people look to enhance their own skills and knowledge to increase their personal capacities and, thereby, sense of purpose and meaning, they strategically seek to work with others who are seen as being able to contribute towards this process of ongoing self-formation (Castells, 2000). These workplace networks are created in such a way that individuals attempt to 'avoid those interactions where [they] will spend more benefit than [they] gain, and [they] will pursue those interactions where [they have] a good chance of increasing their level of benefit. [They also tend] to avoid those interactions where their lack of capacity will be apparent' (Allan, 2011: 317). As a result, it is argued that people now tend to want to separate themselves into symbolic or status groups or networks around other workers who are seen as having mutually beneficial knowledge, skills and expertise. It is through a tangible sense of solidarity with others, whose knowledge, skills and expertise are seen to be mutually complementary and beneficial, that the group member now gains the deepest sense of workplace purpose and security.

With this awareness of a natural tendency towards networking through selective solidarity in mind, the leader's attention can be drawn towards gaining the benefits from enabling rather than constraining its occurrence. First, rather than seeing selective solidarity solely as an individualistic phenomenon, the transrelational leader must see it as a natural tendency that can work to the advantage of all. To this end, if left unimpeded or actually nurtured, selective solidarity will cause each person to strive to do his or her best and to keep improving. Quality work emerges out of the individual's need to be seen as worthy by their co-workers. Under such circumstances, people do not have to be deliberately organised so as to work well; they will do so naturally provided that they are not limited, frustrated, suppressed or controlled by their leader.

More specifically, the leader's task in this process is to create dynamic connectedness (Dutton and Heaphy, 2003). This calls upon the leader proactively to build relationships of worth and merit, to maximise opportunities for productive networks to form, and to ensure that each person's perceived worth grows (Holland, 1995; Marion & Uhl-Bien, 2001). Through the creation of dynamic connectedness, the leader is able to expand selective solidarity so that many more people and groups within the particular organisation are willing and able to interact collaboratively to better achieve not only their personal need for solidarity but also the primary focus of the organisation (Regine and Lewin, 2000). In this way, the results of those interactions can produce success and sustainability for the organisation. Moreover, leaders wishing to use the selective solidarity tendency of group members through the creation of dynamic connectedness do not try to direct change or control future outcomes. Rather, they encourage connections and interrelationships among those they are leading in unpredictable, dynamic, strategic, fluid, creative and emergent ways. They seek to create as many co-group member connections as possible, based upon equality, respect, collegiality, support, encouragement and empathy.

Responsibility

The perceived quality of a person's performance in an organisation has been the focus of leadership since Frederick Winslow Taylor introduced scientific management into organisational culture (Hamel, 2007). Simply stated, ever since the introduction of scientific management leadership has been consumed by the need to determine 'how well people are doing their jobs' (Luecke, 2007: 116). In contemporary workplaces, this need is couched in terms of accountability – holding the person accountable for the quality of their workplace performance. The person is held accountable through an explicit performance review process, with the aim of improving 'future work performance by examining how well the person is doing in carrying out their respective elements of the [organizational] plan and their specific tasks' (Macdonald et al., 2006: 152). From a line manager perspective, it is the leader who takes responsibility for both determining what is deemed to be an acceptable level of performance and for establishing the means by which a person's performance can be compared to this expected level.

In contrast, Bauman (1992) argues that the contemporary person's own desire for selective solidarity with others in the form of workplace networks means that they highly value self-determination. Moreover, under such workplace circumstances, people do not want to be distracted or misdirected by externally and impersonally imposed rules, expectations and accountabilities, which are likely to have them working with some others who appear to offer little benefit to the partnership and/or to have them completing responsibilities that do not seem to fully utilise or extend their knowledge and skills. In other words, not only does the person *look to* work with others who reciprocate with perceived benefits but they are also fully aware that every other person is doing the same. The person is conscious of being both a judge of others and the focus of judgement by others. Thus, the person is aware that they must continually self-monitor their performance to ensure it presents well in the judgements of others. It is in this way that personal responsibility, rather than leadership imposed accountability, becomes the fundamental processes for maintaining performance standards. The leader's task is not then to make sure that each group member knows exactly what to do and how to do it. Instead, it is to ensure that there is strong and evolving clarity about what is happening in the organisational environment and what this requires of group members.

Simply stated, it is important for the leader to ensure that group members are not just looking at themselves and one another but also able to comprehend what is happening around them. This is not about the leader imposing an image of the environment upon each group member but more that the leader is able to describe that environment and to draw the attention of the group members to the acknowledged purpose of the particular organisation within that environment. This helps to create a discourse concerning what challenges lie ahead while not mandating how these are to be addressed. It is about trusting in the commitment, creativity, ingenuity, determination and personal responsibility of the group members to begin to move towards meeting any new knowledge and skill requirements, and to start to invent ways to overcome the challenges.

When the emphasis is on transrelational leading, achieving performance expectations thus becomes the responsibility of the group member supported and guided by the leader. This contrasts with a line-managed situation in which achieving performance expectations becomes mandated through formalised review and accountability procedures. Transrelational practices empower the group member; line-managed practices dis-empower the group member. Transrelational leadership provides the group member with the opportunity to dwell on the meaning ascribed to their work so as to discover common issues and problems that are deemed significant and addressable. Then responsibility becomes personal and spontaneous. Although we see responsibility at the material level, we also see how processes that are immaterial generate it. Thus, leadership must look for these invisible relational processes rather than the accountability regulations and policies that they seem to engender. It must look for those processes that give rise to meaning. It must look beyond the traditional ways of achieving performance expectations to utilise the processes that give them birth and value. As explained by Wheately (2006),

> When leaders honor us with opportunities to know the truth of what is occurring and support us to explore the deeper meaning of the events, we instinctively reach out to them. Those who help us center our work in

deeper purpose are leaders we cherish, and to whom we return love, gift for gift. With meaning as our centering place, we can journey through the realms of chaos and make sense of the world. With meaning as an attractor, we can re-create ourselves to carry forward what we value most. (p. 133)

With meaning and purpose as motivators, group members do not need to be held accountable; they just need the freedom to become responsible.

In conclusion

The impetus for this chapter was the widely recognised tensions inherent within the role of middle leaders in higher education. Our view is that it is organisationally and morally inappropriate to continue to ignore this common situation. First, it is essential to acknowledge that tradition and expediency will not maintain organisational efficiency and longevity in today's highly complex and competitive organisational world. Organisational success now depends on maximising each person's contribution. Unless the practice of the middle leader in higher education is changed, the tension and stress it regularly engenders will diminish the role holder's contribution, and their willingness to remain in the role will also be reduced. The continual turnover of middle leaders must ultimately adversely affect the functioning of the organisation. Second, it is morally iniquitous to continue to appoint people to positions that are known to be fraught with stress and tension caused by seemingly incongruous and competing responsibilities, especially if there is an alternative and achievable means of practice. Hence, this chapter has described an alternative means of practice. Rather than claiming that middle leadership in higher education necessitates a different form of leadership, this chapter argues that leadership theory itself requires an adjustment, a reconceptualisation. In this way, the nature and practice of leadership, and especially middle leadership in higher education, becomes unified and coherent.

This description of transformational leadership is not promoted as a replacement leadership theory but rather as an additional consideration within our understanding of leadership. In other words, to Burns's (2010) two broad styles of leadership – transaction and transformational leadership – this chapter adds the third style of transrelational leadership. Figure 10.1 illustrates this understanding by showing how the level of commitment of the leader to their relational association with each member of the group they are leading ultimately determines their style of leadership. The more relational the leader, the more they are likely to be transformational and, ultimately, transrelational. Here, relational power, rather than coercive power, is the source of their influence upon their group members. What is more, this chapter has argued that transrelational leadership is not just an additional style of leadership: rather, it is the primary, or fundamental,

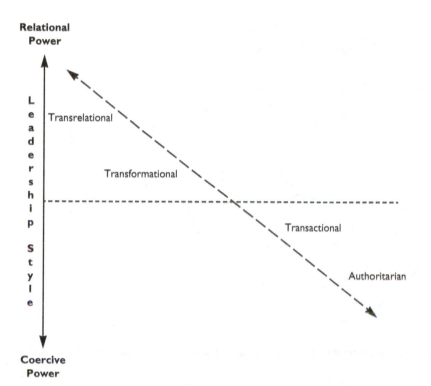

Figure 10.1 An illustration of the relationship between various styles of leadership.

component of leadership. Simply, each of the aforementioned styles of leadership has their genesis in transrelational leadership as shown in Figure 10.2.

This is to argue that all leaders require a certain level of initial credibility. They
must possess an acceptable level of professional knowledge and skills in order to be
able to successfully complete the basic requirements of their position. However,
beyond these basic requirements it is their leadership acumen that enables them
to become the leader of a group. As has been proposed in this chapter, becoming
the leader starts with being accepted as an authentic member of the group. Then
the complexity of such a leader has been described in terms of developing the
practices of transrelational leadership. Once the leader has been accepted into the
group by such means, each group member will willingly embrace transformative practices. They will readily become engaged, committed and responsible.
Moreover, if necessary, the group member is more likely to accept a mandated
direction, an outcome of transactional leadership, from a leader that they trust
and accept.

Although this chapter has highlighted the multiple benefits gained from
unifying the practice of middle leadership in higher education from a focus on

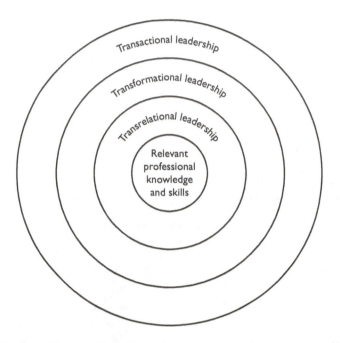

Figure 10.2 An illustration of the interconnectedness amongst various styles of leadership.

transrelational leadership, it must be acknowledged that this cannot happen in a vacuum. There is an essential need to address the influence of organisational culture on leadership practice. The chapter highlights the interdependency, the seemingly indivisible juncture, between leadership practice and organisational culture: one cannot be changed without simultaneously changing the other. While a line manager perspective treats leadership practice and organisational culture as discrete phenomena and discusses their interplay in a differentiated manner, a transrelational perspective respects their incorporated mutuality. Any move towards a more transrelational approach to middle leadership necessitates a simultaneous move towards a more learning-centred organisation.

References

Abel, C. F. (2005) 'Beyond the mainstream: Foucault, power and organization theory', *International Journal of Organization Theory and Behavior (PrAcademics Press)*, 8 (4): 495–519.

Allan, K. (2011) *The Social Lens: An Invitation to Social and Sociological Theory* (2nd edn). Thousand Oaks, CA: Sage.

Alvesson, M. (1996) 'Leadership studies: from procedure and abstraction to reflexivity and situation', *Leadership Quarterly*, 7 (4): 455–485.

Alvesson, M. and Sveningsson, S. (2003) 'The great disappearing act: difficulties in doing "leadership"', *The Leadership Quarterly*, 14: 359–381.

Bauman, Z. (1992) *Intimations of Postmodernity*. London, England: Routledge.

Bauman, Z. (1999) *In Search of Politics*. Cambridge, England: Polity Press.

Bennett, N., Woods, P., Wise, C. and Newton, W. (2007) 'Understanding of middle leadership in secondary schools: a review of empirical research', *School Leadership and Management*, 27 (5): 453–470.

Branson, C. M. (2009) *Leadership for an Age of Wisdom*. Dordrecht, Netherlands: Springer Educational Publishing.

Branson, C. M. (2014a) 'Maintaining moral integrity', in C.M. Branson and S.J. Gross (eds) *Handbook of Ethical Educational Leadership* (pp. 263–281). New York, NY: Routledge.

Branson, C. M. (2014b) 'Deconstructing moral motivation', in C.M. Branson and S.J. Gross (eds) *Handbook of Ethical Educational Leadership* (pp. 294–312). New York, NY: Routledge.

Branson, C. M., Franken, M. and Penney, D. (2015) 'Middle leadership in higher education: a relational analysis', *Educational Management Administration and Leadership*: 1–18. DOI: 10.1177/1741143214558575

Burns, J. M. (1978) *Leadership*. New York, NY: HarperCollins.

Burns, J. M. (2010) *Leadership*. New York, NY: HarperCollins.

Cangemi, J. (1992) 'Some observations of successful leaders, and their use of power and authority', *Education*, 112: 499–505.

Castells, M. (2000) *The Rise of the Network Society* (2nd edn). Oxford, England: Blackwell Publishers.

Clarke, M. and Hennig, B. (2012) 'Motivation as ethical self-formation', *Educational Philosophy and Theory*, 45 (1): 77–90. DOI: 10.1080/00131857.2012.715386

Davies, B. and Harré, R. (1999) 'Positioning and personhood', in R. Harré and L. Van Langenhove (eds) *Positioning Theory* (pp. 32–52). Oxford, England: Blackwell Publishers.

de Certeau, M. (1984) *The Practice of Everyday Life*. Berkeley, CA: University of California Press.

Dutton, J. and Heaphy, E. (2003) 'The power of high quality connections', in K. Cameron, J. Dutton, and R. Quinn (eds) *Positive Organizational Scholarship*. San Francisco, CA: Berrett-Koehler.

Evers, C. W. and Lakomski, G. (2001). 'Theory in educational administration: naturalistic directions'. *Journal of Educational Administration*, 39 (6): 499–520.

Evers, C. W. and Lakomski, G. (2012) 'Science, systems, and theoretical alternatives in educational administration: the road less travelled', *Journal of Educational Administration*, 50 (1): 57–75.

Foucault, M. (1997) 'Technologies of the self' (R. Hurley and others, Trans.), in P. Rabinow (ed.) *Ethics, Subjectivity and Truth* (pp. 223–251). New York, NY: New Press.

Hamel, G. (2007) *The Future of Management*. Boston, MA: Harvard Business School Press.

Hammersley-Fletcher, L. and Kirkham, G. (2005) *Distribution, Collaboration and Collegiality: Issued for Primary Middle Leaders*. Paper presented at the British Educational Research Association annual conference, University of Glamorgan.

Harré, R. and Moghaddam, F. (2003) 'Introduction: the self and others in traditional psychology and in positioning theory', in R. Harré and F. Moghaddam (eds) *The Self and Others: Positioning Individuals and Groups in Personal, Political, and Cultural Contexts* (pp. 1–11). Westport, CT: Praeger Publishers.

Harré, R. & Slocum, N. (2003). 'Disputes as complex social events: on the uses of positioning theory', in R. Harré and F. Moghaddam (eds), *The Self and Others: Positioning Individuals and Groups in Personal, Political, and Cultural Contexts* (pp. 123–136). Westport, CT: Praeger Publishers.

Harré, R. and Van Langenhove, L. (1999) 'The dynamics of social episodes', in R. Harré and L. Van Langenhove (eds), *Positioning Theory* (pp. 1–13). Oxford, England: Blackwell Publishers.

Haslam, S. A., Reicher, S. D. and Platow, M. J. (2011) *The New Psychology of Leadership: Identity, Influence and Power*. Hove, England: Psychology Press.

Hersey, P., Blanchard, K.H. and Johnson, D.E. (2001) *Management of Organisational Behaviour* (8th edn). London, England: Prentice-Hall.

Holland, J. H. (1995) *Hidden Order*. Reading, MA: Addison-Wesley Publishing.

Lakomski, G. and Evers, C. W. (2011) 'Analytic philosophy and organization theory: Philosophical problems and scientific solutions', in *Philosophy and Organization Theory*, 32: 23–54. DOI:10.1108/S0733-558X(2011)0000032004

Lapp, C. A. and Carr, A. N. (2006) 'To have to halve to have: "being" in the middle in changing time's space', *Journal of Organizational Change Management*, 19 (5): 655–687.

Luecke, R. (2007) *Manager's Toolkit: The 13 Skills Managers Need to Succeed*. Boston, MA: Harvard Business School Press.

Lynch, R. A. (1998) 'Is power all there is?: Michel Foucault and the "omnipresence of power relations"', *Philosophy Today*, 42 (1): 65–70.

Macdonald, I., Burke, C. and Stewart, K. (2006) *Systems Leadership: Creating Positive Organisations*. Farnham, England: Gower Publishing Company.

Marion, R. and Uhl-Bien, M. (2001) 'Leadership in complex organizations', *The Leadership Quarterly*, 12 (4): 389–418.

Marshall, S. G. (2012) 'Educational middle change leadership in New Zealand: the meat in the sandwich', *International Journal of Educational Management*, 26 (6): 502–528.

May, T. (2006) *The Philosophy of Foucault*. Chesham, England: Acumen.

O'Connor, E. (2008) *'There Is a Lot to Be Learnt': Assistant Principals' Perceptions of Their Professional Learning Experiences and Learning Needs in Their Role as Middle Leaders in Irish Post-Primary Schools*. An unpublished doctoral research study. London, England: Institute of Education, University of London.

Perloff, R. M. (2010) *The Dynamics of Persuasion: Communication and Attitudes in the 21st Century* (4th edn). New York, NY: Routledge.

Regine, B. and Lewin, R. (2000) 'Leading at the edge: how leaders influence complex systems', *Emergence*, 2 (2): 5–23.

Sergiovanni, T. (1992) *Moral Leadership: Getting to the Heart of School Improvement*. San Francisco, CA: Jossey-Bass.

Verderber, R. F. and Verderber, K. S. (1992) *Inter-act: Using Interpersonal Communication Skills*. Belmont, CA: Wadsworth.

Wheatley, M. J. (2006) *Leadership and the New Science: Discovering Order in a Chaotic World* (3rd edn). San Francisco, CA: Berrett-Koehler Publishers.

Widder, N. (2004) 'Foucault and power revisited', *European Journal of Political Theory*, 3 (4): 411–432.

Yukl, G. (2006) *Leadership in Organizations* (6th edn). Upper Saddle River, NJ: Pearson-Prentice Hall.

Yukl, G. A. and Becker, W. S. (2006) 'Effective empowerment in organizations', *Organization Management Journal*, 3 (3): 210–231.

Chapter 11

From studying educational inequalities to building equitable educational environments

Hugh Mehan

This chapter is an account of how, throughout my 40-year career as an educational researcher and professor of sociology and education, most recently at the University of California, San Diego, I have tried to live my values of justice and equity in practice. These values permeate my story, which is presented here as two halves. The first half, broadly spanning 20 years, focused on uncovering the roots of the seemingly inexorable social fact of educational inequality in US K-12 education, mainly through studying some of the policies and practices that produce those inequalities. My findings showed consistently that students of colour from low-income backgrounds did not fare as well as their middle-income 'majority' contemporaries. For reasons I describe below, I decided, for the second 20 years, to change my focus from searching for the roots of educational inequalities to building educational environments that might produce more equitable possibilities for underprivileged young people.

Parts of the story have been told elsewhere, as in, for example, Mehan (2012) and Mehan and Chang (2010). Here, however, I adopt a new perspective, that of focusing on the values base of what colleagues and I do in our research and work. In our view, appreciating the values base of research has to be seen as a core value both of higher education and of efforts to establish equitable possibilities. This commitment has inspired the story, told now from this fresh perspective.

All my work has been influenced by the concept of constructivism (or constructionism), a term used widely in ethnomethodology (Mehan and Wood, 1975). In *The Rules for Sociological Method*, Durkheim (1982) explained how social structures become immutable and independent of social action, yet in turn constrain social action. Like-minded colleagues and I therefore began to ask how it was that social structures became structured and thereby immutable and constraining of social action, and how these structures stratify and thereby construct inequality in social interaction. If we could find this out, we reasoned, we would be better informed about how to disrupt and change the stratifying machinery in order to construct more equitable educational environments that would allow the research and workplace values of freedom and personal-social entitlement to be realized in action. The clarion call by Durkheim, Weber and Marx to social scientists to make research relevant for social policy exemplifies this value orientation. This idea unfortunately, has not been widely adopted

Documenting stratifying practices

Here are three examples of the kinds of insights I developed from my empirical research into how stratification can be structured in K-12 education.

Stratifying social inequality through educational testing encounters

The conduct of educational testing exemplifies the way in which unequal social structures are created through social interaction but are then portrayed as independent of that action (Mehan, 1974, 1978; Mehan and Wood, 1975). The dominant models of educational testing are premised on a technical rational form of logic that perceives reality as fixed and organized according to specific rules. I saw this model in action when I videotaped elementary school students performing IQ tests as part of routine psychological evaluations and then read the results of those same students' IQ tests displayed in aggregated, numerical form. On the videotapes, I observed how tester and children took turns in speaking. I noticed especially how the tester actively structured the students' answers and consequently the production of their IQ test scores by phrasing questions in certain ways, pausing or adding hints and cues. I observed also how this process morphed into the construction of a student's identity. The values being displayed at this point were those of domination and control, as also discussed by Erickson (2004) and Erickson and Shultz (1978) who explain how a construction of 'co-membership' can influence counselors' interactions with community college students. These interactions can then influence which next steps a student will take along their professional learning pathways: whether, for example, to transfer from a two-year to a four-year college. It became evident to me that the technical rational forms of school sorting practices both structure educational inequality and produce stratifying effects. These ideas are explored also by Giddens (1979), whose concept of 'structuration', parallel to my idea of 'structuring social structure', also emphasizes elements of control. 'Structure is both medium and outcome of the reproduction of practices and "exists" in the generating moments of this constitution', he comments (1979: 5): social structures shape people's practices, and people's practices in turn constitute (and reproduce) social structures. People are not given the freedom to create their own identities as they wish.

Stratifying social inequality through classroom interactions

Courtney Cazden, internationally renowned expert on children's language development (1965), invited me to evaluate the quality of her teaching of low-income young people in urban settings, in light of her doctoral research into the nature of language development. My colleagues and I became daily observers in Courtney's classroom and videotaped nine reading lessons. This experience led to *Learning Lessons* (Mehan, 1979), *Classroom Discourse* (Cazden, 2001), and a recent retrospective (Mehan and Cazden, 2015). *Learning Lessons* became one of the earlier landmark qualitative studies of classroom discourse, describing the basic structures of classroom lessons (Initiation–Reply–Evaluation and Extended Sequences) and turn-allocation procedures (Individual Nomination, Invitation to Reply, and Invitation to Bid). Teachers use these procedures to structure, and thereby control the flow of classroom discourse. Also, the students who internalize those structures as normative are enabled to be seen as legitimate members of the classroom community who may thereby make contributions that will be taken seriously by teachers and peers. Again identity is manufactured according to the views of the dominant participant in the interaction.

Stratifying social inequality through tracking and streaming

The practice of *tracking* or *streaming*, used widely in education, can have stratifying consequences (Oakes, 2005). This often takes place when some students are placed in high-track classes aimed towards college entry. Here the main form of instruction is abstract and symbolic, grounded in a value of objectification. Other students are placed in less demanding 'low track' or 'career technical' courses, similar to the European model of Vocational Education and Training, where they are schooled in ways that prepare them for the world of practical work, with a stronger emphasis on relational values. Further, the distribution of students in different tracks tends to correlate with their ethnicity and socioeconomic status. Children of colour from low-income households are more likely to be assigned to low-ability groups or special education programs, whereas those children from middle- and upper-income families will more probably be assigned to high track and 'gifted and talented' programs (Oakes, 2005). This may be construed as a manifestation of the parallel relationships between the values and practices of domination and control.

Also, students in these different tracks and programs receive *differential treatment* (Cicourel and Mehan, 1985; Varenne and McDermott, 1998). While an elementary classroom teacher might instruct high- and low-ability groups in the same class, students in different groups within the class are instructed differently. Those in low-ability groups are attended to less frequently, and the teacher exercises greater control over their actions, whereas the opposite is the case in high-ability groups, where high-flyers are afforded considerably greater freedom. Consequently, high-ability groups often progress more rapidly and cover much more curriculum material over the course of a school year. These processes have a cumulative effect, and usually continue into secondary school: low-track classes are given less exposure to more demanding topics whereas high-track classes are required to engage with more complex material.

These effects may be most obviously seen within the context of research on the perhaps-unintended negative consequences of tracking. Here my colleagues and I studied how the identity of special education students can be systematically constructed (Mehan et al., 1986). In several episodes we observed, teachers notified the principal that a particular student was displaying what appeared to be symptoms requiring a special education designation. Standard procedures then followed: the referred child went to the school psychologist who administered a battery of tests. On their recommendation, the referral was passed on to a special education committee, comprising educators and the referred child's parent(s). However, on analysing these testing sessions, we found the replication of earlier findings: the tester's phrasing of questions and their pauses, hints and cues all contributed to and subtly structured the students' answers. Also, an analysis of some special education committee meetings showed that specific organizational constraints such as state and federal laws and financial incentives and disincentives influenced decisions. A major consideration even appeared to be the number of students already in those special education programs to which new students were assigned: if programs were 'full', having reached the maximum number eligible for state and federal funding, students were referred to similar programs elsewhere. Ironically but not surprisingly, the placing itself thereby came to define the student. Studying such organizational practices led us to conclude that the construction of students' identities was as much a function of institutional arrangements as of the presenting symptoms of the children referred to special education programs (Mehan, 1993; Mehan et al., 1986).

My research focus temporarily shifted between 1998 and 2002 to the study of international conflict (see, for example, Mehan and Skelly, 1988). When I returned to educational studies, my focus shifted again, now to studying 'larger' or 'macro' institutional structures. For example, my colleagues and I followed the effects of efforts to repeat a successful education program developed in one educational context (New York City) in an entirely different educational context (San Diego) (Hubbard et al., 2006; Mehan et al., 2003). We reported how potentially worthwhile reforms were undercut by some business leaders' insensitivity to local community values and needs, their lack of appreciation of the historically grounded nature of organizational procedures, and a desire for the rapid implementation of the program. This was yet another example of how dominant values can transform into power-constituted relationships.

Employing design research to advance an equity agenda

The reason for this shift to larger macro structures came, in part, from an acknowledgement that the close analysis of face-to-face interaction we had been using was not having significant influence in either sociological or social policy communities; more importantly, it became increasingly clear that the dominant form of thinking and theorizing used by those communities continued to contribute to social inequality. This constituted a denial of my values as an educator and a researcher. It was also depressing to see, again and again, the same outcomes in people's lives of the practices of tracking, ability grouping, and standardized testing. I therefore decided now to focus specifically on finding ways to create more equitable educational environments and explain the processes involved, so that others might learn from our research. This reorientation led to my adopting a version of 'design research' (see Brown et al., 1999), a term denoting a variety of collaborative research agendas that share a family resemblance, including action research (McNiff, 2013; Penuel et al., 2011; Riel, 2012). This approach shifts the responsibility for conducting research exclusively to the practitioner (teacher, nurse, doctor, office worker). Its goal is three-fold: improvement of the individual's practice, deeper understanding of organizational change, and personally-directed development of a researcher identity. The stereotypical university-based researcher fades into the background, appearing occasionally as faculty advisor. Action researchers frequently reject the term 'participatory', saying that everyone – teacher, doctor, university researcher, office worker – is automatically a practitioner-researcher by researching his or her own practices. Similarly, Burawoy (2005) calls for a form of sociology that involves collaboration between professional social scientists and the lay public, thereby equating design research with 'organic public sociology'.

This kind of design research suits me, informed as it is by the values of emancipation, participation and cooperation. It requires university researchers and workplace practitioners to work together, often for extended periods of time, in order to improve complex social systems; it therefore goes beyond the currently dominant 'research–development–dissemination–evaluation' (R-D-D-E) model. This model aims simply to show the links between research and practice, and is grounded in inequitable, power-constituted relationships between researchers and practitioners. The task of researchers, it is assumed, is to study 'important educational issues' and, through their publications, to communicate their findings to practitioners in districts, schools and classrooms. The expectation then is that the practitioners will put the researchers' findings into practice. Further, practitioners are often positioned as objects of study rather than as research partners who are equally capable of interpreting results.

Traditional policy researchers often take these dichotomies as standard and as core institutional values. They put in place institutional reward systems for basic research, grounded in abstract mental work, and this comes to be seen as more valuable than a commitment to research-informed public policy formation. Researchers, from a traditionalist perspective, are expected to engage in 'discovery research', to remain separate from the objects of their research, and to produce research reports. Practitioners are involved only insofar as they provide data.

This situation does not lead to social benefit, which, in my view, is what research should be about. Policy documents, as in Brown et al. (1999: 29) advise that researchers should accept responsibility for making their research useful; they also advise that practitioners, too, should accept responsibility for evaluating practices and explaining how those practices may be seen as useful. If researchers and practitioners agree to share responsibility for research and practice, then they can imagine and try out new ways of improving unsatisfactory situations.

CREATE – the Center for Research on Equity, Access and Teaching Excellence – was created at the University of California, San Diego, in response to the elimination of affirmative action in college admissions to investigate inequitable educational environments and contribute to the construction of more equitable ones. This groundbreaking effort enabled my colleagues and myself to instantiate our version of design research, where workplace practitioners and university researchers collaborate at each phase of the research process: they mutually define research problems, gather research materials, analyze them, and make them public through joint presentations and/or publications. We recognized also that the aim of reducing educational inequality requires sustained commitment. This meant we had to move towards a more engaged form of research where all participants were involved as co-researchers in describing and interpreting events. We saw this as a critical form of ethnography that documented and made people's experiences of oppression publicly available.

Thereafter, CREATE colleagues and I became actively involved in contributing to the reconstruction of educational environments. We began to see our work as enabling practitioners and researchers to work collaboratively to improve complex systems and produce cogent explanations and theories regarding how and why programs, designs, or ideas do or do not work.

Trying to construct equitable educational environments

Against this brief discussion of design research, I now present some examples from recent work that shows how university researchers and practitioners can work collaboratively and thereby create productive learning environments for low-income students of colour. It should also be noted that the projects described here did not proceed smoothly from planning to implementation: they were caught up in political conflicts that required skillful negotiation and political astuteness.

Creating a model system for expanding diversity and improving students' life choices

The first design research project was inspired by a devastating and far-reaching political event when, in 1995, the Regents of the University of California refused to recognize race and gender as factors in University admissions. Our response, as a small but committed group of UCSD faculty, community members, and students led by Thurgood Marshall College Provost Cecil Lytle was to propose that UCSD open a 6–12 grade college-preparatory school on campus for low-income students to ensure they would be well prepared for admission to any UCSD college or other four-year college (Lytle, 2007; Mehan 2012).

I participated actively in this effort, attending weekly meetings of the UCSD Outreach Task Force during 1997. This led to the formation of CREATE and a model school (The Preuss School, as below). I served as Director of CREATE from 1999–2012. However, our initial 1997 proposal for a model school on campus was not supported either by the full faculty or the campus administration (Lytle 2007; Mehan et al., 2012). Later that same year, however, the combined forces of public outcry, negative press reports and pressure from the Regents persuaded the campus administration to reconsider. More public meetings were held to discuss the possible sponsoring and development of a charter school, with the result that community members broadly supported the concept, insisting, however, that the school be located on the UCSD campus.

CREATE and the new charter school – The Preuss School – opened in Fall 1999, as part of a more comprehensive outreach plan approved by the chancellor and the academic senate in November 1997. Both CREATE and Preuss came into being, partly through the lengthy and contentious public debate during which the values that inspired the concept of the charter school as well as the values regarding the nature and purposes of the university itself became contested objects of inquiry (Rosen and Mehan, 2003).

The work of CREATE involved the following: coordinating campus-wide outreach initiatives; widening and developing partnerships with struggling K-12 schools; conducting basic and design research on matters of educational equity; and supporting schools as they adapted principles developed at The Preuss School to their own circumstances. The responsibility of the on-campus Preuss School was to provide a wider range of options to prepare under-represented minority students for entry to four-year colleges and universities, while also avoiding positive discrimination.

The Preuss School admissions policies were constructed carefully to conform to state laws. The school accepts applications only from students from low-income households (earnings are less than twice the federal level for free- and reduced-cost lunch eligibility) and whose parents or guardians are not graduates of four-year colleges. Students are selected randomly, by lottery. Now in its fifteenth year, the school prepares approximately 800 low-income students from across San Diego for college.

The theory of action (what we call 'detracking') that CREATE colleagues and I developed to inform the development of The Preuss School, and that communicates its values base, came from contemporary thinking about effective schooling and cognitive development. Among others, Darling-Hammond (2010) suggests that distinctive features of successful schools in the US, Europe, and Asia include a rigorous curriculum and extended learning time, recognizing that specific arrangements vary across countries. Students in the US attend school for 165–180 days, while it is normal for students in Europe and Asia to attend school for 190–220 days, accompanied, in some countries, by extra test-preparation classes after school. Similarly, Preuss extends the school year by 18 days; this provides further opportunities for students to develop skills and deepen understandings.

The values base of the school stems from the idea that all normally functioning humans are capable of significant levels of high school achievement provided courses of study are accompanied by appropriate social, relational and academic supports, thus preparing them adequately for college and the world of work (Bruner, 1986; Cicourel and Mehan, 1985; Mehan et al., 1996; Meier, 1995; Cole, 1999; Oakes, 2005). The school offers only college-preparatory classes, many in the Advanced Placement category. Its curriculum fulfils or exceeds the University of California and California State University entrance requirements.

Acting from its articulated values base, educators at the school have put in place a range of academic and social supports or 'scaffolds' to prepare students for the rigorous study required to qualify for four-year colleges and universities. As well as extending learning time by 18 days, students who need immediate help are offered additional tutoring sessions before school, during advisory periods, after school, and on Saturdays. Careful selection procedures ensure that only those instructional staff will be appointed who appreciate the need for personalized interactions with students, and the need to develop an academic identity while also maintaining a neighborhood identity. Preuss's college-going culture is further supported by the appointment of UCSD students who serve as tutors and informants about college life.

Since its inauguration in 1999, The Preuss School has achieved an impressive record: the average student enrollment in four-year and two-year colleges from 2004–2013 is 99 per cent. The average enrollment in four-year colleges during that same period is 85 per cent (742 of 871 graduates). This figure compares favorably with national data, showing that 31 per cent of low-income youth enroll in college in the fall after graduation (NCES, 2014). It also compares favorably to the college enrollment record of students who applied to Preuss but were not accepted through the lottery. Strick (2012) estimates that between 40 and 64 per cent of that comparison group enrolled in four-year colleges in the fall after their graduation. The school has also accumulated a number of accolades, including being named the 'most transformative high school in the United States' by *Newsweek* for three consecutive years. These data provide concrete evidence that low-income students of colour can close the achievement gap and be prepared for college when provided with rigorous instruction accompanied by an extensive system of scaffolds.

While the school was being built, the founding Preuss principal and I frequently made joint presentations about its origins and development at educational conferences (see Alvarez and Mehan, 2004, 2006). CREATE researchers collaborated with Preuss teachers to document the academic performance of Preuss students in high school (for example, McClure et al., 2006). Preuss educators were also interested in students' lives once they enroll in college. This interest led to a Preuss teacher's dissertation and a joint publication describing some of the challenges that students face, especially those from low-income families, while trying to reconcile their 'home identities' with their new 'academic identities'

(Mehan and Mussey, 2012). Preuss teachers developed other research interests, too, such as whether the tests students took before entering the school predicted later academic performance. These teacher-generated research questions have led to joint reports by Preuss and CREATE, that, in turn, have fed back into Preuss school policy and practice.

Restructuring and reculturing a neighborhood school

The successful outcomes of the coalition of UC San Diego faculty, community activists, elected officials, and generous philanthropists in creating The Preuss School on the UCSD campus now led to a coalition of parents and teachers. The aim was to re-form Gompers High School, a local failing neighborhood school, into Gompers Preparatory Academy, a college-prep high school modeled on The Preuss School. Thus a community relationship emerged as a guiding value.

Gompers Secondary School was originally an urban 7–12 school located in Southeastern San Diego. It had operated for over 50 years in a community with a high crime rate and a lengthy history of gang-related violence. In 2004–2005, Gompers was divided into a 6–8 middle school and a 9–12 high school. Unable to meet its *No Child Left Behind* performance targets for six consecutive years, district leaders planned to close the high school as soon as the nearby newly constructed Lincoln High School was completed and to restructure the remaining Gompers Middle School.

The situation in Gompers Middle School was serious. When it opened in 2004 there were 18 teacher vacancies out of a 50 teacher staff; six vacancies remained in math and science in January of that school year. Teacher attrition rates were over 70 per cent. This meant that students were faced with a stream of substitute teachers, a situation that militated against high-level learning and the achievement of *No Child Left Behind* annual progress goals. Teacher and student absences were high; the average daily attendance rate hovered near 90 per cent. The physical plant was deteriorating. Teachers openly expressed their dislike of students, violent fights occurred regularly, and over 1,000 students were suspended annually (Kenda, 2008).

A task force of parents, teachers, administrators, and community leaders (notably from the Chicano Federation, The United Front, the San Diego Organizing Project, and the Urban League) formed to discuss options for restructuring Gompers Middle School. It was decided, following the successful intakes at Preuss of students from the Gompers neighborhood, to invite UCSD to join the conversation. Professor Cecil Lytle and I were asked to consider whether UCSD could 'take over' Gompers and form a UCSD-managed charter school, similar to The Preuss School. We agreed to serve on the task force. However, in light of the UCSD administration's reluctance to sponsor another charter school, Lytle and I recommended forming an independent (501c3) charter school, this time not managed by UCSD.

Gompers parents liked this idea, given that more than seventy had at least one child at Preuss. Confident that their students could be academically successful, Gompers parents supported the proposed re-formation of Gompers into a college-prep charter school in partnership with UCSD and community groups.

I as director and Lytle as associate director of CREATE pledged material resources, including UCSD students to serve as tutors as well as our extensive understanding of the requirements for teacher professional education, parent education and research and evaluation. Of possible greater importance was the intellectual and political capital the university provided in terms of a values-oriented theory of action for the new Gompers, and political capacity for interacting with community members and district leaders.

According to California charter school law, a majority of parents hoping to enroll their children in a new charter school are required to sign a petition for its approval. Parents and teachers joined together in leading the petition drive. They walked the streets around the school to explain the background and intent of the school; this resulted in a substantial majority in support of the conversion. Support was also offered by influential organizations: the California Charter Schools Association provided pump-priming funds as well as advice on preparing relevant documentation and other political matters; funding was provided by another local foundation for the first Gompers 'culture camp' (see below). Following several other political forays, including confrontations with the teachers' union, approval was granted for the Gompers charter proposal on March 1, 2005. Opening day was scheduled for September 5, 2005, so the newly hired school leaders, together with Lytle and myself set about hiring. A teaching staff of 47 was soon in place, along with a senior leadership team and resource teachers in math, English language arts, and science.

The leadership team initiated 'culture camp', a two-week professional development activity aimed at bringing staff together to negotiate and agree a common culture, especially an agreed philosophy of how to engage collaboratively with students. This philosophy was sustained and reinforced through regular refresher sessions throughout the school year. There is now a commonly agreed framework for assigning and receiving homework, classroom organization and the conduct of the school day and lessons, and how to deal with absences, latecomers and students' movements between classes.

Gompers posts motivational signs and other symbols around the school to reinforce its commitment to a college-going culture of learning. College pennants adorn classroom and hallway walls, and students enter the school through 'the Gates of Wisdom'. A banner underneath the sign reads, 'GOMPERS IS A UCSD PARTNERSHIP SCHOOL'. The school motto, 'REACH' (Respect, Enthusiasm, Achievement, Citizenship and Hard work) is visible everywhere. Teaching and administrative staff dress 'professionally' while students wear school uniforms. The intention is to signal to students and the community that Gompers is about serious learning for college entry.

Like Preuss, Gompers offers a college-prep curriculum to students, and has similarly instituted practices for supporting rigorous student learning. When it first opened, many incoming students were below state and federal recognized grade level. Class times were therefore allocated variously across academic subjects. Math and English language arts were offered in 90-minute slots, five days a week. Afternoon classes were organized as 90-minute blocks to enable the teaching of science, social science, language and PE on alternating days. Subject matter teachers assisted the math and English teachers in the morning and roles were reversed in afternoon classes.

As at Preuss, learning time was extended. Gompers' solution was to add minutes to the school day. This meant that school times tallied with those of other local schools, and accommodated student families' vacation and travel plans (many Latino families travel to Mexico for an extended Christmas break). The last 30-minute period of each day was flexible: students who were performing well could participate in an extracurricular activity, while additional tutoring sessions were made available for students who were not performing so well. Extracurricular activities and tutoring both continued into after-school hours.

It is recognized at Gompers, as at Preuss, that professional education occurs most effectively on site, especially when embedded in actual everyday classroom practice (Darling-Hammond, 1997, 2010). Time was therefore made available during the school day to enable teachers to meet in grade level or department teams to take stock of progress, plan and assess lessons, and negotiate the curriculum.

A Family Support Center operates where staff interact with parents (using English or Spanish, as appropriate), to familiarize them with the school and its values and policies. Staff also provide support for parents regarding logistical issues such as how to secure immigration papers, transportation, health care and child care.

Gompers has expanded from a 6–8 middle school to a 6–12 high school. Now named 'Gompers Preparatory Academy' to signal its college-preparatory orientation, like The Preuss School, Gompers added one grade level at a time, starting in 2008 with a 9th grade. The school enrolled 1,000 students, with approximately 140 students at each grade level when it reached maturity in 2013.

The school regularly engages in self-evaluation strategies, and has also made steady progress on state-mandated tests, improving from 540 (of a possible 900) in 2004 to 686 in 2013. One hundred per cent of Gompers seniors graduate. This compares favorably to other high schools in San Diego's low-income neighborhoods. Thirty-five per cent of the first graduating class enrolled in four-year colleges. This rate rose to 45 per cent in 2013 and 46 per cent in 2014. The remaining students enroll in community colleges: this enables Gompers to celebrate its pledge to 100 per cent graduation and 100 per cent college enrollment (Parsons, 2014).

Mutual benefits and limitations for researchers and practitioners

These brief reflections serve to show how CREATE's interventions provide disadvantaged students with access to the kind of knowledge and resources that will help them develop a critical stance toward educational inequality. At this point, however, one can only speculate whether these kinds of scenarios can be sustained. While our research shows that Preuss and Gompers students can turn their high school academic and social skills into successful college enrollment, it remains a point of conjecture whether graduates will be able to convert their newly acquired cultural capital into economic benefits such as well-respected jobs. It may be that, once they leave school and move away from those intensive academic, relational and social supports, they will lose their accumulated cultural capital in the face of pressures from the external technical rational-oriented social world.

It should also be remembered that when researchers participate in and research an activity, their actions partially constitute them (Cicourel, 1964). Because of its real-world nature, design research makes explicit its own ethical stance. Any ethnographic study of any organization, and especially of oneself as one consciously tries to engage in change processes, foregrounds ethical considerations. It will also inevitably expose gaps between values-inspired intentions and socially-constructed actions.

However, it is not easy to 'decolonize' research (Wood, 1999). While the egalitarian ideal of co-theorized and co-written ethnographies might extend sociology (and other social sciences) in interesting new directions, the traditionalist academy still exerts pressure on researchers to do 'scientific' research. This works against involving participants as co-researchers or co-producers of publications. Further, practitioners and researchers often work from different values perspectives. Naturally enough, practitioners want to showcase the positive aspects of their organization and students' learning; they want to show how their learning has benefited their local situation. University-based researchers are more likely to wish to abstract generalizations from local circumstances and focus on knowledge and theory generation. Consequently, differences of opinion emerge about which aspects of a research project to make public. It also has to be remembered that doing research is never value neutral. Even to declare notional value neutrality is to adopt a political position. Researchers do not simply observe and report 'reality'; they construct reality through their interpretations. Therefore, in order to avoid potential missed opportunities, any collaborative arrangements aimed at improving the quality of teaching and learning, or at organizational improvement, need to be planned and negotiated from the start.

Conclusion

My colleagues and I have deliberately made ourselves more sensitive to many challenges facing educators engaged in school improvement. Teachers in classrooms are undoubtedly constrained by uncontrollable external social forces. Federal mandates governing the use of Title I funds (as under *No Child Left Behind*) require them to prioritize some subjects (math and English language arts) at the expense of others (notably social science, art and music). The timing of school days frequently does not allow for the teaching of higher order thinking skills; instead time is given over to the preparation of students to take the timed tests that measure rote learning. Teachers are subjected to federal mandates, reinforced by state and district directives. These are all seemingly intractable problematics, though our research shows that they can, at least in part, be penetrated.

We continue to support teachers and their professional learning in spite of the difficulties involved. Speaking for myself, by engaging in design research on the origin of Preuss, Gompers, and the development of Preuss School students' academic identities, I have learned how to work systematically with practitioners to co-construct basic knowledge while attempting to build progressive policy and practice. Thus, in making the shift from documenting inequality to attempting to construct equitable educational environments, I have not abandoned an equity agenda; I have refocused its orientation.

References

Alvarez, D. and Mehan, H. (2004) 'Providing educational opportunities for under-represented students', in D. Lapp (ed.) *Teaching all the Children* (pp. 82–89). New York: Guilford.

Alvarez, D. and Mehan, H. (2006) 'Whole school detracking: a strategy for equity and excellence', *Theory into Practice* 45 (1): 82–89.

Brown, A., Greeno, J.G., Resnick, L.B., Mehan, H. and Lampert, M. (1999) *Recommendations Regarding Research Priorities: An Advisory Report to the National Educational Research Policy and Priorities Board*. New York: National Academy of Education.

Bruner, J. (1986) *Actual Minds, Possible Worlds*. Cambridge: Harvard University Press.

Burawoy, M. (2005) 'For public sociology', *American Sociological Review* 70 (1): 4–28.

Cazden, C.B. (1965) *The Acquisition of Noun and Verb Inflections*. Unpublished Doctoral Dissertation. Cambridge, MA: Harvard Graduate School of Education.

Cazden, C.B. (2001) *Classroom Discourse: The Language of Teaching and Learning* (2nd edn). Portsmouth NH: Heinemann.

Cicourel, A.V. (1964) *Method and Measurement in Sociology*. New York: Free Press.

Cicourel, A.V. and Mehan, H. (1985) 'Universal development, stratifying practices and status attainment', *Social Stratification and Mobility* 4: 3–27.

Cole, M. (1999) *Cultural Psychology*. Cambridge MA: Belknap.

Darling-Hammond, L. (1997) *The Right to Learn: A Blueprint for Creating Schools That Work*. San Francisco: Jossey-Bass.

Darling-Hammond, L. (2010) *The Flat World and Education: How America's Commitment to Equity Will Determine Our Future*. New York: Teachers College Press.

Durkheim, E. (1982) *The Rules for Sociological Method*. New York: The Free Press.

Erickson, F. (2004) *Talk and Social Theory*. Cambridge: Polity Press.

Erickson, F. and Shultz, J. (1978) *The Counselor as Gatekeeper: Social Interaction in Interviews*. New York: Academic Press.

Giddens, A. (1979) *Central Problems in Social Theory*. Berkeley: University of California Press.

Hubbard, L., Mehan, H. and Stein, M.K. (2006) *Reform as Learning: When School Reform Collided with School Culture and Community Politics in San Diego*. New York: Routledge Falmer.

Kenda, A. (2008) Interview with Gordon C. Chang. November 13.

Lytle, C. (2007) *The Burden of Excellence*. La Jolla: RELS.

McClure, L J., Morales, C., Strick, B. and Jacob-Almeida, R. (2006) *The Preuss School at UCSD: School Characteristics and Students' Achievement*. San Diego: University of California.

McNiff, J. (2013) *Action Research: Principles and Practice* (3rd edn). Abingdon: Routledge.

Mehan, H. (1974) 'Accomplishing classroom lessons', in A.V. Cicourel (ed.) *Language Use and School Performance* (pp. 76–142). New York: Academic Press.

Mehan, H. (1978) 'Structuring school structure', *Harvard Educational Review* 48 (1): 32–64.

Mehan, H. (1979) *Learning Lessons*. Cambridge MA: Harvard University Press.

Mehan, H. (1993) 'Beneath the skin and between the ears: a case history in the politics of representation', in S. Chailkin and J. Lave (eds), *Understanding Practice: Perspectives on Activity and Context* (pp.241–268). Cambridge: Cambridge University Press.

Mehan, H. (2012) *In the Front Door: Creating a College Going Culture of Learning*. Boulder, CO: Paradigm.

Mehan, H. and Cazden, C. (2015) 'The study of classroom discourse: early history and current developments', in L.B. Resnick, C. Asterhan and S. N. Clarke (eds) *Socializing Intelligence Through Academic Talk and Dialogue* (pp. 13-36). Washington DC: AERA Publications.

Mehan, H. and Chang, G. (2010) '"Is it wrong for us to want good things?" The origins of Gompers Charter Middle School', *Journal of Educational Change* 12: 47–70.

Mehan, H. and Mussey, S. (2012) 'Changes in students' aspirations and conduct', in H. Mehan (ed.) *In the Front Door: Creating a College Going Culture of Learning* (pp. 91–115). Boulder CO: Paradigm.

Mehan, H. and Skelly, J. (1988) 'Reykjavik: the breach and repair of the pure war script', *Multilingua* 7 (1/2): 35–66.

Mehan, H. and Wood, H. (1975) *The Reality of Ethnomethodology*. New York: Wiley Interscience.

Mehan, H., Hubbard, L. and Stein, M.K. (2003) 'When reforms travel: the sequel', *Journal of Educational Change* 6 (1): 1–33.

Mehan, H., Hubbard, L., Villanueva, I. and Lintz, A. (1996) *Constructing School Success: The Consequences of Untracking Low Achieving Students*. Cambridge: Cambridge University Press.

Mehan, H., Meihls, L.J. and Hertweck, A.J. (1986) *Handicapping the Handicapped: Decision Making in Students' Educational Careers*. Stanford: Stanford University Press.

Meier, D. (1995) *The Power of Their Ideas: Lessons for America from a Small School in Harlem*. Boston: Beacon Press.

NCES (2014) College Enrollment Statistics. Washington DC: National Center for Educational Statistics Digest of Educational Statistics.

Oakes, J. (2005) *Keeping Track: How Schools Structure Inequality* (2nd edn). New Haven, CT: Yale University Press.

Parsons, J. (2014) *Self Study*. Prepared for WASC. San Diego: Gompers Preparatory Academy.

Penuel, W. R., Fishman, B. J., Cheng B. H., Sabelli, N. (2011) 'Organizing research and development at the intersection of learning, implementation of design', *Education Researcher* 40 (7): 301–337.

Riel, M. M. (2012) *Understanding Action Research*. Center For Collaborative Action Research, Pepperdine University, accessed online on October 15, 2014 from http://cadres.pepperdine.edu/ccar/define.html.

Rosen, L. and Mehan, H. (2003) 'Reconstructing equality on new political ground: the politics of representation in the charter school debate at the University of California, San Diego', *American Educational Research Journal* 40 (3): 655–682.

Strick, B. R. (2012) 'Equitable access to college: evidence for the influence of school context', *Education Policy Analysis Archives* 20 (35). Retrieved May 28, 2014, from http://epaa.asu.edu/ojs/article/view/1047.

Varenne, H. and McDermott, R. (1998) *Successful Failure: The Schools America Builds*. Boulder, CO: Westview.

Wood, H. (1999) *Displacing Natives: The Rhetorical Production of Hawai'i*. Boulder, CO: Rowman and Littlefield.

Index